MW00643075

Other Books by Paul Hellyer

Agenda: A Plan for Action (1971)

Exit Inflation (1981)

Jobs for All: Capitalism on Trial (1984)

Canada at the Crossroads: A Liberal Agenda for the 90's and Beyond (1990)

Damn the Torpedoes: My Fight to Unify Canada's Armed Forces (1990)

Funny Money: A Common Sense Alternative to Mainline Economics (1994)

Surviving the Global Financial Crisis:
The Economics of Hope for Generation X (1996)

Arundel Lodge: A Little Bit of Old Muskoka (1996)

The Evil Empire: Globalization's Darker Side (1997)

Stop:Think (1999)

Goodbye Canada (2001)

One Big Party: To Keep Canada Independent (2003)

A Miracle in Waiting: Economics that Make Sense (2010)

Light at the End of the Tunnel:
A Survival Plan for the Human Species (2010)

The Money Mafia: A World in Crisis (2014)

HOPE RESTORED

My Life and Views on Canada, the U.S., the World & the Universe

An autobiography by PAUL HELLYER

HOPE RESTORED: AN AUTOBIOGRAPHY BY PAUL HELLYER
COPYRIGHT © 2018 PAUL T. HELLYER

Published by:
Trine Day LLC
PO Box 577
Walterville, OR 97489
1-800-556-2012
www.TrineDay.com
publisher@TrineDay.net

Library of Congress Control Number: 2018951076

Hellyer, Paul T.
−1st ed.
p. cm.

Epub (ISBN-13) 978-1-63424-185-4
Mobi (ISBN-13) 978-1-63424-186-1
Print (ISBN-13) 978-1-63424-184-7
1. Paul Theodore Hellyer (1923-)--Autobigraphy . 2. Canada--History--20th
Century. 3. Canada--History--21st Century . 4. Unidentified flying objects
-- Sightings and encounters. 5. Human-alien encounters. I. Hellyer, Paul T. II.
Title

Credos Books is a TrineDay imprint.

FIRST EDITION
10 9 8 7 6 5 4 3 2

Printed in the USA
Distribution to the Trade by:
Independent Publishers Group (IPG)
814 North Franklin Street
Chicago, Illinois 60610
312.337.0747
www.ipgbook.com

ACKNOWLEDGMENTS

First I would like to acknowledge the role played by my friend Patrick Boyer, former Canadian Member of Parliament who finally convinced me that I had a responsibility to write my memoirs as a public duty. Thank you Patrick.

Thanks also to Noel Cooper, Kent Hotaling. and James Maclean for reading part or all of the manuscript and for making numerous important suggestions as to how it might be improved.

I am deeply indebted to Courtney Brown. Without him Chapter Twenty-Two would have been impossible.

Once again my long-time, faithful assistant Nina Moskaliuk typed the manuscript and studiously assisted in preparing the footnotes. My special thanks to Nina.

Next, I must pay tribute to my mentors in the field of ufology and the extraterrestrial presence on Earth. I begin by thanking my sponsors Mike Bird and Victor Viggiani who provided the forum for my declaration on September 25, 2005 that: "UFO's are as real as the airplanes flying overhead." Then to Dr. Steven Greer, Stephen Bassett, Richard Dolan, Paola Harris, Linda Moulton Howe, Dr. Michael Salla, Dr. Carol Rosin, and many more who have shared their knowledge and insight. I am not a ufologist, and never will be. But I have learned a great deal from each of these students of the subject.

To my editor, Carol Bonnett, words are inadequate to express my gratitude. Her painstaking efforts, brilliant suggestions for improving the manuscript, and extraordinary wisdom have been a real blessing.

My publisher, Kris Millegan, is the one who has made it all happen. A man of peace, Kris has risked everything to publish the truth in many books about America's darkest secrets. Thank you Kris for being a real patriot of the U.S. and the world.

Last on the list but first in my heart is my dear wife Sandra. Three times in our brief 13-year marriage she has sacrificed much to accommodate the urgent demands of "the book." May Heaven reward you greatly, my love.

TABLE OF CONTENTS

INTRODUCTION

The first fifteen chapters of this book are the memoirs of my personal and political life from early youth until the spring of 2004, when I left partisan politics completely. The final ten chapters are of direct and immediate importance to everyone everywhere, including and, perhaps, especially Americans. In these chapters, I expose the truth about the lies, deceptions, misinformation, and disinformation that the U.S. government has presented to its citizens beginning on July 4, 1947, right through to the end of 2017. Actually the government I refer to here is not the one that was elected, rather it is the alternate government or shadow government that became the *de facto* U.S. government more than a half-century ago, which slowly but surely transformed the United States into a police state under its control.

Hope Restored is the third book in a trilogy of books inspired by a higher power. My role has been that of messenger. The first book, *Light at the End of the Tunnel: A Survival Plan for the Human Species*, listed many of the world's problems including the Israeli-Palestinian conflict, and the dismal record of organized religions fighting each other instead of working cooperatively to build a world of peace, justice and hope.

It also introduced the concept of the "Broader Reality," and the fact that sentient beings from other planets and star groups had been visiting Earth for thousands of years and influencing human development. The United States for certain, and quite possibly the U.S.S.R., made agreements with one or more of these species that have had far-reaching and unforeseeable consequences.

The second book, *The Money Mafia: A World in Crisis* was not on my agenda but became essential when I became privy to very disturbing information. The German Nazis had not accepted defeat in 1945. They simply surrendered to end that war, and began planning a new strategy for another attempt to establish a Fourth Reich. Through a stroke of incredible good luck they were able to resume their military build-up in the United States under a blanket of near-total secrecy.

In that second book, I also outlined the Nazi revival as I understood it, and made a number of suggestions as to what could be done to change the course of history. I am grateful to the thousands of people who read either one or both of these books and have written letters of support and encouragement. But all of us are only a drop in the bucket. The power structure in the U.S. is such that to the best of my knowledge no one in a position to help has responded to the call issued in these first two books.

Hope Restored is the unexpected end to the trilogy. It repeats, in considerably shortened version, all of the principal arguments of the earlier books. In addition, however, it introduces very important new revelations including the origin of the cosmos, the nature of God the Creator, and the spiritual battle that is inherent in the Nazi struggle for supremacy as well as the antidote, which is a non-sectarian spiritual revolution. It also introduces the practice of remote viewing that some people may find upsetting, but in that case you can skim over that section and come back to it as your perspective broadens.

I apologize to feminists for referring to the Creator God, also known as the Source, the One, the Great Spirit and more in the masculine gender. This is simply to accommodate convenience and custom. I believe the Creator God is the mother and father of us all.

Finally, for those of you who haven't read *The Money Mafia*, I am repeating the last two paragraphs of Chapter One entitled "The New World Order." They emphasize the "End Game" of our life or death struggle in the current crisis.

"James Warburg, son of the Council on Foreign Relations' founder, Paul Warburg, and a member of Franklin D. Roosevelt's "brain trust," which was made up of individuals from outside government, including professors, lawyers, and others who came to Washington to advise him on economic affairs, delivered blunt testimony before the Senate Foreign Relations Committee on February 17, 1950: "We shall have world government whether or not you like it — by conquest or consent."

And most tellingly, in an address to the Bilderberg Group at Evian, France, May 21, 1992 — and transcribed from a tape recording made by a Swiss delegate, Michael Ringier, Publisher and CEO of Ringier Inc. — Henry Kissinger said, "Today, Americans would be outraged if UN troops entered Los Angeles to restore order; tomorrow, they will be grateful. This is especially true if they were told there was an outside threat from beyond, whether real or promulgated, that threatened our very existence. It is then that all people of the world will plead with world leaders to deliver them from this evil. The one thing that every man fears is the unknown. When presented with this scenario, individual rights will be willingly relinquished for the guarantee of their well-being granted to them by their world government."

The scary attack from beyond is not going to be an alien invasion. It is just going to be another "Red Flag" deception like that of September 11, 2001, but designed to persuade innocent victims to accept martial law and a Nazi world government, which based on their record in the 1930s, would be a fate worse than death.

So consider the present to be a third strike. Will it be a home run, or game over for humanity.

CHAPTER ONE

GROWING UP ON A GINSENG FARM

I was blessed at the outset to have such wonderful parents. They were a kind, compassionate, God-fearing and innovative couple who exercised a positive impact on our community, as well as on my older sister, Hazel, and me. We lived on a farm in the province of Ontario, about half way between the city of Brantford, where Wayne Gretzky would later be born, and Port Dover, a little fishing town on the north shore of Lake Erie, one of the Great Lakes separating Canada and the United States.

Our farm was bisected by the Nanticoke Creek that began in Waterford, the nearest town to our place. The creek flowed east for two miles, and then took a 90-degree turn as it wound its way to Lake Erie. My creative father built a dam to generate electricity before it was available from a public source. This was essential for the ginseng business that became the farm's principal crop. The dam created a pond, which became the habitat for a fascinating variety of fish and animals.

The farm was occupied by two Hellyer families, one on each side of the creek. My Uncle Russell, his wife Lillian, and their four children Shirley, Mildred, Walter and Editha lived in the original farmhouse on the west bank. Their home had been beautifully refurbished and boasted a rock garden that cascaded gently down toward the powerhouse. It was surrounded by a barn, the ginseng dryer and a fruit orchard. Russell had been teaching school in Saskatchewan when my father asked him to come back home and form a partnership of Hellyer Brothers to manage the ginseng business.

Our house was on Cockshutt Road about 1,000 yards east of Uncle Russell's. It was a four-bedroom brick building with a covered veranda. A matching two-car garage defined the end of the vegetable garden.

That was the setting into which I arrived on a steamy hot August 6, 1923, just as the threshers were leaving the field to wash up for supper. My mother, Lula Maude Hellyer, had summoned my father, Audrey Samuel Hellyer (yes, that was his name, it is not a typo) to call the doctor just minutes before she delivered me in the downstairs den which had been converted into a temporary bedroom. Second-hand information indicates that my six-year old sister Hazel was very pleased by my addition to the family.

I mentioned the threshers, as we also grew crops such as wheat, oats, and enough hay for the horses, with a little to spare in case of emergencies, which were rare. Normally, the grassy meadows along the creek provided sufficient forage for the young beef cattle that arrived in the spring to be sold in the fall when they were all fat and beautiful. We also had a few apple and peach trees, and lots of pears. Not long before I left the farm I helped plant 4,500 pear trees. All of these had a niche to fill, but none could produce the kind of revenue necessary to build a beautiful brick house. It was ginseng, when the price was high, that had made that possible.

GINSENG WAS OUR TRADEMARK

Very few of my friends and acquaintances knew that ginseng is indigenous to North America. It was Canada's first or second export to the Orient in the eighteenth century.

In 1714, The Royal Society of London, England, reprinted a letter entitled *"The Description of a Tartarian Plant, Called Ginseng; with an Account of its Virtues."* This document was written in 1711 by Father Jartous, a Jesuit who had been working in China. This document, which had been sent to his Procurator General, described the habitat, harvesting, value and medicinal characteristics of the herb in fascinating detail, and was accompanied by an accurate drawing of the plant and its root. Legend suggests that a copy of the *Royal Society Journal* was sent to Father Francois Lafiteau in Québec City. He showed the sketch of the Manchurian root to a group of Mohawk Indians who recognized the similarity to one they revered as a tonic. They directed Father Lafiteau to a place near Montréal where ginseng was abundant.

The Iroquois Nation was the first known user of the root in North America. They considered the ginseng sacred, calling it "Garent-Oquen," which means "man's thighs and legs separated." "The similarity to the Chinese name of the plant, Jin-shen, which means 'man root' is noteworthy, for the American Aboriginal ancestors were believed to have migrated from North-East Asia by way of the Bering Straits."[1]

Father Lafiteau sent samples of the Canadian root to France where Jesuit botanists verified that it belonged to the ginseng family and classified it as Panax Quinquefolium (five leaved) or North American ginseng. As soon as the analysis reached Canada, samples were sent to Peking where "the roots were found to be of excellent quality and were sold for their weight in gold. The news of this sale soon spread and precipitated the 'ginseng rush' of 1715."[2]

Shipping masters made deals with trappers and Aboriginals to hunt for the roots. They also petitioned France for the exclusive trading rights with China. Their request was granted and the "Company of the West Indies" obtained a monopoly that prospered until the middle of the century when it was subject to some harsh economic realities. When the price rose to five dollars a pound, greedy individuals dug roots out of season, and dried them hastily and carelessly around campfires, ovens and fireplaces. The company refused the badly prepared and scorched product but private entrepreneurs sent the rejects to China "and the market for Canadian ginseng was ruined."[3] A fundamental lesson that the world's farmers, foresters and fishermen might learn from this early experience was that the product was becoming extinct. Roots had been gathered before the seed matured so rather than being a renewable resource, the wealth was just harvested on a one-time basis.

The New England colonies and territories as far west as the Mississippi were beneficiaries of the Canadian malpractice. "Between 1744 and 1766, the ginseng trade between New England and China grew rapidly. George Washington, on a trip west to his lands on the Kanawha River in Virginia, noted in his journal: 'I meet with many mules and packs laden with ginseng going east over the Forbes-Braddock Road.'"[4] The first American ship to trade with China, the 360-ton *Empress of China*, carried a cargo of ginseng which "yielded over 300 percent profit on the amount originally invested."[5] As a result the trade flourished for a while until the Americans proved that they were unable to learn from the Canadian experience. "By the end of the 1890s, the ginseng supply dwindled rapidly and the plant was approaching extinction."[6]

That was just about the time that enterprising farmers on both sides of the Canada-U.S. border attempted to grow the root domestically, one of the early pioneers being the Fromm Brothers of Wisconsin. My great uncle Clarence must have read an article, including pictures, of their operation which enabled him to recognize the plants growing in the hardwood forests not far from the farm he was about to sell. He picked the seeds and persuaded my grandpa Albert to plant some in partnership on the farm where I was born. The orchard environment they chose proved relatively inhospitable to the early experiment. In addition, they had to learn by trial and error that seed harvested in the fall does not germinate in the spring, but must lie dormant for 12 months.

It was left to my father to carry on where the initiators had left off. This gave him the distinction of being the real pioneer of the Canadian domestic ginseng industry. Instead of relying on the natural shade of woods or orchards, he moved his gardens into open fields and covered them at six-foot height with wooden lath slats to block out two-thirds of the sunlight, in simulation of the forest. The fledgling business grew rapidly and, as I said earlier, Dad recruited his younger brother Russell to join him in a partnership that endured for decades.

Hellyer Brothers dominated the Canadian ginseng market but, during the 1920s, when profitability was at its peak, dozens of smaller growers were attracted to the business. Their timing couldn't have been worse. In the 1930s the price dropped as low as Cdn. $2.25 a pound, which was well below the cost of production, so nearly all of the small growers either abandoned their crop or went bankrupt. My family proved an old adage attributed to British economist John Maynard Keynes who said, in effect, that if you owe your bank one hundred pounds, you have a problem. But, if you owe a million, it has. Hellyer Brothers owed the tiny Waterford, Ontario branch of the Bank of Montreal so much money that the bank couldn't afford to foreclose. It was better to pretend that the loan was active.

With the outbreak of World War II the price began to creep back up but following the Japanese attack on Pearl Harbor, nothing could be shipped to China and we had a truckload of ginseng root sitting on a New York dock from November 1941 until almost the end of the war. This almost proved disastrous as a result of a rigid tax regime that insisted on taxing a crop the year in which it was sold, rather than the year it was grown. A little flexibility on the part of the tax authorities renewed bank confidence and the day was saved. The Hellyer Brothers emerged from the war with a virtual monopoly which was not to last very long in a changing world.

Father had hoped that I would take over the business, but that was not meant to be. I was simply too tall at six feet and three inches to work in the gardens without wreaking havoc on my head. More important, I had my heart set on politics where I hoped that I would be able to accomplish something worthwhile for the common good. So when Dad retired, my cousin Walter took over the family farm and became Canada's largest grower. My brother-in-law, John Race, incorporated Race-Hellyer Ginseng Growers, a company in which I was a shareholder. About two decades later, in 1980, my oldest son Peter, with the able assistance of his brother David, established Peter L. Hellyer Ginseng Growers. Peter was able to operate profitably for quite a few years until what was first a trickle became a tidal wave of new entrants flooding the market.

One farmer after another planted a few acres. Then Chinese and Korean immigrants, familiar with the ginseng trade, began planting enormous gardens and the supply increased exponentially to an extent that the market became saturated and the price, once again, fell below the cost of production. Peter decided to exit the business and harvested his last crop in 2006. It was a bit sad after almost 110 years of family involvement in the ginseng business. The market, however, dictated the decision.

Throughout the years few subjects have been more controversial than ginseng's medicinal properties. Many years ago I had a small dictionary that was categorical: "Ginseng: a worthless herb prized by the Chinese." A more restrained view came from Dr. Omand Solandt, the first chairman of Canada's Defence Research Board who, with a generosity untypical of his medical colleagues, simply said: "It must have something or the Chinese wouldn't have used it for so long."

In recent years the skepticism has changed remarkably. Ginsenosides, the active ingredient, have attracted wide attention. The Soviets, who conducted controlled experiments as far back as 1948, gave it to their cosmonauts and Olympic athletes to enhance their performance. More recently, Canadian scientists have developed a ginseng product known as Cold-FX® that many people, including myself, have used and found helpful in preventing colds in the early stages by boosting the effectiveness of the immune system.

LIFE ON THE FARM

Farms are wonderful places for children to grow up. There is so much freedom to move around and go to the barn with its many attractions – petting, feeding and learning to drive the horses and milk the family cow. At a little later age I learned to drive a tractor and the farm truck. It was usually fun to help with the various chores and combine play with exploration in a way that is not available to city kids. It is sad that "big Agro" is buying up so much land and making it so difficult for small farmers to survive. The very large decrease in the number of farms is robbing thousands of young people of the many blessings that were routine for those of my generation.

I only had one pet when I grew up, a beautiful German Shepherd named Peter. I loved him so much that one day when a careless workman left the top off a can of paint, I took advantage of the opportunity to convert Peter's beautiful brown fur into bright green. I don't think my decorating skill was fully appreciated either by the dog or my parents.

Unfortunately Peter came to an untimely tragic end. He was so diligent in guarding and protecting me that some of the neighbors came to mistrust him, and one of them poisoned Peter. Many tears were shed, and I have never had another pet.

The farm was a great place to develop entrepreneurial skills. I manufactured bath salts that I used to fill the most exotic bottles I could find before putting them in my little wagon to peddle to the neighbors. My wagon also came in handy when father drained the pond to make some repairs to the turbine. There were a number of large carp left stranded in the shallow water and I was able to get my hands on a number of them and sell them to neighbours of European extraction for five cents each. They obviously knew a bargain when they saw one!

I came up with other initiatives as diverse as selling magazine subscriptions, and trapping muskrats in the pond. I would skin and dry the pelts and sell them to Boehner Bros. in New York. They were fur brokers who bought our ginseng for resale in the Far East.

My principal business project, however, was market gardening. My products were peaches, pears, apples, elderberries and acorn squash. I always put the larger fruit in the bottom of the basket and the smaller ones on top, a practice which appeared to give me a slight advantage over some of my competitors. I would begin loading the family truck at about 5:30 a.m. every Saturday morning and, because I was not yet old enough to have a driver's license, my sister Hazel was kind enough to drive me to either the Hagersville or Brantford farmers' market.

Anyone who is interested in subjects like inflation may be interested to know that the price of peaches, pears and apples was invariably 20 cents for a six-quart basket, and the wooden basket was included in the price.

I was also blessed by an unexpected opportunity to learn a little bit about leadership. My father was the president of the local softball (now known as fastball) league for all of my formative years. There were traditionally about six teams in the local league but in 1939, when I was 15 years old, three were unable to field teams due to the war. Father invited the league executive committee to a meeting to plan for the season. It was held in our living room so I was allowed to listen in. When they agreed to prepare a schedule for three teams, I spoke up and said "four." At first they just ignored the interruption but when I persisted they finally agreed that I could try to put together a team in Townsend Centre, the name of the four corners of our township.

I called a practice but four of the best players from previous years didn't show up, each claiming that due to the uncertainty, they had made other plans for the summer. So I was stuck with the less experienced players who were, however, eager to pitch in. No one was surprised when we lost our first game. But a few eyebrows were raised when we tied the second game, and won the third and fourth. Curiously (although not really), one by one the four experienced players, including a star pitcher, phoned me to say that their plans for the summer had changed, and they would be available after all – everyone wants to be part of a winning team. Our team wound up in first place at the end of the season, and took possession of the trophy.

We topped the league again the next year in 1940. In 1941 I was in California, but the team topped the list for the third consecutive year, a feat that had never happened before in the long history of the league. The prize for this achievement was that the Townsend Centre team was given permanent possession of the John S. Martin Trophy.[7]

I learned a great deal from mother and dad. They were both Sunday school teachers, and both sang in the Villa Nova Baptist Church choir. Dad was the church treasurer and responsible for counting the collections. He taught me to tithe, (give 10% of one's income to a church or charity) a habit that has persisted to this day with more than a little bit added to that original percentage. They both walked the talk and this was demonstrated by the generous and compassionate way they treated their employees, and also neighbors, who occasionally had special needs beyond their ability to cope.

My parents' actions were such that decades after they were gone, whenever I would visit the sites of my childhood, I would be approached by people who sang their praises and in more than one instance confided that my parents had exercised a more positive influence on their lives than their own parents.

My Experience at School

I wish I could say that my academic record was on a par with what I learned at home. Alas, it was a slippery slope from positive to mediocre. I didn't have far to go to the little red schoolhouse on the hill about a thousand yards from home. This was a blessing because some of my schoolmates had to walk as far as two miles. It was a one-room school where one overworked, over-stressed teacher had to cope with 35 to 55 youngsters in eight different grades.

As my grades reflected, I wasn't a good student. There were a few real excuses such as taking quite a bit of time off due to health problems. A bout of scarlet fever, for example, resulted in a four-week quarantine. Also, I was alleged to have a weak heart (a weak heart that has kept on ticking for 94 years to date), which periodically kept me bedridden for a few days at a time. The list was long. Despite these illnesses, the real problem, I regret to admit, was the fact that the word "homework" was not part of my vocabulary when I was young.

I must have misbehaved at school on two or three occasions because I remember being strapped several times. It was routine that if I got the strap at school, the punishment would be repeated at home on the assumption that I must have deserved it. Mother, who was the family disciplinarian, would open the top cupboard door in the bathroom where the strap was kept, and say: "This is going to hurt me as much as it is going to hurt you." I strongly suspected there was something missing in her logic.

When I was 12 years old, mother taught me to drive a car. We were on the way home from Brantford and just after we did a 90-degree turn near the village of Oakland she said: "Would you like to drive from here?" So I got behind the wheel of our 1931 Auburn sedan, a really special car, and never looked back. Perhaps mother was demonstrating foresight. The next year I was enrolled in Waterford High School, which was more than two and a half miles from our place, and the only way to get there was to drive.

Sadly, Waterford High burned to the ground before the school year began so my early semesters were spent in the old abandoned Wax Flower Building on the main street of our town. The experience of improvising was unforgettable but there was genuine relief when a beautiful building was completed on the site of the old high school. The new school sported amenities such as a large gymnasium that could be used as an auditorium when required, a large outdoor playing field, and new physics and chemistry laboratories.

I had little difficulty achieving passing grades while maintaining my "no homework" policy. I always came up with some lame excuse such as having to milk the family cow each night. The only exceptions to the passing grades were languages – I flunked out of both Latin and French. I held the teachers partly responsible because neither one was a star performer. Of course I can't vouch for the objectivity of that assessment, which might have been just a cop-out. Still, I am convinced that if our future principal, Ken Richardson, who had his own special gift of penetrating the fog, had been teaching Latin I might have paid greater attention and scraped through with a passing grade.

I did much better in extracurricular activities. Since I was quite tall, I played some basketball. In addition, I earned a school letter each year in track and field events like shot put and javelin throwing. I enjoyed taking part in school plays such as *The Bishop's Candlesticks*, a stripped-down version of *Les Misérables*. Finally, I sang in the school choir. By 1939 I was studying voice with P. George Marshall, the school music teacher, and I was asked to sing a solo, "There'll Always Be an England." The audience liked this demonstration of patriotism and encouraged an encore. The second time through I cracked on a B-flat, providing a good lesson in humility.

In the spring of 1940 I completed four years at Waterford High and received my graduation diploma. My grades weren't very good, in part because I was an average student, and also because I missed so much time – fully half of my final year – due to various illnesses. Still, there was nothing to prevent me from continuing with Grade XIII, as there was a fifth year in high school at that time. But I didn't because I had another bee in my bonnet.

I had been mesmerized by the American Airlines DC3s which flew majestically, like golden birds on their regular schedule along the railway line from Detroit to Buffalo, and had developed a passion for aeronautics. I thought it would become a tremendously important field for a big, sparsely populated country like Canada. Unfortunately, no Canadian university offered a course in aeronautical engineering, but I had seen advertisements for U.S. schools offering concentrated courses in the subject. The most attractive, in my view, was the Curtiss-Wright Technical Institute of Aeronautics in Glendale, California. Its curriculum included all the basic requirements of engineering without wasting any time on languages, history or philosophy. That seemed like a great idea to me because I had not yet developed a genuine appreciation of the liberal arts. There was a stunned silence from my parents when I raised the subject at dinner one evening, but a few weeks later my trunk was loaded on a bus at Simcoe, Ontario, and I was on my way.

CHAPTER TWO

California, Here I Come

My declared reason for going to California was to attend Curtiss-Wright Technical Institute of Aeronautics in Glendale, a suburb of Los Angeles. My interest in aeronautics was genuine but there was another powerful motive. I had a crush on Deanna Durbin, a beautiful young Hollywood star with the voice of an angel, not that I am an expert on angel voices but I had a lively imagination.

I had been a member of Deanna's fan club and had two or three letters from her signed by her own hand. That was in the days before movie starlets and politicians began using machines that were able to simulate genuine autographs. My dream, of course, was that I would have the opportunity to meet her personally. The odds of that happening would be greatly improved if I lived just over the hill from Hollywood.

The bus trip from Simcoe, Ontario, to Los Angeles in September 1940 was long and tedious, broken only by the occasional pit or food stop. The most interesting aspect of an otherwise uneventful trip was crossing the Rocky Mountains by moonlight. That's the romantic stuff of which movies are made. The Los Angeles dawn, in contrast, was a let-down. L.A., as it is known, was just another big, sprawling city unremarkable except for the Spanish influence on its architecture. Pasadena, Glendale and Hollywood looked very much like other suburbs, although separated by coastal hills.

Curtiss-Wright Technical Institute, located at the edge of Glendale's Grand Central Air Terminal, was very much as I had pictured it. A big, no-nonsense education factory, where students were immersed in each subject for intensive six-week periods, with no time off in between. There were separate academic and trades training wings but engineering students were required to do one six-week stint in the shop where we were exposed to the rudiments of welding, "tin-bashing" and low humor.

The school directed me to a boarding house at 530 E. Cypress Street which was to be my home away from home. It was situated on a steep hill abutting Forest Lawn Memorial Park, the star-studded sanctuary for Hollywood's dearly departed. There were eight students and our landlady, Betty, a well-preserved middle-aged widow, who loved us all dearly but ran a tight ship. Rooms had to be kept neat as a pin, and no food could be wasted. That posed a challenge to someone like me whose diet had been strictly the basics. My first exposure to Swiss steak, loaded with onions, contained all the elements of an initiation ritual.

Still, it was a congenial place and although there wasn't much time to play, there were a few hilarious exceptions. The most memorable occurred Halloween night after one of the boys bought a Model A Ford sedan and decided to give it a trial run down Hollywood Boulevard. We were in a party mood, which may have been our undoing. The car had no roof so we would alternately sit or stand, holding on to the frame intended for the canvas canopy – singing very loudly all the way. Suddenly, people began throwing things at us from the sidewalk, oranges, avocados, tomatoes, anything they could get their hands on. Before long a motorcycle policeman, erroneously convinced we had started the melee, pulled alongside and ordered us off the boulevard.

We would have complied, but were unable to as we were in the center lane of solid traffic and no one would yield to let us through. We were trapped and our predicament was complicated by the necessity of ducking or catching the red, green and orange missiles directed at us from all sides. The irate cop must have radioed for help because we soon had one motorcycle policeman on each side of our fenders, sirens screaming, escorting us the half mile or so to the nearest exit leading back to Glendale. We finally made it and were just chugging up the hill to Betty's when the main bearings dropped out on the pavement. Manpower was substituted for horsepower but no one seemed to care, least of all the car's owner. He said it was a small price to pay for "taking Hollywood by storm."

Generally speaking, Hollywood was a bust. Like other youngsters my age I had stardust in my eyes, and was infatuated with Deanna. But if a secret part of my motive for choosing Curtiss-Wright over eastern schools was the hope of seeing and meeting her, it was in vain. I enjoyed visiting famous places like Grauman's Chinese Theater, with its sidewalk punctuated with the footprints of the famous, and the truly fabulous Hollywood Bowl. However, the studios were spread far and wide, out of practical bounds to busy students. Linda Darnell gave me her autograph when she visited the school and I almost climbed into a taxi already occupied by Lana Turner, but that was the limit of my direct exposure to the goddesses of glamour.

Ironically, the movie stars I met personally, I encountered at church. Soon after my arrival in Glendale, I began attending First Baptist Church which was within easy walking distance of Betty's. The parishioners, like most Westerners, were extremely friendly and both the pastor, Dr. Jim Brougher Jr., and his father the pastor emeritus were good preachers. Additional marks can also be awarded for a first-class choir with professional soloists like John Raitt, who later appeared in a number of movies.

The morning services were quite traditional but at night there were guest appearances by Hollywood celebrities such as Mary Pickford, Buddy

Rogers, the Morgan Family and Leo Carillo, who played the role of Pancho in *The Cisco Kid*. There were other guests like composer Albert Hay Malotte, who wrote popular arrangements of the Lord's Prayer and the 23rd Psalm. This was something of a culture shock, but I wasn't unduly distressed until one of the Hollywood starlets sang, "I don't want to set the world on fire, I just want to start a flame in your heart." That disturbed me.

I raised the subject with Dr. Brougher Sr., whose reply was simple and straightforward. "In the morning, we cater to habitual church-goers. At night, we try to attract the younger, less committed crowd who might not come otherwise. Different fish, different bait." I got the point, but it certainly was a far cry from Villa Nova Baptist.

I soon found another attraction at the church. Most Sundays, although not always, there was one extraordinary, long-haired beauty in the soprano section of the choir. The reality of Deanna being just as distant on the other side of the hill as she would have been across the continent had now long been accepted, and I found my eyes drawn to this lovely stranger like iron to a magnet. I didn't know her name and it must have been fear of rejection that deterred me from finding out. It was just another love at a distance. That was just as well, perhaps, because I was able to put my full energy into my studies with good, positive results.

There was a bit of unexpected drama one morning when the school principal came to my desk and asked if I would come with him. There were some gentlemen who would like to see me. You can imagine my surprise when I learned that the visitors were four FBI agents dressed in their fine black suits.

They asked me my name and I told them. They then asked me if I ever used another name? I sheepishly admitted that I did. Part of my adolescent fantasy had been to adopt a pseudonym, Donald M. Darwin, which just happened to have the same initials as Deanna May Durbin. I had used it with my voice coach, Stanley Vermilyea, who knew me by that name, and probably with a few others.

I was then given the classic lecture to the effect that using a pseudonym was not illegal as long as it was not used for fraud. No one had suggested that I had acted illegally so I was allowed to return to my classes, but it was a day to remember.

Christmas 1940 was the first I had spent away from home. Californians played the same music and exchanged familiar greetings, but there was also something a little bit weird about shorts-clad people playing tennis one minute, and singing carols the next. Irving Berlin subsequently captured the mood exactly for the movie *Holiday Inn* with the Christmas classic "White Christmas."[1]

As the months rolled by, and my studies seemed well under control, I decided to enlarge my extracurricular activities. This involved more cash than

15

my allowance provided, but fortunately the school had a program of part-time work for just such "emergencies." I donned sweeper's overalls to earn a little freedom to undertake other activities and I also sent my parents an SOS for help with the voice lessons and flying instructions I hoped to arrange.

As well, after much adoration from afar, I decided it was time to stop playing the fool and try to meet the girl of my dreams. There was no problem arranging an introduction at the next church social. I formally met Margaret Elizabeth Nelson and learned that she was pleased to make my acquaintance. My protracted interest had not escaped her attention and she left no doubt that the attraction was mutual. After coffee I walked her home, just a couple of blocks away, and we agreed to meet again the next day. We saw each other often and would walk, talk, go to movies or concerts. It didn't matter where we went or what we did, we enjoyed each other's company.

Our courtship was facilitated by the fact that one of my two closest friends at Betty's owned a reasonably reliable car that he was willing to lend me whenever I asked. So Margaret and I were able to tour the L.A. area, enjoy its parks, feed the deer and revel in its many attractions. The most memorable time was a concert we attended at the Hollywood Bowl. At the end of the performance we were asked to take a match from our pocket or purse and have it ready. The lights were turned down and a signal was given to light the matches. Spectacular doesn't begin to describe the scene. It was wondrous. It was novel at that time and probably wouldn't pass the fire marshal's test now. But it was one more step down that enchanted trail of falling in love.

By November 1, 1941, I had completed the required curriculum and just had a few weeks to put in prior to graduation. The time was right to enrol at Joe Plosser Air College, just across the airfield from Curtiss-Wright. It was a young man's dream come true. My first "bird" was a two-seat in tandem Columbia with a Franklin engine and my first flight was on November 10th. In subsequent sessions my instructor put me through all the standard maneuvers including take-offs, landings, turns and spins. The only one that bothered me was the power stall. That is the one where you pull back on the stick and point the nose to the sky. The plane gradually loses speed until it comes to a dead stop and falls over like a rock plummeting down to earth. When that happened I felt as though I'd left my stomach hanging on a cloud.

In the four weeks before training ended abruptly there was only one really close shave. The Columbia was a tandem dual with the instructor ensconced behind the student. He would tap my shoulder when I was to fly and again when he wished to take over. On this scary occasion, the instructor had taken control as we approached the airport but for some reason we continued on toward the hill separating the Glendale field from Hollywood. I thought he was just testing my nerves as part of one of his routines. We got closer and closer and finally, at white-knuckle range I broke and applied full left stick and rudder, clearing the treetops by a handful of leaves.

"What in hell do you think you're doing?" he bellowed from the rear.

"Me!" I yelled back, defensively. "You were flying and I thought you were testing my nerves."

Each of us had thought the other was in control when, in fact, nobody was. The plane had been pilotless! The miracle was that we both applied full left at precisely the same instant. Any disagreement at that point would have seen us becoming ornaments for the hardwoods.

My first solo flight was December 4th, for nine minutes. The landing wasn't the smoothest on record, but my mentor came to the rescue with that immortal consolation: "Any landing you can walk away from is a good landing." I was up alone again for 25 minutes the next day and 70 minutes on the 6th. On the 7th, I took off again and headed for the San Fernando Valley to practice spins. It was a beautiful day and I was in luck because I didn't see any of the film makers' orange balloons restricting use of the airspace.

I gave the old lady a good workout for more than an hour but when I got back to Grand Central and made my approach I saw some seemingly distraught person madly waving a yellow flag. It had to signify an emergency of some kind so I gunned the engine and did another circuit. When I got back in position the flag performance was repeated so I went around again. The third time, I was getting low on gas so I landed in spite of the flag and got the balling out of my life. What I had interpreted as "emergency – don't land" really meant "emergency – land at once." But how could I have known. I would have set down the first time if the madman hadn't run out in front of me, and no one had included that flag in the list of do's and don'ts.

The reason for the turmoil was soon explained. The Japanese had attacked Pearl Harbor and everyone was in a state of panic. Traffic was diverted away from the airport region to protect the big Lockheed factory that had been turning out bombers for the Royal Air Force. The confusion that followed was such that the most interesting flight I had undertaken wasn't even recorded in my logbook.

I planned to leave L.A. in time to be home for Christmas but that wasn't soon enough for my mother, who had been caught up in the press hysteria. "How about you coming right home" she wrote on December 10th. "I don't like the thought of you being in a danger area. They haven't said much tonight about your district but they did this afternoon. Things don't look so good do they?"[2] From my vantage point, and also in retrospect, her concern was ridiculous but it was a measure of the media's incredible capacity to exaggerate.

Ironically, as I was packing, I received a message inviting me to take a screen test at Universal Pictures. It had been arranged by my singing teacher, Stanley Vermilyea, a close friend of one of the producers. It was too late. Margaret was sad to say "au revoir" but the world was at war and I had a responsibility to do my part.

CHAPTER THREE

THE WARTIME YEARS – 1941-1945

When I returned home to Canada from California in December 1940 I was gung-ho to join the air force. For an adventurous 18-year old who loved to fly there seemed to be no alternative. But over the Christmas holiday my family, unencumbered by any military tradition, urged me to at least consult "the powers that be" in Ottawa to get the official word on where I could best serve. So a letter was dispatched to the Deputy Minister for Air. The response was prompt and unequivocal. Industry was the priority due to the desperate shortage of engineers. With that information in hand, parental pressure became irresistible.

A colleague from Curtiss-Wright, Doug Zeller, who had already joined Fleet Aircraft at Fort Erie, wrote and told me that the company was looking for additional help to build the Cornell aircraft that had been selected as the primary trainer for the Royal Canadian Air Force (RCAF). About life in the border town, he said, "We like it very much except for a few things, living conditions are lousy and transportation worse."[1] I applied, was interviewed and hired. Meals were taken in the company cafeteria, or at a local restaurant famous for its friendly atmosphere and the acrobatics of its cockroaches. I didn't mind the roaches playing games along the walls, but when one pretended to be an alphabet in the vegetable soup, I was more than a little bit put off! The transportation problem was solved by buying a used 1938 Buick, with hydraulic transmission, the prototype for hydramatic drive which was introduced in Oldsmobile the following year. The transmission was a pain, but the car, which was painted a flashy two-tone with maroon bottom and cream top, was a godsend as a carpool to get to work, as well as for off-hour activities across the Niagara River in Buffalo.

Fleet Aircraft was a congenial place and the engineering department in particular, was pretty much one happy family, including future notables such as Ian Gray, who became Chairman and Chief Executive Officer of Canadian Pacific Airlines. My early assignments consisted primarily of "change orders," which meant re-drawing aircraft parts to make them stronger, lighter or easier to manufacture. On the bright side, Fleet was just beginning to gain momentum and I had the satisfaction of watching the first complete plane move out of the hangar door to be put through its paces by the legendary Tom Williams, our chief test pilot, and then seeing production increase until it reached eight planes a day, a Canadian record.

Fort Erie was not exactly a cultural center, but it did have the advantage of being close to the renowned Crystal Beach Amusement Park, several good swimming quarries and the Peace Bridge across from Buffalo. That allowed me to join the Buffalo Philharmonic Choir, directed by Franco Autori, as well as the one at Asbury Delaware Methodist Episcopal Church, where I sang a number of baritone solos.

On the weekends that I went home to the farm, I took a few more flying lessons at the Brant-Norfolk Flying Club and got my spin certificate from Tom Senior, who must have certified a few thousand pilots in his day. That enabled me to apply for a private pilot's license but unfortunately, the government decided to discontinue tests before I was able to get mine.

Meanwhile, my sister Hazel joined me at Fleet. This made life more agreeable as we were good friends and enjoyed doing things together. She was there to witness my biggest blunder. The Chief Engineer, George Otter, asked me to draft a new set of leading-edge curves for the Cornell wing. When I was finished they went directly to the plant without being checked. Luckily, for me, the shop foreman decided to do a hand-made mock-up before making templates. The finished product bore more resemblance to a snake's tail than the leading edge of an airplane wing and panic struck. I was given the crash assignment of doing the job all over again.

I worked virtually non-stop day and night until it was done, including my own thorough double-check. With the project complete, I disappeared for 24 hours' sleep before returning to pick up my walking ticket. To my astonishment, instead of being fired I was promoted. They must have concluded, perhaps correctly, that anyone guilty of such a grievous error is unlikely to do a repeat performance.

My Courtship of Margaret Nelson Continued

Margaret Nelson and I corresponded regularly and each chided the other if the intervals were too great. In the late summer of 1943 I invited her to come to Canada for a visit, which she joyfully accepted. Mrs. Teal, my landlady, graciously agreed to make a room available for her at her boarding house.

I met Margaret at the Fort Erie Railway Station and we were soon on our way to a gravel quarry that was a very popular place to swim. Wow, could she swim! This was just the first of a long list of adventures that included visiting the mighty Niagara Falls, Niagara-on-the Lake, Buffalo and other attractions on both sides of the Canada-U.S. border.

As the days rolled by my parents suggested that she extend the visit and spend Christmas with us at the farm. She agreed, and I wish you could have seen the look on her face when it began to snow. A snowball fight began, ending in a draw. My parents fell in love with Margaret at first sight and the bond grew stronger as she added her lovely soprano voice to the Hellyer chorus of Christmas carols around the fireplace. I took advantage of the opportunity to ask Margaret to marry me and was delighted when she agreed.

TIME TO MOVE ON

As the war dragged on I became increasingly restless and longed to be more directly involved. There was no doubt that what I was doing by late 1943 was of value. I had been promoted to the "Stress Section" as one of three engineers, each in charge of an eight-hour shift. If someone dropped a hammer through the plywood wing it was my job to design a patch, supervise the installation, and approve it as satisfactory, a fair responsibility as there was often an emergency of some sort. But as Cornell production began to taper off, and the company was about to tool up to manufacture Lancaster wings, I decided it was time to leave.

Several Curtiss-Wright graduates enlisted in Montreal and were commissioned as engineers. They were subsequently allowed to transfer to aircrew without losing their rank. I thought the procedure sounded a bit cumbersome and time consuming. Also I had a penchant for doing things the hard way, and preferred to go through the ranks. Syd Britton, a future member of the renowned Avro Iroquois engine team, and I, decided to enlist together.

When I arrived at the RCAF's Hamilton Recruiting Centre there was none of this "fellow worker who had been doing his bit" stuff.[2] I was received with about as much grace as would have been shown to an enemy subversive emerging from the bush. I was told my application would be filed because there were no openings – which was not the truth! A few weeks later I tried again and was passed along to the medics who checked all my working parts and pronounced me fit. The following morning Flying Officer Anderson administered the oath of office. Syd, meanwhile, was called up by the Royal Navy, with whom he had filed an application a year earlier.

My reporting date to No. 1 Manning Depot was set for April 14, 1944, giving me almost a month of time off, so I opted for a fast trip to California. I mischievously didn't advise Margaret in advance, so when her mother told her I was at the door, she was incredulous and shut it in my face. A second later, shock gave way to joy and all was forgiven. Margaret's sister Madelyn and her husband, Don Young, let me stay at their place and Don granted me generous use of his car which enabled me to pick Margaret up after work and get a head start with the evening's plans. We had 10 wonderful days together and talked about the possibility of marriage when the shooting war was over. On the final weekend, we went sailing on Balboa Bay. It was a fantastic day, although I got a nasty sunburn as a result of ignoring Margaret's advice to wear a shirt. Time ran out and she took me to the station to see me off. She wrote in a letter the next day: "As soon as you kissed me goodbye and then turned around and waved for the last time, something inside of me seemed to fade away."[3]

By the time I got to the Manning Depot on Friday, April 14, 1944, the sunburn had developed into a nasty cold. A group of us were trucked to the Canadian National Exhibition (CNE) Coliseum, affectionately known as the "cow palace." The next day I was issued an ill-fitting uniform that was barely good enough for Sunday's church parade. On Monday I traded it for an outfit that came close to fitting, had my immunization shots and began training. By nightfall, I felt like the wrath of God and my temperature was 103.2 F when the Orderly Sergeant insisted that I go to the depot hospital. There, despite my protest that the pink on my chest was sunburn, and that I had a bad flu-like cold, Flight Lieutenant O.E.A. Stephens diagnosed my problem as scarlet fever and had me wheeled along to the isolation ward.

Tuesday morning a group of half a dozen doctors confirmed F.L. Stephens' opinion and I was shipped to Riverdale Isolation Hospital. I hated the idea of being cooped up for 28 days and getting behind in my training, so I protested my innocence on arrival at "admitting." My stretcher was parked on the floor until a very distinguished, gray-haired gentleman arrived on the scene.

"What's the matter, son?" He inquired.

"Sir," I said, "I have already had scarlet fever; this pink is a sunburn I got while sailing in California."

"Stick out your tongue and say ahh."

"Ahh."

"You're right. You haven't got scarlet fever."

"But who will sign his rejection slip?" asked one of the worried-looking officials.

"I will," replied the elderly doctor, as he scrawled his name and disappeared as abruptly as he had come.

I returned to basic training with a vengeance. I was the troop marker, probably because I was the tallest recruit, and really threw those arms up and down. Keeping in step was easier when we had a band, and there was always something especially stimulating about the Royal Air Force march. The compact schedule presented no real problems with the exception of the obstacle course, where I had some difficulty getting my lanky body up and over the vertical wall. But somehow I did, and finished stage one with a good report. Then it was on to Selection Wing.

This was to be the big test. A year earlier, the air force wouldn't take anyone who didn't agree to be a pilot, but an official had gone to England to check Air Chief Marshal Harris' casualties and concluded the requirement for aircrew was considerably overstated. The RCAF cut back its intake, especially for pilots. Air gunners were still in short supply so the aAir Force adopted the neat trick of asking each trainee if he would like to be an air gunner. Anyone who said "no" was automatically washed out on the grounds of "poor attitude."

The devil must encourage amateur psychologists to prepare questions of this sort which encourage people to lie. The whole camp knew the ruse so I was well prepared in advance. I was much too tall to be selected as an air gunner, so the question was really academic.

"Is there any aircrew position you wouldn't want?" The interviewing officer inquired. "Not really, Sir, though I'm not too keen about wireless," I replied in a futile attempt to protect both my future and my reputation for truthfulness.

"Isn't that a coincidence," he replied. "Your only poor mark is in Morse code. You did exceptionally well on the Link Trainer. I think you would make a good pilot."

I was elated! Especially when I learned that only three of us had made pilot out of the 300 airmen interviewed. I was therefore in high good spirits when I was posted to Camp Borden awaiting posting to Initial Flying Training School. A few weeks of useful employment, more accurately dubbed "useless duties," was a small price to pay for such a big step along the way.

As the weeks rolled by, I became more and more impatient. I wanted to get on course but when that seemed uncertain I was paraded to the commanding officer to ask if I could be sent overseas in another trade.

"You're aircrew and you're stuck," was his blunt reply. Then to underline his firmness, despite the inconsistency, he added: "And if you bother me again, I'll wash you out of aircrew and put you back in the mess as general duties."

A diversion, although not a happy one, was singing at funerals. Those of us who built the Cornell Trainer had placed a little warning plaque on the instrument panel indicating the maximum diving speed. Every once in a while, some student refused to believe us, with disastrous results. Invariably I was drafted to participate in the memorial service. After two or three of these dreadful assignments, I dreamed up a ruse to get out of the mess where I was working. I warned the padre that if he intended to call on me again he should do his best to get me out of the kitchen because the grease was affecting my voice.

It seemed ironic, not to say perverse, that the only person on the base with any experience in aeronautical engineering should be flipping eggs instead of repairing airplanes. I couldn't go back to the commanding officer and suggest the switch without getting my wings clipped but I assumed he would be more considerate of the padre. He was, and like magic it was done. Toward the end of September I was transferred to the big hangar full of unserviceable planes and handed some tools. My part in patching an An-son wing earned me the only "flip" of my air force career, a test flight over Manitoulin Island when the leaves were at their glorious best. The kaleido-scope of color was as thrilling as any I have seen, which was reason enough to make the occasion memorable. Earning 75 cents flying pay to boot made it doubly so.

Little did I dream that the Mackenzie King government was being shaken by an internal crisis at that same time in the fall of 1944. The Ca-nadian Army was desperately short of reinforcements and although a referendum had given King the authority to send conscripts overseas he stubbornly refused for fear of offending his hard-core Liberal support in Quebec. Defense Minister James Ralston resigned in disgust to precip-itate a crisis which came close to toppling the government. Part of the fallout from this debacle was a decision to release 4,200 surplus aircrew – presumably in the hope that many of us would wind up in the army and help relieve the pressure.

I was sent back to the CNE for discharge. Confusion reigned supreme and it took six weeks to do what should have been done in three days. It was six weeks that had an unanticipated impact on my life.

AN UNEXPECTED TURN OF EVENTS

Whiling away the time was alternately pleasant and painful. It was pain-ful to see valuable manpower being wasted in a way that was frivo-lous bordering on subversive. I came to understand the maxim that wars are won by the side that is least incompetent. On the positive side, the "make-work" projects designed to re-prove Parkinson's Law did not include kitch-en fatigues, and the after-hours activities were more varied and entertain-ing than those at outpost Borden. Most evenings were spent at the Active Service Canteen on Adelaide Street East. It offered magazines, tickets to movies, concerts and galleries.

There was also dancing and the canteen provided carefully selected hostesses under the watchful eye of some wonderfully dedicated supervi-sors such as Irma Patterson and Peggy Jennings. There was often a "Paul Jones" to mix everyone up and give the more timid types a chance. Once, when the music stopped, my eyes met those of an extraordinarily beautiful blonde in the opposite corner of the room. There are two distinctly differ-ent versions of what happened next, though the outcome is the same. It was our dance. No doubt the fact we were the tallest man and woman on the floor was part of the attraction. After several sets we retired to the lounge for conversation and coffee. We were soon deeply involved in a discussion of religion which was just entering its most fascinating stage at closing time. For understandable reasons, the girls were not allowed to meet servicemen outside, but we decided that the seriousness of the subject justified an exception and agreed to continue the debate over hot chocolate.

We met at Diana Sweets Tea Room at Queen and Yonge Streets. Ellen Jean Valentine Ralph was both surprised and delighted to find that I had a car, an exception in those days. I learned that the name "Valentine" had been a last minute addition when, like Jack Benny, she had been born on the 14th of February. When it was time to leave, I insisted it would be less than gallant not to drive her home, and she reluctantly agreed.

"Go along College to Bay," she suggested, "then north on Bay to Dupont." At that point she directed me under the railway bridge and "along Davenport Road to Christie." Then it was "north on Christie to Tyrrel. Our house is number 62, first from the corner," she said.

I couldn't believe my ears! Had she just told me where we were going I could have driven there with my eyes shut. Ellen lived next door to the Chute residence where I had stayed every time I had been in Toronto overnight since my childhood. She was the proverbial "girl next door," although I had never before set eyes on her. The scene was reminiscent of a movie where credulity is stretched by a far-fetched coincidence. At least it was more than reason enough to meet again.

It was a casual relationship, at least at first. I don't think either one of us took it very seriously, which was just fine because, after all, we were both engaged to someone else. As the weeks rolled by there was just sufficient spark to light a small fire and keep us coming back for more. We would meet at the Active Service Canteen where we could talk and dance. Ellen danced beautifully and this proved to be an irresistible attraction. When we were together it was like putting on a new pair of gloves and finding they fit perfectly.

Our date on the 11th of December was probably our most memorable. It was the evening of the legendary 20-inch snowstorm and getting from Tyrell Avenue to Loew's Theatre on Bay Street, required considerable ingenuity. Secondly, Ellen's father, Henry, was furious. A long-time Regimental Quarter-Master Sergeant with the 48th Highlanders, "Harry" Ralph thought that if the storm had been bad enough to keep his daughter from going to work at R.L. Crain Ltd., it was certainly bad enough to prevent her from going out with me.

The next day I finally got my discharge from the RCAF. It was a classic case of now you see it, now you don't. I was handed my release with one hand, and my draft call with the other. An editorial in *Torch*, the Canadian Corps Association magazine, said perfectly: "Airmen treated as zombies."[4] I wasn't interested in going back into industry, so I resolved the question by taking the holiday off and then joining the army, where I was assigned to the Royal Canadian Artillery (mobile) because my mathematics was above average. Shortly thereafter, I was posted to "C" Troop, "D" Medium Battery, Canadian Army Training Corps at Camp Petawawa, on the Ottawa River.

The whole process was so absurd that I didn't know whether to laugh or cry. It involved new documentation and new "dog tag". Then there was drill, which was learning to march. When I mentioned that I was fully trained in the art of forming threes, I was told "that was Air Force drill." Next was gas drill. The mask was the same but the technique was just different enough that previous experience could be contemptuously dismissed as "Air Force gas drill." The final indignity occurred when a doctor came by and ordered, "Roll up your sleeve." The fact that I was already fully immunized brought a slightly scornful, "Ah yes, but those were air force shots (inoculations)."

I can't say that my service experience was a significant factor in my decision as defence minister years later to unify the three forces but it must have had an effect on the subconscious. It was of no real import that airmen slept between sheets and soldiers didn't. These differences were superficialities. But I did resent the fact that soldiers were treated as second or third-class citizens. And I abhorred the reality that, although the army overseas was desperate for reinforcements, grown men indulged in silly games that wasted valuable time. There was little effective cooperation between the services when each concentrated almost exclusively on its own interests.

In Petawawa, once again due to my height, I was chosen as marker (the man on the left side of the front row who sets the pace for the troop) and it wasn't long before I was given the acting rank of Lance Bombardier. H.A. White of Kapuskasing, was given the other slot of our "C" troop. We each got 10 cents a day additional pay. One of my extra duties was an occasional stint in the orderly room where a notation on my file suggested "make good officer." Days later, an order came from Ottawa directing that no further officer candidates would be accepted from the ranks. The next time anyone saw my file the original notation had been erased and replaced by "make a good NCO," (non-commissioned officer.)

Meanwhile, I exchanged letters with Ellen, who was one of the most talented correspondents I have ever known. Her letters were always bright, witty and often provocative. I enjoyed them immensely and, about Easter, we agreed to marry even though she insisted the idea was a little bit insane. What made it even more insane was that we were both engaged to someone else. That meant we had to go through the excruciatingly difficult task of writing our "Dear John" letters with the knowledge that we were breaking other people's hearts. Looking back I am convinced that it was only a bit of divine intervention that kept our plan from unravelling.

Of course, soldiers couldn't marry without permission, so Ellen got a splendid letter of reference from Ivor Lewis, her sister Vida Watson's husband's uncle, who was a director of the T. Eaton Company. Ivor was best remembered for sculpting the well-known statue of Timothy Eaton. Armed with such impeccable credentials, Colonel K.H. Tremain was quick to grant us permission and we were married June 1, 1945 at St. Columba's United Church, on St. Clair Avenue in Toronto.

We spent the night at the first class Royal York Hotel followed by a couple of days in Niagara Falls and then a few more days in Cleveland with relatives. On route, I gave the bride some driving lessons, a practice that I would not recommend for honeymooners. We returned via Waterford where we were given an old fashioned charivari, that delightfully grotesque ritual when neighbors wait until you should be in bed and then show up with a barrage of shotguns, tooting horns, and banging washtubs, staying until you reward them with cake, coffee and ice cream. We were equally amused to learn that the party lines, where several families share a telephone line, had been buzzing with busybodies wondering aloud if there was "any news," an unsubtle and totally unwarranted inference that our hasty marriage was in some degree influenced by the exigencies of family planning. It was in fact two years before our first child was born.

CHAPTER FOUR

PREPARING FOR POLITICS

After, Germany surrendered, and the war in Europe was over, we were asked to volunteer for service in the Pacific. My buddy L.B. White agreed, was promoted to sergeant and sent to Florida for further training. I refused on a point of principle. After volunteering for active service twice, once with the air force and once with the army, I felt that any government worth its salt should just send its manpower where they were required and I found it downright insulting to be asked to go through the ritual of volunteering yet a third time.

Standing on principle is not without its cost and, for me, it meant losing my only stripe and being subjected to authentic zombie-type treatment for the balance of my time in uniform. I was posted to Alberta to guard prisoners of war and to witness more weird military practices. I had applied for an audition with the Army Show and when the opportunity finally caught up with me, the commanding officer wouldn't let me go because losing one more man from the nominal roll would drop his rank from colonel to lieutenant colonel. An experience at another base was even more bizarre. An order was posted for two soldiers to take a short course in aeronautical engineering in order to act as liaison with the RCAF. Naturally, I applied. One morning our parade commander asked for two volunteers to step forward without giving any indication of what they would be volunteering for. After some hesitation, two men finally did and were promptly advised that they were being sent on the course for liaison with the Air Force. Incredible! The only plus was a first, wide-eyed glimpse of Western Canada including a weekend trip across the mountains to Vancouver at its glorious sunny best.

I applied for farm leave which, when granted, gave me the advantage of being close to my wife and permitted some serious thought about the future. In November, I answered an advertisement for baritone soloist at Parkdale United Church in Toronto and landed the job. The choirmaster and organist, Roberts (Bobs) and Kay Williams, were a husband and wife team who were both good musicians and wonderful fun. Unlike many of their peers, they were able to achieve results with good humor and it was double good fortune to work for them and get paid for it. The other members of the quartet were equally congenial and it was the Parkdale connection that launched my long association with the United Church of Canada, which had been Ellen's church since birth.

I had decided to go to university to broaden my education, which had been too narrowly technical. That meant settling in Toronto where available housing of any kind was virtually non-existent. Ellen and I ploughed through the rental ads every day and scoured the city for leads but always to no avail. Veterans had to double up with relatives or settle for life in attics or basements.

In desperation, we considered the idea of buying a store with an apartment overhead and spent many evenings looking for opportunities with appropriate accommodation. Father had agreed to help with the financing, which gave us a little flexibility. Finally, we settled on Mari-Jane Fashions, a ladies ready-to-wear shop on the south side of Bloor Street West between Dufferin and Brock. It included a nice three-bedroom apartment with a separate entrance. We overpaid, of course, due to our inexperience. Still, we might not have been able to do much better as good leases were hard to come by.

We were lucky to have a roof over our heads by the time I got my discharge from the army in April 1946. But life was not all a bowl of cherries. We had neither an ice box nor a refrigerator, and storing some ham in the bread box produced an early miracle of multiplying maggots. Ellen's washing machine was a tub with a scrub-board and brush. On the positive side, she got her clothes wholesale and enjoyed the responsibility of buying garments and working in the store. She was blessed by the fact that Rae Anger, an experienced saleslady who had worked for the previous owner, agreed to stay and teach us the tricks of an extremely competitive business.

In the summer of 1946, Ed Whittaker, who was the tenor at Parkdale United Church, and I, joined the stock company at the Royal Alexandra Theatre where we sang in popular Broadway perennials such as *The Chocolate Soldier* and *New Moon*. After rehearsal, or a performance, we often took Ellen and Ed's wife, Eileen, to Lichee Garden to replenish our calories with fantastic Chinese food.

By the fall, I was ready to enrol at the University of Toronto. The subjects I chose were those I considered essential to a proper balance. English was a must, as were political science and economics. Psychology sounded intriguing as a balance to physics and mathematics.

On June 26, 1947, our first child, Mary Elizabeth, was born. As a portent of things to come, I couldn't be found at the critical time, so Ellen had to take a taxi to the hospital. She was joined by her sister-in-law, Betty Ralph, a nurse who volunteered to help. Thank goodness, because as things turned out she was desperately needed to assist with some tricky complications. When it was all over Betty called to say a baby daughter had arrived safely and both mother and daughter were doing well. I made a beeline for the hospital and experienced that indescribably beautiful moment when heaven and earth are in perfect tune.

A few days later, I got a summons for going through a red light that I didn't recall, and so I decided to appear in court to object. When the magistrate asked for my side of the story I simply said: "It was the Sunday morning my daughter was born. I was on my way to the hospital and I have no recollection of going through a red light," which was the truth. "No, you wouldn't have, case dismissed," he ordered with unusual compassion.

In addition to attending university, I studied voice. My teacher was Ernesto Vinci, an Italian-born medical doctor whose true love was music. Accepting me was a unique act of kindness on Dr. Vinci's part. I candidly explained that my primary interest in life was politics and singing was just a hobby. He must have been intrigued because he made an exception to his strict rule that only serious students of music were eligible. By the fall of 1947, he thought my voice showed sufficient promise that I should join the opera school that Dr. Arnold Walters had set up as a corps of singers for an opera company he hoped would be established in Toronto. Dr. Vinci's recommendation was enough to get me in.

That November, when we were rehearsing the "Prisoners' Chorus" from *Fidelio*, the phone rang. Virginia (Ginny) Lippert answered and then whispered something in conductor Nicholas Goldschmidt's ear without him losing a beat. When we finished, "Niki," as everyone called him, said the message had been for me to call home but I had to use the phone in the hall. When I dialled the line was busy, and after repeated attempts I called Ellen's sister, Lorna Holmes, to ask if she knew what it was all about. "Yes," she said, "you had better get home pretty darn quick because your place is on fire."

By the time I got there, it was all over. Ellen and the baby had escaped as the flames licked through cracks in the glass risers of the apartment stairs. They probably owed their lives to Jacob Gold, our Jewish *basso profundo* cantor neighbor, who persisted in banging on the door when Ellen, who was feeding Mary Elizabeth, believed it was just a salesman or perhaps the paper boy. The store was a shambles, a stinking, charred, water-soaked mess. One sleeve had been burned off every dress, suit and coat in stock when the flames roared around the bins.

Needless to say the extra workload, in the middle of the school year, ended my operatic connection. The next few months were sheer hell. The fire had come at the worst possible time – after the Christmas stock had arrived but before the Christmas rush – and we were only 40 percent insured. The adjuster bent over backward to help, but it was still a Herculean struggle rebuilding the store while redecorating and refurbishing the apartment, which had been almost completely gutted.

In accord with the maxim that it never rains but it pours, everything seemed to go wrong at once. Soon after the fire forced us to move in with

Ellen's parents, her father became ill and died. Then Betty Ralph, our angel nurse in white, wrecked my car. But a kind man who was good enough to give me a lift when I was hitchhiking to school reminded me that no one is ever so badly off that there aren't others who are worse off. It was a bit of homespun philosophy that has stuck with me all of my life.

The strain of re-opening the business, in addition to raising a family, studying music and singing professionally, effectively prevented me from making much contribution to university life, one of my few regrets. It was only in my final year that I felt free to join the Hart House Glee Club. Apart from that, and membership in the Liberal club, it would have been a near wipe-out except for one unexpected opportunity. The Students Administrative Council's final concert at Convocation Hall included Gabriel Fauré's *Requiem* sung by the All-Varsity Mixed Chorus with orchestra. The baritone soloist, John Blair, bowed out at the last moment and I was asked to pitch in, which I did with reluctance because I was totally unfamiliar with the work. Reviewing the concert in *The Telegram* the following day, Rose Macdonald noted, "Paul Hellyer undertook the assignment with three days' notice and brought to it a voice of rich, smooth quality and sang with dignity. Given more adequate time for preparation, his performance indubitably would have had an even greater confidence."[1] In *The Globe and Mail*, Court Stone reported, "Baritone solos were sung by John Blair,"[2] an early hint of the reliability of some newspaper coverage.

SEEKING A LIBERAL PARTY NOMINATION

Superimposed on all other activity that year was my relentless pursuit of my "Holy Grail," a Liberal nomination for the 1949 federal general election.

Although I had been interested in politics at a very young age, I never dreamed of getting involved so early in my life until I studied economics at the University of Toronto. It was the subject that really grabbed my attention. I was a child of the Great Depression and saw poverty in its rawest form. But I had always wondered why depressions were necessary.

So when I got the opportunity I asked my economics professors if recessions and depressions were really necessary. I was dismayed by their response. In effect they were an intrinsic part of a cyclical system. All further discussion of why the system was cyclical ran into a brick wall of resistance. I refused to accept such a morbid "theology" and decided to do my own analysis.

Influenced by the work of the great Yale professor, Irving Fisher, and his "money equation," I was soon convinced that the Great Depression reflected the ultimate folly of our entrenched establishment. It didn't need to happen. So, by extension, there had never been a recession or depression that needed to happen. They had all been monetary phenomena caused by erratic changes in the rate of expansion of the money supply, a practice subject to manipulation by highly leveraged banks and bankers.

I felt as if I had been called to try and do something about this phenomenon that sometimes benefited the banks, especially the large ones, but were a curse on ordinary people. When my professors began to predict another depression, with a capital D, for 1950 I felt compelled to try and do something about it. For me, that meant trying to get elected to the House of Commons. When I told my Liberal friends that I wanted to run for Parliament it was taken as something of a joke. But they were very polite and provided the names of key people I should meet with. I would make an appointment and spend the best part of an evening pouring my heart out on the twin subjects of housing and Canada's future. I always received a sympathetic hearing which ended by being told that I was talking to the wrong person. It was someone else that I should see.

After numerous appointments, the president of the Parkdale Riding Association levelled with me and explained the political facts of life. Parkdale was already taken. The candidate would be Lt. Col. John W.G. Hunter who was "boss" McNish's hand-picked choice, and no further search was being considered. McNish was the voice of Ottawa in Toronto.

I thanked the president for his candor, and as we parted, and very much as an afterthought, he suggested that if I was really interested in running I should try in my own riding of Davenport. It was a better bet than pursuing an unwanted courtship.

Parkdale Riding No: Davenport Maybe

Davenport was my riding? That was news to me. The riding maps were misleading, but a check with the returning officer confirmed that we were indeed in Davenport. One ballgame was over before the end of the first inning, but here I was contemplating another one. The problem was that all the postwar roots I had put down in my adopted city were in Parkdale. The choir job had been the focus of both our church and social activity. A move to Davenport meant pulling up those roots and starting all over again. There was no other choice.

Ellen, good scout that she was, agreed. So I gave up my very enjoyable soloist job and we set out to look for a new church home. We attended a service at Westmoreland United one evening when the choir sang the anthem *a cappella*. It was excellent, so we decided to look no further. After the service I had a chat with the choirmaster Alice Wilson. I was quite candid about my reasons for being there but she assured me I would be welcome in her choir. It was the beginning of a long and warm association. What we didn't know was that we had been inducted into a bastion of conservatism. There were only six Liberals in the whole congregation.

When we applied for membership in the Davenport Liberal Association there was no immediate response. Unlike the situation in Parkdale, we had no friends in the inner circle and the executive was hyper-suspicious. We later learned that after they made inquiries in Parkdale and were reassured, we received our cards. Only days later the association held its annual meeting when, to my astonishment, I was nominated and elected treasurer to become the custodian of a bank book showing a credit balance of $5.83. Need I say that something is better than nothing?

Mrs. O.H. Dunn was re-elected as president, apparently for the umpteenth time. A tall, robust woman of middle years, she was the leader of a group of Irish Catholic ladies who were the heart of the association. It isn't really unkind to say that they appeared to be more interested in controlling the paid jobs as enumerators, deputy returning officers and revision officers at election time than they were in electing candidates. After all, Davenport was one of the most Tory of Toronto ridings and the results were always a foregone conclusion. The thought of electing a Liberal had never seriously entered their minds.

When it became obvious that I was seeking the Liberal nomination the same game I had played in Parkdale began anew. Mrs. Dunn insisted that the choice was not one for the association alone. She and the executive had to be guided from "downtown" and when my name was mentioned to boss McNish the reception had been something less than wild enthusiasm. Despite this, discreet inquiries disclosed that the party brass really had no one else in mind. Carrying the Liberal banner in Davenport was not a prize to be coveted.

My quest was frustrating to the point of exasperation. Especially as the process consumed hundreds of hours of valuable time that friends and family thought might be more usefully spent in the library studying for my final exams. Unwilling to give up, I turned in desperation to the returning officer, William S. Rosen, for advice.

Rosen was very proper and explained that once appointed as returning officer he had to be strictly non-partisan. Nevertheless, as a friend, he would be happy to give me some helpful hints. First and foremost, he explained, Mrs. Dunn was the key, notwithstanding the contrary impression she had given me. What she said would carry the day with the executive that she controlled. Her reluctance to consider me, he added, was probably due to some well-known hang-ups. As far as she was concerned I was just a college student, and she was not convinced that I could fight a respectable campaign.

Rosen advised me to see Mrs. Dunn again in order to review developments and bring her up-to-date. He then recited word-for-word what I should say. I was to tell her that some of my business friends had been canvassed and that I was convinced we could raise enough money to put on an effective campaign. Due to her wide experience and intimate knowledge of the riding I would like her to act as my campaign manager, and although she would prefer no doubt to do this on a voluntary basis, I appreciated that she was a widow of modest means and would therefore like her permission to reimburse her for out-of-pocket expenses to the extent of $50 a week, with an equal amount as bonus should we win. "At that point," said Rosen, "she will throw up her hands in horror, but then she will agree with your assessment and accept your generous offer."

I phoned Mrs. Dunn for an appointment and memorized my lines like an actor rehearsing for a one-act play. When we met, I followed the script precisely and the results were as Rosen predicted, including raising her hands in objection, right on cue. From that moment on there was no further question. I was to be the candidate. I phoned my father at the farm to tell him about the breakthrough and that I expected to be the Liberal candidate in Davenport. His response was forthright: "You run in Toronto! You crazy?" That was the end of the conversation.

A couple of days later Doug McNish phoned to see if we could meet. We did and he said he understood that I was interested in Davenport, sounding as though the news had just recently come to his attention. During the brief interrogation, Doug was not a man of many words; he asked how many local organizations I belonged to, presumably those such as the Kiwanis, YMCA, and Bloor Businessmen Men's genre. "Sufficient," I replied quickly. It was a good thing he didn't continue with the cross-examination. Although my response turned out to be literally true, a more precise answer, at the time, would have been "none." I doubt that there were 50 people in the riding who knew my name.

McNish admitted that I would be an acceptable candidate. He was, after all, a realist and withdrew his opposition once he realized that Mrs. Dunn was in my corner and that I was going to be the candidate with or without his blessing. He had taken the precaution, as I learned months later, of phoning Senator William H. Taylor of Norfolk County, who was well acquainted with my family. Taylor confirmed that the Hellyers hadn't stolen any sheep and that there were no skeletons in the closet that would be likely to embarrass the party. Thus reassured, McNish adopted me as his own and reported to Ottawa that his flock of candidates included a bright, young, sacrificial lamb for Davenport. The last official hurdle was over and the subsequent vote was just a formality, thanks to Mrs. Dunn.

THE JUNE 27, 1949 ELECTION

By that time the election, called for June 27, 1949, was well underway and only five of the 13 weeks remained to execute "mission impossible." The prelude had been a hectic period that included those dreaded final exams, and here I was up to my ears in an election campaign before the results were in. I knew that the studies had suffered, and I had nightmares about flunking, but I didn't. My luck held and the only day off during the entire campaign was graduation day.

Other obstacles were equally formidable. There was no organization to speak of. Mrs. Dunn and her ladies staffed the committee room but much of their energy was consumed lining up polling places, deputy returning officers, and so on. The ranks of the old-time Liberal volunteers were so thin that I only heard from one male member of the association from nomination night until after the election results were in.

Getting my name known, "name identification" as it is called in the trade, was a major problem. In those days there was no party affiliation on the ballots so voters had to know who they wanted to vote for by name. We took on the challenge with vigor, the aim was saturation coverage.

Sports fans attending football games at Lansdowne Park were exposed to the name Hellyer on their way in, during the game and on their way out. Sound trucks blared my name both going and coming; balloons and blotters, the rage of that long by-gone era, were handed out as they entered; and Leavens Bros. flew "VOTE HELLYER" banners back and forth across the sky.

Not everyone followed football, however, so we had to take the message into people's homes. I couldn't do much canvassing personally when saddled with the jobs of publicity chairman, organization chairman and finance chairman. So I hired three university students to do some of the legwork. Terry Doidge, Ray Tower and Louis Hertzman did a thorough door-to-door canvass, and this was several years before Stephen Lewis was credited with inventing the idea. They faithfully reported the reactions they were getting and it appeared that we were making progress, but that there was still a considerable gulf between our level of support and the victory we hoped for. With nowhere in particular to turn for help, I decided to lock myself in a room for a couple of days and think the problem through.

I knew that would put Mrs. Dunn into a big flap. "Where is he?" she repeated constantly to anyone who would listen. Her dilemma was real. How does a campaign manager explain a candidate who disappears? I sympathized, but something more had to be done and there was no evidence that she would come up with anything positive. She had adamantly opposed the Leavens aerial banner, for example, on the grounds that the only other person she knew who had used one had lost. So I would lose. Nor did she like the idea of hiring university students to knock on doors. She didn't say so directly but I suspected the real objection was that they were being paid and she thought if there was any more money to be passed around it should be reserved for some of the faithful members of the executive. Whatever the reason, she invariably reacted negatively to the projects I considered vital, so my conscience gave me the green light for time out to think.

I started leafing through every book that might be relevant. Perhaps the experience of well-known politicians should have offered some clues but none were apparent. Eventually, I picked up an introduction to psychology where, in bold relief, I was reminded that an appeal to the emotions was undeniably more powerful than an appeal to the intellect. That was it! Until then the campaign had been a rather straightforward effort to publicize my name, set out policy, and identify likely supporters. What was needed was a good tug at the heartstrings. I drafted the following letter to voters from our two- year-old daughter:

Wednesday, June 22, 1949

Dear Friends of Davenport:

I am writing to you on behalf of the children of this riding. Many of them, like me, have no garden to play in – no grass, no trees, no flowers. Others don't even have a place to live! That's why my daddy is so interested in housing – that's why he has spent the last three years in housing research. Last summer he travelled all over the country, at his own expense, visiting housing projects, finding out the best and soundest way to get houses built for all the people in Canada who need them! These houses would have recreation rooms in the basement and gardens with grass and trees and flowers, and behind this a common playground – everything for children. If these houses are built and financed according to the plan (even at present prices) they could be purchased by anyone on a monthly payment basis and without a subsidy – not one cent of extra taxes. It is a wonderful plan which can be achieved only by a young man with boundless energy.

Daddy is the only candidate in Davenport who would have a chance to do anything about housing, if elected, because he is the only one who would be a member of the Government. He has worked hard in an all out effort to be given the opportunity to help us children. We can count on my daddy and I know we can count on you to help.

Yours for a better Canada,
Mary Elizabeth Hellyer

The next step was to print the letter bearing Mary Elizabeth's picture, a blotter listing my seven-point platform alongside a family photo and the standard "YOU VOTE AT …" cards giving the polling subdivision number and the address of the polling place. The three pieces would be stuffed in individually addressed and stamped envelopes to be mailed first-class. There would be no indication on the outside of the envelope that it contained election material so people would be sure to open it, one of the tricks of the trade that I had learned in promoting our annual sales in the dress business.

Mrs. Dunn was apoplectic when she heard about the first-class postage. The thought of spending almost a thousand dollars for three-cent stamps, the largest single item in the campaign, by far, was more than she could bear. It was never done! She groped for words to describe the enormity of the extravagance. Insult was then piled on injury when her volunteers were asked to help address the envelopes and lick the stamps.

From her perspective, the president's reaction was quite legitimate. She knew that the party had only given us $1,500 for the whole campaign and there would be no more. "We simply do not have that kind of money," McNish had assured me when I argued that we were entitled to at least double that amount. It was my first exposure to the kind of off-white lies that politicians tell, especially to the uninitiated. The truth, as experienced partisans well know, is that the big money is reserved for the sure and marginal ridings. The amount is scaled down to a token minimum for the "write-offs," of which Davenport was one.

My perspective was a pole apart from that of Mrs. Dunn. I wasn't sophisticated enough to understand that Davenport couldn't be won. I was already deeply in the red for a campaign that wasn't quite good enough, and obviously in need of a powerful last minute boost. The gambler's instinct inherited from my father took over and I concluded that I might as well be hung for a sheep as a lamb.

By Thursday, June 23rd, just four days before polling day, the envelopes were all stuffed and ready to go. I took them to the post office personally, to make sure that they didn't get lost in the shuffle. They were all delivered the following day, the last possible day to be of any effect. The prompt service, which was pretty well taken for granted at that time, was much appreciated.

The letter did its intended job. When Tower, Doidge and Hertzman returned from their canvassing Friday night they reported a significant, almost dramatic improvement in the electoral climate. The upbeat mood continued into Saturday and brought a fresh flurry of activity at headquarters. It was timely too, because that was the day the Ontario campaign chairman, Col. Harry Hamilton of Sault Ste. Marie, dropped by for the usual, one-time, perfunctory courtesy call. He was sufficiently impressed that he went back to headquarters, said we would lose, but that we had put on such a good show the party should reward us with another $1,000. That sum was delivered in cash, later in the day, to be available on Monday.

On Sunday there was nothing further that could be done to influence voters, but we still had work to do. We had no organization for election day. Davenport Liberals had never had one so no one had given the question much thought until then. Especially when there were so many other urgent things to do. We opted for a crash project and called in friends and relatives who rallied magnificently to our aid. Ellen's brother, Al Ralph, manned the phone while his wife, Betty, ran a continuous coffee and refreshment service for the dozen or so people involved. As each of us thought of someone who might help we handed the name to Al to do the recruiting. The longest list came from George Grant, a theological student at St. Augustine's Seminary, who had dozens of friends in St. Anthony's Parish. He even drafted several of his fellow seminarians. It was a high-pressure, non-stop operation and by midnight we had enough people to man about 70 percent of the polls both inside as scrutineers, and outside as poll captains to get the vote out.

Election day I bowed to custom and visited a representative cross-section of polling stations. The turnout, I was told, was about normal for general elections. Later, I went to our tiny campaign office on Dupont Street, near Dufferin, to wait for the results to come in. Someone reported that gamblers at the local pub, allegedly dry that day, were giving odds of 15 to one against me.

June 27, 1949, Election Day

When the polls closed the tension soared. Those 20 minutes or so waiting for the phones to ring, put my stomach in tighter knots than at any other time from the outset of the campaign. When the results began coming in it soon became obvious that we were actually in the running, so the tension continued unabated. When it was all over I had won by 955 votes. Hellyer (L) 11,431; MacNichol (PC) 10,476; Archer (CCF) 7,366. Davenport had elected a Liberal for the first time since Canada's Confederation in 1867.

Pandemonium broke loose and it was congratulations and embraces all around. In thanking my workers, I gave generous credit to Mrs. Dunn and her tiny band of stalwarts for pulling it off. After all, it wouldn't have been possible without them and suddenly we were just one big happy family. Any differences there might have been disappeared into the woodwork.

We adjourned to our Bloor Street apartment for cakes, cokes and sandwiches leaving only a sentry to direct the "slow counters" to join us immediately after they reported in from their polling stations. The press, who hadn't counted on a call at our headquarters, elbowed their way through the crowd for interviews and pictures. Ellen and I were feeling the kind of pure, unadulterated joy that one experiences rarely in a lifetime.

A spontaneous parade was organized. Cars were decorated with surplus balloons and slightly used veranda signs and we were driven around the riding in a maroon convertible, waving and acknowledging the congratulations of bystanders who appeared magically caught up in the enchantment of the moment.

After the election, I got a call from Sen. Peter Campbell, King's Counsel, who was the Liberal Party "bag man" for English Canada. The senator was so delighted by my win that he said he was going to do what parties never did and something he, personally, had never done before. He was sending me a cheque for $2,000 to assist with the deficit. So the party that "didn't have that kind of money" had upped the ante from the initial $1,500 to a total of $4,500, leaving me with a shortfall of less than $2,000.

The story would be incomplete if I didn't point out that I was elected in a Liberal sweep. Prime Minister Louis St. Laurent was a very popular father figure and much of my ride was on his coat tails. And from behind, I got a boost from the Conservative leader George Drew's unpopularity. Unlike his early days in Ontario politics when he was more of a populist, he was then perceived as a cold and arrogant autocrat, not a man of the people. This combined pull and shove had elected 190 Liberals nationally including seven in Toronto, six more than ever before, and I was one of them.

Dave Croll was expected to win big in Spadina. J.W.G. "Jake" Hunter, Lionel Conacher, and A.J.P. "Pat" Cameron were considered "possibles" in Parkdale, Trinity and High Park respectively. Charlie Henry had been a long shot in Rosedale and James Rooney won, despite McNish's disapproval, in St. Paul's. Winning in Davenport was considered "mission impossible" but we won anyway. In retrospect it appears to have been a minor miracle. There is no doubt in my mind that it was the letter signed by Mary Elizabeth that put us over the top. She received a number of replies and one, in particular, said it most poignantly. "Yes, Mary Elizabeth, after receiving your letter I voted for your daddy." Signed, "An old Turncoat." He couldn't have been the only one or the numbers wouldn't have turned out the way they did.

CHAPTER FIVE

LEARNING THE INS
AND OUTS OF POLITICS

When the First Session of the Twenty-First Parliament began in September 1949, I checked into Ottawa's Lord Elgin Hotel because the price was right. It had a special deal arranged by one of the Liberal owners under which Members of Parliament paid only $2.50 a night. That meant that commuters like me only had to pay $10.00 a week. The more affluent MPs bunked at the Chateau Laurier which charged $4.50 daily, a sizable sum in an era when politics was not considered a full-time occupation and the $4,000 sessional indemnity wasn't enough to live on.

The workings of Parliament put me on a fast learning curve as I experienced both the good aspects and the limitations of life in this new venue.

I knew the Parliament buildings from previous visits to Ottawa but my first walk up "The Hill" as an MP was an especially proud one. Somehow the stately Gothic structures looked even more magnificent and it was a thrill to see the flag at the top of the Peace Tower fluttering bravely against the northern sky. The joy of that walk was a great beginning to my parliamentary career.

But when I entered the Centre Block, I was directed to Room 613. There the dawn of reality came quickly. No one told me what to do and, worse, no one seemed to care. Instead of being a "Mr. Somebody" I was just a very, very small cog in a big impersonal machine. Backbenchers were stacked two to an office which was about the size of a small bedroom.

My room-mate was Ralph Campney, King's Counsel, the newly elected MP for Vancouver Centre, and the doubling up must have been quite an adjustment for him. Campney had served as one of Prime Minister Mackenzie King's secretaries and, when elected, was the senior partner in one of Vancouver's largest and most prestigious law firms. This was the beginning of a long and comfortable relationship that continued through the years as my footsteps followed his up the rungs of National Defence.

Being with Ralph was a stroke of luck because he knew Ottawa well from his days with the former prime minister. Frequent visitors to our office included H.R. MacMillan, the lumber baron, Ralph's partner Jack Cline, who became chief executive officer of H.R.'s company years later after serving as a B.C. Superior Court Justice, and also John Connolly, a prominent Ottawa lawyer and Liberal, who had been one of Ralph's friends from the days when they both worked in political offices. Connolly, one of the most gentle and thoughtful men I have ever met in public life, also became my friend.

Being in Parliament gave me opportunity to be in the presence of Louis St. Laurent, C.D. Howe, and James Gardiner, who were members of both His Majesty's Canadian and U.K. Privy Councils. Other household names included Douglas Abbott, Brooke Claxton, Lionel Chevrier, Paul Martin Sr. and Stuart Garson. Of them all it was the PM for whom I had the greatest affection. "Uncle Louis" was another of the nicest, kindest, most gentle and thoughtful of the great men I have known. He was truly of the old school and I was proud to be associated with him and his many accomplishments. Of these three deserve special mention.

The Prime Minister and his Minister of External Affairs, Lester B. Pearson, were leading proponents of the North Atlantic Treaty Organization (NATO), which was primarily responsible for maintaining peace in Europe for decades following World War II. Newfoundland joined Canada as its tenth province in 1949 following negotiations between Prime Minister St. Laurent and Joey Smallwood, the Premier of Newfoundland and Labrador. And later the Canadian PM was ultimately responsible for universal hospital care, the precursor of Medicare first introduced in Saskatchewan by Tommy Douglas.

BACKBENCHERS HAVE LITTLE INFLUENCE ON POLICY

My limitations were not immediately obvious but I soon learned what some of them were. Although I was a backbencher in the purest sense of the word, my first seat in the House of Commons was in the front row on the government side in a section called "Little Chicago." But it was so far from Mr. Speaker that binoculars would have been helpful.

For the first two sessions I seldom spoke in the Commons. It made sense to listen for a while and find out what my seniors were saying. Equally compelling, I couldn't catch the Speaker's eye. That is an euphemism for the government's reluctance to let backbenchers sound off and hold up passage of its legislation – especially those of us who were the most junior. So, even when the Whip allowed my name to be put on the Speaker's list, the debate would invariably end before I made it to the top of the list. At first, the roadblock was accepted with good humor but it soon became a standing joke that whenever I prepared speeches, they wound up in a special drawer that soon became filled with them.

One of the first rules of politics is that newly elected MPs seldom have any influence on policy, and that was especially true in the case of finan-

40

cial policy. Still, in my case, it was impossible to forget the reason I had made such a terrific effort to get elected. Therefore I would raise the subject and state my concern to anyone who would listen. The response of my colleague Pat Cameron, MP for Toronto High Park was typical. "Young man, you don't remember the Great Depression," he explained, not unkindly, but in a way that said anyone my age wouldn't understand what made the world go 'round. I did remember the Great Depression very well, and that was the powerful memory that became my driving motive; however, I was learning that in the realm of economics everyone is an expert and I had not yet earned the right to have a voice.

My luck at influencing people outside the House had been equally unimpressive. All Toronto MPs were invited to be present on 9 September, 1949, when the first pile was to be driven to begin construction on the Yonge Street subway line. It was an historic event followed by a reception and harbor cruise aboard the ferry Sam McBride. I spent quite a while in the wheelhouse badgering the Toronto Transit Commission (TTC) Chairman W.C. McBrien about extending the line farther north than Eglinton, perhaps to Wilson Avenue. The Yonge line was an experiment, he told me, and there were no plans for extensions at that stage.

Stymied on that front, I suggested buying the right-of-way before land prices rose further, so it would be available later when required. Again, the answer was no, and with a firmness proportionate to my lack of sensitivity in raising questions of that sort on a day of celebration. No doubt it was stupid of me to take advantage of that occasion but I didn't often have an opportunity to talk to the chairman. In any event his close-mindedness cost the taxpayers a pretty penny, because when the Yonge line was extended the TTC paid as much as $250,000 an acre for land that could have been bought, in 1949, for less than $400.

I continued to learn that no matter how good your ideas might be, it is very difficult to convince those in power to listen.

In looking back on the positive aspects of being in the Parliament, I immediately recall the friendships that developed with other backbenchers. Some of these freshmen included my Toronto colleague Jake Hunter, Johnny James of Bowmanville, Harry Cavers of St. Catharines, and Colin Bennett, the MP for Grey North.

It was Bennett, the small town Meaford lawyer, who became my closest confidante and friend. This was more than a bit ironic because, as a former Group Captain (Colonel), he was the highest ranking RCAF veteran in the Commons and, Leading Aircraftsman (LAC) Hellyer, the lowest. Colin was a constant kidder and whenever the subject was discussed he would remind everyone within earshot that the promotion from Aircraftsman Second Class (AC2) to LAC had been automatic. On other occasions he referred to me as "junior," because I was the baby of the House. It was a label that stuck until the day I was appointed to the cabinet, when it was dropped as abruptly as it began. Colin insisted that it was no longer appropriate.

Even though I had no voice in Parliament on economic matters I still fussed about the ominous economic clouds and the new depression that had been predicted. Then, suddenly, the Korean War began on June 27, 1950, a year to the day after my election. Fear of an economic downturn quickly abated as the same conservative financiers who lacked the wit to keep the economy afloat in peacetime, "found" the money to ensure that the war effort was adequately financed.

In retrospect, the Korean conflict saw us through the period of greatest economic danger and by the time the armistice was signed the ideas of the great English economist John Maynard Keynes had penetrated the halls of academe. Then, for the first time in more than 150 years since the Industrial Revolution began, the economic textbooks bore some workable relationship with the real world. Although there was another tiny little inflation thundercloud barely visible on the horizon, we were to be spared long enough to enjoy 15 years of unprecedented prosperity when capital and labor both reaped handsome rewards for their inputs.

SPECIAL SESSION OF PARLIAMENT TO END A RAILWAY STRIKE

In the summer of 1950, Parliament was recalled for a special session to settle a railway strike. This led to a comic incident. The announcement ended any hope that Ellen and I had of getting a few days holiday and we were forced to settle for a long weekend at a small rustic tourist resort called Arundel Lodge, in Muskoka, which we had discovered in 1947. We were just nicely settled in when an Ontario Provincial Police (OPP) cruiser arrived on the scene. The face of George Paish, the proprietor, turned ashen. The place wasn't licensed for alcohol but George Paish usually kept a case of beer in the basement in the event thirsty guests arrived at night or on weekends and he had to lend them a few bottles until they could get into Gravenhurst or Bala for some of their own. It was just a convenient customer service, but of borderline legality, and George suspected that some disapproving rat had squealed.

"Do you have a Paul Hellyer registered here?" the constable inquired. The relief on George's face was visible for 50 yards as he pointed in our direction. Our concern vanished when it was explained that the OPP were cooperating with Mr. Speaker in rounding up Ontario MPs. There was no phone at Arundel so they had come to see if we would like a float plane to pick us up and fly us to Ottawa. We thanked the officers for their concern and assured them they could report that we would be arriving in the capital under our own steam.

The drive through Algonquin Park was very pleasant and we arrived in Ottawa on time. The session lasted 10 days and the debate was quite fascinating. It was my first exposure to the pros and cons of legislated settlements, an issue that is about as far from definitive resolution today as it was then.

I had found my second session in the spring of 1950 quite instructive and I managed to put in my two-cents worth on the Alberta Natural Gas Bill extending the pipeline to British Columbia for the ultimate sale of natural gas to the United States. I also spoke about the budget. The special summer session was a new experience, but by the time the third session got underway I was acutely conscious of the repetition. Some MPs made the same speech every time. Stanley Knowles, the veteran MP for Winnipeg North Centre, always spoke on pensions. John Blackmore, of Lethbridge, inevitably explained the intricacies of monetary theory and deplored the international bankers' conspiracy to rob the poor. Several other Western MPs spoke about wheat so often, and for so long, that poems were written about it. This was another lesson on the ineffectiveness of many words that produce no action even when spoken in the most prestigious legislative hall in Canada.

One can only digest so much of anything, whether wheat or codfish, and I noticed my attendance in the House dropping from near 100 percent to 90 and then 80 percent depending on the subject under discussion. My learning curve was falling sharply when it was suddenly revived by an accident of fate that got me into the house building business. I will discuss that challenge in detail in Chapter Seven.

The Coronation of Her Majesty Queen Elizabeth II

Just when a June election in 1953 seemed certain, Her Majesty Queen Elizabeth II announced that she would be officially crowned in Westminster Abbey on the 2nd day of the month. PM St. Laurent wisely decided to postpone the election until after the coronation.

Each Commonwealth country was given a quota of invitations to the Coronation. I had a few dollars in the bank from selling a little bit of ginseng father had grown for me, so Ellen and I decided to put our names on the list. To our surprise, there were more spaces than takers so we got the nod. Needless to say, there were some raised eyebrows when it was learned that we were buzzing off to London when an election was imminent, but the prospects in Davenport had improved dramatically in four years and I was reasonably confident. When I reported my "reading" to Mr. Howe, the minister responsible for Toronto ridings, he replied, "Yes, that's what I hear too." It was the street assessment.

On May 20, 1953, we left Toronto by train for Quebec City. True to form, I was still dictating letters to my secretary, Joan Dool, when I should have been at the station. Mercifully, Ellen had gone ahead to greet well wishers including my entire Senior Bible Class from Westmoreland United

Church. My eleventh hour arrival allowed only seconds for handshakes and kisses to the echo of "all aboard."

Our foursome included my sister Hazel and her husband, John Race, and we all set sail the next day aboard the Cunard Liner *RMS Scythia*. Fellow passengers included the Minister of Labour Milton Gregg, V.C., and his wife. They were on their way to an International Labour Organization meeting in Geneva following a stopover in London for the big event.

The Cumberland Hotel in London which became our home away from home was just opposite Marble Arch and Hyde Park's famous Speaker's Corner. Fellow guests were Canadian and Commonwealth visitors including Ottawa's flamboyant mayor, Charlotte Whitton, replete with flowing scarlet gown and gold chain of office. It was a fantastic scene and almost beyond description. We were indiscriminately rubbing shoulders with Lords and Ladies, barmaids and bootblacks and everyone was in high spirits, especially the Bobbies, whose unfailing good humor bordered on the saintly.

We were privileged to have seats in the Abbey where we could watch the actual ceremony. Ellen looked stunning in an ankle-length turquoise chiffon gown with a veil, which was mandatory in the absence of a tiara. Woolworth's were sold out of tiaras so we had to get by with the next best thing. John and Hazel, well situated in bleachers opposite the Abbey, had a much better overview of the pageantry as guests from four corners of the globe arrived in costumes as varied as their origins. A disadvantage of being inside was sitting still for seven hours. Tiny portable "Johns" were hidden in the rafters but we were too shy to use them and it was a tribute to our youth that we met the test of endurance. It was worth it. The service was reverently majestic against a background of truly magnificent music. Only in Britain would they organize such a truly grand spectacle.[2]

We knew there would be no time for summer holidays when we got home so on the 7th of June we flew to Geneva for three nights at the Hotel de la Paix. Then it was on to Paris for a two-day stopover that provided our first exposure to the fabulous city on the Seine and its wide spectrum of culture ranging from the incomparable Louvre at one extreme to the Place Pigalle and girlie shows at the other. We became acquainted with both, and our stay included a visit to the Sphinx Club where the dancers wore G-strings and tiny stars in strategic locations. Ellen's most vivid memory was of the holes in the soles of the dancers' shoes.

RUSHING HOME FOR THE 1953 ELECTION

By the time we got back to England the election had been called and we had to book the first available flight for home. Our flight on the June 22nd was truly unforgettable. Friends of Ellen's family thought we might be hungry enroute so they insisted that we share "high tea," which in less ambiguous language would have been called dinner including fresh strawberries with clotted cream. Thus fortified, we drove to Heathrow where we said goodbye to John and Hazel and boarded a big Boeing Stratocruiser, which was to the air, what the *Queen Mary* was to the sea.

As soon as we broke through the cloud above London's haze we were engulfed by a glorious sunset, a marvellous backdrop for the eight course champagne feast that we needed about as much as an extra thumb. We nibbled gamely at the gourmet fare, but the real thrill was in the sky. We followed the great circle route past the tip of Iceland where it was a continuous sunset until we reached the Gulf of St. Lawrence and dusk faded into dawn, 14 hours of magnificent ever-changing reds, pinks and purples. It was the first and only time that we have ever witnessed anything like it.

My good and loyal friend George Grant was my campaign manager in 1953. He was ably assisted by most of the 1949 workers as well as a younger group from his circle of associates. My private secretary Marg Bulger played a key role, as did Ron and Elaine Heydon. My PC opponent was Harold McBride. Harold was a stalwart of Westmoreland United Church who must have felt that my 1949 win was an aberration and that given a fresh chance, voters would return to the proper Conservative fold. At the church, everyone was delighted that good friends were opponents in the election and seemed quite oblivious of the inevitable tensions.

When the polls closed, I had won handily, and the St. Laurent majority was still impressive, but reduced from its 1949 peak as had been widely predicted.

THE FIRST SESSION OF THE 22ND PARLIAMENT

In late September, Gordon Graydon, the Tory MP for Peel, died. His funeral was a sad occasion for me. Not only had he been one of the group that met at Murray's Restaurant for cornflakes after the House adjourned at 11:00 p.m., he was a friend. He had given my housing speech a good report in his weekly column, but far beyond that, he was, to the best of my knowledge, the first person to put in a good word with Mr. St. Laurent on my behalf. According to second-hand reports he said: "I know that if he were in our party we would certainly give him the chance to shine and move toward center stage." A compliment like that from someone who has nothing to gain is appreciated and not quickly forgotten.

Gordon's death raised an issue of wider import. After he died, it was alleged that his wife was left destitute, even though the couple had faithfully served their electors and the people of Canada for 18 years. The province of Ontario eventually came to the rescue and gave her a job but the whole episode was deeply disturbing. It was really the catalyst that led to the consideration of pensions for MPs.

A big plus from the 1953 election were the two new Liberal members from the Toronto Metropolitan area. One was Al Hollingworth, an up-and-coming young lawyer from York Centre who defeated the mighty Roy Thomson, whose money and prestige were rejected by the voters. The other was York Scarborough's Frank Enfield, another superb young lawyer genuinely dedicated to public life. Frank, who was as easy to get along with as anyone could be, became my new room-mate. He decided we should both take French lessons and made arrangements with Aline Rattey, a Parliament Hill habitué. The project didn't last long due to the pressures of our parliamentary schedule, but I was eternally grateful to Frank for sparking my interest in Canada's other official language.

THE QUESTION OF A CABINET MINISTER FOR TORONTO

The post-election era saw an intensification of interest in the question of a cabinet minister for Toronto. It was one of the most talked-about issues of the day. Especially when the government rubbed salt in the open wound by appointing two parliamentary assistants for the regions to the east and north-west of Metro my friends, Dr. Fred Robertson of Cobourg and Colin Bennett from Meaford.

David Croll was the obvious choice for Toronto. His qualifications were impressive and included seniority in the House, distinguished wartime service, municipal experience as mayor of Windsor, and cabinet experience in Mitch Hepburn's Ontario government. Croll had earned the respect of his colleagues as well as the press, yet he was still cooling his heels on the backbench after nine years as a Toronto MP.

Any other pretenders to ministerial rank had to be realistic. No one could compete with Croll's credentials. Furthermore, he was the key log in a massive logjam and none of the rest of us had any hope until he was taken care of. Our Toronto caucus met, without Croll, to map out an action plan. We decided to send a joint request to the prime minister recommending that he appoint our senior member. It was a sincere submission because we could not have agreed on anyone else.

Months went by without a reply. Word from my sources was that Mr. St. Laurent was more than willing to name Croll but there were several considerations he had to take into account. One of these was the fact that Ontario already had more ministers than Quebec and the government didn't want to increase the imbalance. At one of the meetings with Toronto MPs, Walter Harris asked if we wanted him to resign to make room for a Toronto minister, his way of emphasizing the dilemma.

An even greater restraint on the PM's freedom of action was opposition from Liberal insiders, including Ontario's most powerful minister, C.D. Howe. Whether Howe's concern was legitimate or not didn't really matter.

He was St. Laurent's senior and most powerful "Anglo" minister and there was no way the PM would overrule him on this issue.

THE PRIME MINISTER'S RETURN FROM HIS WORLDWIDE TRIP

The political scene in Ottawa was never the same after the Prime Minister returned from his gruelling around-the-world trip. He had been well received wherever he went, in London, Paris, Bonn, Karachi, New Delhi, and Tokyo, and earned the title "world statesman," subsequently attributed by his biographer Dale C. Thompson.[1] But lumbering around the globe in the RCAFs C-5 aircraft with its cruising speed of 240 knots, was enough to sap the strength of any man. The trip was a diplomatic success but Uncle Louis came home March 9, 1954, physically and emotionally exhausted from his six gruelling weeks of overcrowded schedules and frequent time changes.

A few days later he rallied for a special dinner given by Liberal senators and members of Parliament in honor of the occasion. The scene was charged with emotion as we presented him with a globe tracing his route and inscribed "…in appreciation of his service to Canada in promoting better understanding and goodwill in the world." In reply he told us that in making the journey, he had tried to convey the message that He who is Our Father in Heaven is indeed "Our Father" to all people the world over, "and that Canada hoped His will would truly be done on Earth as in Heaven, and that mankind, His children all over the world, would be able to arrange their affairs that all could live in peace."[2]

It was a joyful, family party, tailor-made for the Prime Minister and for Madame St. Laurent, who had not accompanied her husband and had missed him terribly while he was away. The program included their favorite French and Irish songs, and I was honored to be one of the entertainers. In the afternoon when Laurie Virr, the Commons treasurer, who accompanied me to the empty parliamentary dining room to rehearse, the waitresses appeared out of nowhere, one-by-one, to lean against the pillars and listen to the music. The scene was a dead ringer of one from a Deanna Durbin movie. It had seemed so phony and contrived when I had seen it on the screen; yet, here it was, re-enacted in real life before my own eyes.

The mood of the dinner ensured an equally warm response but a few days later, Walter Harris took me aside for a little fatherly advice. "Young man," he said, "the time has come for you to make up your mind whether you want to be known as a singer or a politician." The point was well taken and worth pondering.

CHAPTER SIX

WINNING THE PRIZE
BUT LOSING THE WAR

I had never seriously considered pursuing a career in music because I felt my greatest contribution to the general welfare could be made in the political arena. To achieve anything of significance, however, depended on getting promoted to a position where my ideas were more likely to be taken seriously. The key would be a combination of hard work and good luck.

There had been major changes in Cabinet in July and when I had time to reflect on them I realized they had been more profound than they appeared. Three of St. Laurent's most trusted and best-known colleagues, Brooke Claxton, Douglas Abbott, and Lionel Chevrier, had retired to pursue other careers. They were among the Liberal Party's brightest lights and their departure created a major chasm. To fill the void, Walter Harris went to Finance, Jack Pickersgill took Harris's place as Minister for Citizenship and Immigration while Ralph Campney moved up from Associate Minister to Minister of National Defence.

The key move was Harris to the prestigious Finance portfolio. He had been St. Laurent's parliamentary assistant in External Affairs at the end of the Mackenzie King era and had been re-appointed when his boss took over as prime minister. The bond between the Ontario Baptist and the Quebec Catholic was very strong, which made Harris the prime minister's most trusted colleague and lent credence to the rumor that he would be next in line for the leadership of the Liberal Party of Canada. It was inevitable that the unofficial leadership race would be a factor in the choice of a minister for Toronto.

THE RACE TO CHOOSE A CABINET MINISTER FOR TORONTO

Early in 1956, Ottawa was buzzing with gossip as the old Cabinet shuffle rumor mill worked three shifts. On January 17th, the grapevine reported that there was no decision yet and I only wished they would make up their minds. On February 2nd, word came out that there was still no decision but on the 7th, Alex Hume, the *Ottawa Citizen* reporter who had the best pipeline to the prime minister, reported that the prospects were poor for me. My heart sank. It was the kind of news that made it difficult to concentrate on other subjects. I bounced back on the 8th when Alex advised that my prospects were brighter and "tomorrow is critical."

On the 9th, Cabinet met at lunch and my first hint of how things might have gone came when I met C.D. Howe on his way to the House. "Hello Paul," he said, with just a trace more warmth than usual, although it could have been my imagination. That afternoon, Gib Weir, the government Whip, phoned to say I should be in the Commons Chamber at 5:45 p.m. Just before 6:00 p.m. the prime minister asked leave to read an Order-in-Council which named me as parliamentary assistant to Defence Minister Ralph Campney. The die was cast! I was ecstatic. At least I had my foot on the first rung, and I was delighted to be working for someone I knew and liked, and had been my former roommate.

The press reaction was restrained but generally positive. In a February 10th editorial entitled "Toronto's Apprentice Minister" the *Toronto Star* said:

> Since parliamentary assistants have been known to become Cabinet ministers, and since there has been no Toronto member in the federal Cabinet for 20-odd years, the appointment will inevitably arouse some hopes hereabouts. Of course, promotion is not automatic. The apprentice must prove his skills at the trade, which in this case might be described as the defence of the department of defence in Parliament. Mr. Hellyer, a bright and energetic young man, deserves the chance to show what he can do. May he grow in proficiency and wisdom, and surmount the geographical handicap which proved too much for Senator David Croll.[1]

As the *Star* pointed out, an appointment as parliamentary assistant was often a stepping stone to Cabinet. It had been thus for illustrious men like Doug Abbott, Brooke Claxton, Paul Martin Sr., Lionel Chevrier, Jimmy Sinclair and Walter Harris, just to mention a few. But a lot depended on the relationship between the boss and his apprentice. Some ministers treated their assistants as understudies and groomed them for future responsibility. Others considered their PAs as a nuisance to be tolerated.

Campney couldn't have been a better mentor. I knew in advance that the chemistry was right, but he genuinely went overboard to include me in the inner circle. The same was true for his wife, Billy, his executive assistant, J.B. (Jock) Ross and Mary Dudley, his devoted private secretary. They all treated me as one of the family, put my name on the list for all social events, and then took responsibility for giving me a warm introduction to everyone present.

Briefings were arranged by the Naval Board, the Army General Staff and the Air Staff, where each in turn shared their hopes and aspirations to the "top secret" level. No doubt they were seeking an ally to support their pet projects but so much individual attention from so many high-ranking officers was pretty heady stuff.

My first assignment was not glamorous but it was nevertheless useful. I was given a four-inch-thick file concerning a citizen who owed the department $2,000. The debt was uncollectable because the man had no assets and was unlikely to ever have any – facts that had been confirmed by two or three agencies including Dun & Bradstreet. Still, the Treasury Board wouldn't allow the sum to be written off and insisted that we sue even though the Justice Department estimated it would cost about $10,000 in legal fees. No doubt it was my business training but after reading the evidence I couldn't see any point in spending thousands of dollars to obtain a judgment that couldn't be enforced. I wrote a new and stiff submission to the Treasury Board to which they finally agreed.

My most ironic assignment related to the Comet 1 aircraft. Two years earlier I had been worried about the number of unexplained Comet 1 commercial jet crashes which were greater than normal for a new model.[2] My immediate concern was that the RCAF had bought two of the airplanes for VIP flights and I had visions of the prime minister and half of the Cabinet being wiped out in a single crash, perhaps on their way home from attending some MPs funeral. I spoke to the Minister of National Defence, Brooke Claxton, who said he would report back. He did, after officials assured him there was no cause for concern.

Following another crash I was even more alarmed, and refused a ride in one of the airplanes, one of only three occasions I have done so on the grounds of safety. On November 23, 1953, I wrote to the minister referring to our previous conversation. "I would still like to obtain a copy of any reports your department may have pertaining to static and fatigue tests on the Comet wings. As I said at the time, I was not sure that the wing had been given a satisfactory fatigue test since it was redesigned after an earlier failure."[3]

In reply he said: "I have asked the Chief of the Air Staff to have a qualified technical officer call on you to go into this."[4] I received reassuring calls from RCAF technical officers and also from de Havilland's lawyers but these were not enough to convince me so we agreed to get together in Toronto at a mutually convenient time. Before the meeting took place, however, there was yet another crash and the British government, on April 16, 1954, grounded all Comet 1's worldwide. It then ordered one of the most comprehensive investigation in the history of commercial aviation.

Meanwhile, the British government had done a magnificent sleuthing job and found the problem. It was, as I suspected, metal fatigue, but around one of the forward windows rather than in the wings. The required modifications were straight-forward and I was just as enthusiastic about having them reworked as I had been to have them grounded.

Now it was my job to convince the Treasury Board that the two Comet 1 jetliners should be modified and put back in the air. Walter Harris was adamantly opposed and refused to approve the required expenditure. So it fell to the person who had been most fearful for the safety of the aircraft to plead the case for their reincarnation.

Whether it was knowledge of the subject or friendship with Harris that gave me the credentials didn't really matter. All other avenues had failed so I contrived to ride home on the same train and talk to him. Walter's concern, I soon learned, was not the money but the political consequences of a possible crash. I reviewed the history of the planes and assured him they could be made airworthy. Furthermore, the price was right. It would cost 10 times more to acquire VIP planes by other means. Whether it was my eloquence or the pot of hot chocolate we shared that did the trick is not material. Harris agreed, although neither of us could foresee that it would be our political opponents who would be the beneficiaries.

BEDLAM IN THE HOUSE OF COMMONS

In early May of 1956, Walter held a special evening caucus on the controversial subject of the proposed natural gas pipeline. Howe had forced a shotgun marriage of two competing companies. Pipe had been ordered and he wanted construction to begin that spring because he thought it would be an essential stimulus to the Canadian economy. An early start required federal legislation authorizing financial guarantees and both the Tory and CCF parties vowed to oppose it to the end because the merged company was controlled south of the border. They would not tolerate federal backing for the "Yankee Buccaneers."

Even with Howe's tight schedule there were more than three weeks available – ample time for exhaustive debate. But when the opposition adamantly refused to adhere to any kind of timetable the government adopted the extraordinary procedure of invoking closure at the outset, a tactic tantamount to waving a red flag at every political bull in sight. The opposition was outraged, but more importantly, so was the press. Charges of arrogance and dictatorship were leveled at the government as all hell broke loose.

For three weeks from May 14th to June 5th, the Commons was a shambles. My notes record: "May 24th terrible day in the House. May 25th another terrible day. Fleming censured!"[5] Davie Fulton for the Tories and Stanley Knowles for the Socialists used every conceivable trick to block the measure. There were motions to adjourn the debate, motions to adjourn the House and appeals from Speaker's rulings, which were permissible at the time, each consuming an hour or more while the bells rang and members rose one-by-one to record their votes in predictable fashion. More than three-quarters of the total time available for debate was taken up in procedural wrangling.

The day that became known as "Black Friday," June 1,1956, was not only our wedding anniversary, it was one of the worst days of my public life. As soon as the session began the Speaker rose to say that he had been in error the previous day. He ruled that the letter in the Journal did not constitute a *prima facie* question of privilege and that the clock should be turned back to where it had been the previous afternoon when the error was made. Everyone was stunned! Then bedlam ensued as the opposition tried to censure the Speaker and make him abandon his unprecedented plan.

It broke my heart to see the Reverend Dan McIvor, the least partisan and most revered man of God I have known in the House, shouting insults at the Tories. Equally incredible was witnessing the normally gentle J.J. Coldwell standing out in the center of the chamber shaking his fist at the Speaker. It was an unbelievably bad scene and it was something of a miracle that we escaped without a riot. Personal relations were poisoned in a way that I thought impossible and, in my view, the House was never as friendly a place again.

With closure in effect, we sat halfway through the night before the vote was taken. The following Tuesday, we did a repeat performance on the third reading and the bill was passed. Howe got his way and a great project was given the green light. It was almost dawn when the post mortem was adjourned and we left the building to try to snatch a few hours sleep before caucus began at 11:00 a.m. On the way down the Hill we filed past the cleaning women emerging through the haze on their way to work. Judging from their expressions, they must have thought we were out of our minds.

Passing the bill was a technical victory but the government's credibility had been badly eroded. The constant barrage of negative press had penetrated the public consciousness as few issues have.

The political learning curve for me had turned sharply upward with my appointment as parliamentary assistant. There seemed little doubt that Harris had tagged me as his man for Toronto because he treated me as minister for patronage and associated purposes.

DE FACTO PARLIAMENTARY SECRETARY OF IMMIGRATION

December saw unexpected responsibilities loaded on my plate. Thousands of Hungarians had fled their homeland in the wake of the November uprising and the Canadian government decided to admit a goodly number. Jack Pickersgill was in charge but much of the action was Toronto-centered and he didn't have a parliamentary assistant of his own so I was adopted. I became, willingly I admit, acting parliamentary assistant to the Minister of Citizenship and Immigration and for the next few days I almost went crazy with phone calls including innumerable ones from Jack Pickersgill himself.

On December 9th, Arpad Kornel, an assumed name because he was afraid to be identified as Bornemizza, his real name, arrived in Toronto and came to stay with us. Jack had called to say that Arpad was a scout for the University of Sopron Mining School which was being admitted to Canada *en bloc* and hoped to enrol as a group, in a Canadian university. That involved extensive negotiation with several institutions complicated by Arpad's inability to speak English. Fortunately, our Hungarian-speaking Canadian friends such as Gabor Temesvary, George Nagy, and others came to our aid and little time was lost.

Long before dawn on the 13th, Ellen was again ready to head for the hospital for the birth of our third child. The drive downtown surrounded by the Christmas lights was every bit as enchanting as it had been two years earlier when our first son had been born on December 9, 1954. We decided to name him Peter with Lawrence as a middle name in honor of Laurie Chute, one of the finest men we knew. This time when we arrived at Women's College Hospital, Dr. Yoneyama was once again on-hand to deliver our second son, David Ralph, his first name a good Biblical one and the second, by happy coincidence, both Ellen's maiden name and that of my friend and boss, Ralph Campney.

The next few days were chaotic. I shifted gears constantly from visits to the hospital to directing refugee traffic and delivering Yuletide gifts at home. All of this was taking place while I was cutting through red tape on behalf of, and then bidding *bon voyage* to, a plane filled with toys and goodies assembled by the *Toronto Telegram* newspaper's John Bassett for those unfortunate individuals who would be celebrating Christmas in an austere Viennese refugee camp.

A MOMENT OF JOY AS THE END OF THE ST. LAURENT ERA GREW NEAR

Although we were unaware of it, the celebration of Mr. St. Laurent's seventy-fifth birthday was one of the few good days on the 1957 Liberal calendar. On February 2nd, one day after the actual date, the flesh and blood "Who's Who" of the Liberal Party assembled at Quebec City's Chateau Frontenac to honor their chief. The mood was exuberant and even the stoic senior minister, C.D. Howe, must have been infected by the excitement. In his introduction, Howe said, "I have heard him referred to as a second Laurier. These are meant as tributes to our prime minister. But to me, he stands in the shade of no man living or dead."[6] This untypical revelation of Howe's heart brought tears to St. Laurent's eyes.

Predictably, in reply, the prime minister spoke of the Canada he loved. He quoted Laurier's dismissal of separatism: "As for me gentlemen, I do not want any small republics such as San Marino or Monaco ... my ambition is to be a citizen of a great country." French-speaking Canadians were proud of their forebears, St. Laurent added, "Let us have the backbone to stand erect as they did, and our descendants will be able to add us to the long list of those of whom they in their turn may be proud."[7] It was St. Laurent at his inspiring best, an exemplary product of an enriched Canadian duality.

Less than a week later I attended a Cabinet Defence Committee meeting chaired by the great man himself. It provided my initial glimpse of the East Block Cabinet Chamber, the political "holy of holies." The décor was typically nineteenth century and the room was the right size for a sensible Cabinet of 19 or 20 people. It would be quite inadequate for the overblown variety of later years which is one good reason why it is no longer used for Cabinet and is now open to the public.

I wasn't entitled to attend but the subject was the proposed Bomarc missile line, and Ralph considered it important that I sit in. The ramrod straight Chief of the Air Staff, Air Marshall Roy Slemon, was the briefer, and he showed us charts of alternate deployments. One plan excluded any Canadian bases while others included one at La Macaza, Quebec, and another at North Bay, Ontario. Slemon left little doubt that the RCAF preferred a solution that included the Canadian bases. It made more sense, geographically, while allowing our chaps to get in on the action.

I don't recall any decision being taken because it was a preliminary presentation and there was insufficient urgency to require action before the election. Little did any of us dream that the subject would become the center of a raging controversy destined to topple the Diefenbaker government years later.

THE 1957 FEDERAL ELECTION CAMPAIGN

There were times when St. Laurent would have preferred to step down rather than fight another campaign, but as time passed after his tiring worldwide trip, so did his resolve to lead the battle. He was urged to hang in by partisans more concerned with their own affairs than with his. At a late spring caucus there were passionate pleas for him to stay. Jake Hunter spoke for many when he argued that the PM was the only one who could keep the party and the country united and that he must remain for the good of both. It was a direct appeal to the old man's most powerful instincts.

Good intentions were not enough. The rules of politics had changed since 1953 with the introduction of television. St. Laurent made no effort to adapt and refused to wear makeup, presumably on ethical grounds that it would in some way be a distortion of the truth. On the other hand, the opposition Conservative leader, John Diefenbaker, reveled in the new electronic medium that was well suited to his brand of prairie evangelism.

There was some talk of appointing someone from Toronto to the Cabinet but the election was well underway and nothing happened. My PC opponent was nominated. It was once again someone from Westmoreland United Church, this time Doug Morton, Superintendent of the Sunday School and, in that capacity, my Sunday boss. I liked Doug, and his wife Mona, and congratulated him on winning the candidacy, although I wished it had been someone I didn't know. Political innocents said how wonderful it was to have the two of us involved but it was still hurtful to have someone from the church out to skewer me.

Walter Harris and I were at lunch at the Ontario Club on April 25th when he told me I would be getting a call from the prime minister that afternoon. When the phone rang the prime minister skipped the niceties and got directly to the point. "Would you like to join my colleagues and me in the Cabinet as Associate Minister of National Defence?" he asked. "Yes, I would, thank you very much, sir," I responded in an equally business-like fashion. "Then if you will be good enough to come to Ottawa in the morning you will be sworn in at 11:00 a.m.," he added. There was little more said except regards to our respective wives.

The next morning, June 26, 1957, I met the prime minister and Lionel Chevrier who was returning to Cabinet after a stint with the St. Lawrence Seaway, at the Supreme Court building where Chief Justice Patrick Kerwin administered the oath; in my case, first as a Privy Councillor and then the oath of office. For Chevrier, already a Privy Councillor, it was just as President of the Council. I was ecstatic. Toronto finally had a Cabinet Minister after a 22-year drought – the first Liberal minister ever within the city boundary.[8]

Press coverage was extensive and basically factual but editorial reaction was mixed and not too complimentary. Curiously, the conservative *Telegram* was the kindest of the Toronto papers. It described the appointment as "belated recognition" of Metropolitan Toronto's claim to Cabinet representation and concluded that Mr. St. Laurent "had picked a conscientious and experienced minister in Mr. Hellyer."[9]

The *Star* wrote "At Last Ottawa Discovers Toronto" but added that whereas I had said all young people should be radically inclined as a matter of principle that I had hardly been a spokesman for radicalism. In fact a rather quiet member "but surely an effective one, to have gained such notice and approbation from the Prime Minister."[10] The *Globe and Mail* was churlish about the lack of portfolio. It didn't accept Mr. St. Laurent's explanation of my duties and wondered if I were being used as election bait. "If that's the explanation, the appointment is at best a left-handed salute in the direction of Toronto ... Now, this may be out of the doghouse, but only on a probationary basis. That doesn't seem to be quite good enough for election purposes."[11]

Cabinet itself was a new experience. My first meeting was May 9th and "I spoke twice," according to my date book.[12] My sole proposal to Cabinet in those few brief weeks was an imaginative scheme for the disposal of the Long Branch Rifle Range. Although surplus to defense requirements it was a nightmare of a problem because there were four levels of government involved and strings attached to certain parts of the land. I began working on the project soon after being named parliamentary assistant and engaged Eric Hanson of Armstrong, Kingston, Hanson & Associates Ltd. to prepare a plan of subdivision that included something for everyone. Finally I got the politicians together and hammered out a tentative agreement with the powerful support of Metro Toronto's "Big Daddy," Fred Gardiner.

The memo to Cabinet didn't evoke lengthy discussion. Mr. St. Laurent asked for assurance that there was no conflict of interest and, following my affirmation, the item was passed. The plan, which included a 45-acre waterfront park, a 100-acre site for 659 low rental housing units, and a light industry section to appease the township, was unveiled at a joint press conference "attended by Metro Chairman Gardiner, controllers Jean Newman and Joseph Cornish, Reeve Mary Fix of Toronto Township and other township councillors and Alderman Philip Givens of Toronto."[13]

Reaction was almost universally enthusiastic. The election potential wasn't denied but the reason it happened was that for the first time I was in a position to do something about it. After the election I pleaded with George Hees and Howard Green to save the plan but to no avail. The new minister, George Pearkes, VC, let the bureaucrats take over and what should have been a unique beach park became Ontario Hydro's generating plant with its "biggest coal pile in the British Commonwealth."

At the end of the final pre-election Cabinet, under "other business," Walter Harris said the economy was beginning to cool and the Bank of Canada had withdrawn its opposition to a more relaxed fiscal stance. We could announce an extra four dollar monthly pension increase if we wished. St. Laurent sat immobile. The question wasn't discussed. It was as though it hadn't even been raised.

At that stage I don't think it would have made any difference. The damage had already been done. As Finance Minister, Walter had increased the Old Age Pension by six dollars a month, an amount that was considered an insult by seniors. He became known as "Six Buck Harris." The issue had a devastating effect on the election campaign, and this on top of the infamous pipeline debate and the squabble over renewal of the War Measures Act had soured the electorate to a greater extent than I had seen in my lifetime and did not augur well for the Liberal Party.

My pace had quickened measurably after my appointment to Cabinet. Whenever I tried to say "no" to a request from staff it was always "yes minister, that's fine minister, but…" which was always the prelude to a plea to accept one more speaking engagement or attend another function. The party had insisted that I go to Winnipeg, where I learned of C.D. Howe's famous gaffe in telling farmers they had never had it so good, a political bombshell that cost thousands of votes. One invitation accepted for purely emotional reasons was a Trooping of the Colour by the 48th Highlanders of Canada at Exhibition Park on June 1st, our wedding anniversary, and there seemed no more appropriate way to celebrate than with Ellen's father's regiment. It was a pleasant interlude from reality.

When I knocked on doors in my riding the signals were confused. Once, I did what no candidate should ever do – I spent a long time listening to a lady tell me how great I was and what a good job I was doing. Her vote appeared to be in the bag until I stepped off the veranda and she added in parting, "but, I can't stand C.D. Howe." I was just learning the immutable truth that "but" is the most important word in politics. You have to know the "buts" to be sure which way the wind is blowing.

The worst was yet to come. I admit some sense of pride when I picked up the *Toronto Star* and saw a full-page advertisement featuring the prime minister flanked by Harris and Howe, Pearson and me. "St. Laurent to Climax Campaign at Toronto Rally," it proclaimed. The locale was Maple Leaf Gardens and free tickets were available at the *Star* or at Liberal committee rooms. It was to be, "a real, old-fashioned celebration, including bands, girls, the Leslie Bell Singers, and two major surprises."

There were two major surprises, all right, both disasters. The arena was packed, but the mood was somber compared to the joyous celebrations in 1949 and 1953. Some teenagers in the far corner heckled so constantly that any sense of continuity was destroyed. It looked like a spontaneous demonstration but it wasn't. Many years later I met the Tory who organized it. The other surprise was even more damaging. Just before the Prime Minister was to speak a young man rushed up the stairs to the stage where he was intercepted, bodily, by rally chairman Vince Regan. The boy fell backward off the platform and his head hit the concrete with a sickening crunch. Whether he was pushed or just lost his balance was only relevant to future debate. At that moment we didn't know whether he was dead or alive, and the uncertainty descended on everyone like a giant pall. St. Laurent was visibly shaken and his performance, although brave, was lackluster. Instead of the rally ending the campaign with a giant boost it was a monumental dud. We learned after the meeting that the young man was okay.

Ellen and I could feel the ice at church the next morning. A fellow choir member made some wisecrack about us being there. But the unkindest cut of all came just before we left. One of our daughter Mary Elizabeth's classmates told her, "I hope your daddy loses tomorrow." No malice was intended, but a knife couldn't have hurt her as much. The experience helped to sour her on politics in adult life.

My reading of the mood in the country was that the people weren't against the prime minister, although he had received a few spiteful letters from religious bigots in the West. Voters just couldn't stand the image of C.D. Howe and the arrogance of the government as a whole. They wanted to teach the Liberals a lesson even though few expected us to be beaten. Even veteran journalists, who had urged a change, didn't expect a rout and the respected Blair Fraser, who wrote his story in advance because *Maclean's* magazine was going to press, said that the government had been re-elected although it shouldn't have been.

Once the votes were counted the truth was out. When people all across the country decide to "strengthen the opposition" the result is cumulative. As soon as the Newfoundland results were in I predicted a Progressive Conservative minority. The *Globe's* early headline screamed "Harris, Howe, Hellyer losing." In the end Stanley Haidasz was the only Liberal elected in Toronto. Across Canada the PC's had 112 seats to the Liberals 105, while the Co-operative Commonwealth Federation and Social Credit elected 25 and 19, respectively.[14] Undaunted, we had a great election night party in Davenport but we were, in fact, worn out in the morning when the *Toronto Star* came to photograph Ellen and me "exhausted" from sweeping up the debris in the committee room.

The government didn't have to resign until it met Parliament, so Cabinet was called to discuss the issue. For the sake of "decency" the prime minister said no announcement would be made until the Armed Forces vote was counted. Meanwhile Paul Martin and Jimmy Gardiner urged hanging on until the House was convened in the hope of getting minority party support, but St. Laurent would have none of it. The people had spoken and that was that. After 22 continuous years in office it was time to give someone else a chance, a sentiment with which I heartily agreed.

When the military vote was in, the Prime Minister submitted his resignation and the Governor General invited John George Diefenbaker to form a government. On June 21st we trooped to Government House to say farewell and have a final *coupe de champagne* with His Excellency Vincent Massey. An hour later the incoming Cabinet arrived to be sworn in and we were gone.

Back home, the change in pace was profound. Instead of "yes, minister, no minister" there was nothing but silence. The phone stopped ringing. The invitations stopped coming. People would even cross the street when they saw me coming to avoid looking me in the eye, probably because they didn't know what to say. It was just like having the plague. The experience put the whole "business" into perspective and I never took politics as seriously again.

CHAPTER SEVEN

CURRAN HALL LIMITED

The subject of housing had been a top item in my 1949 election campaign and was high on my agenda from the early post-World War II days. Almost all of my friends were aware of my interest and concern in this area. Consequently it was no great surprise when my lawyer Archie Whitelaw phoned and said he had clients whose ideas about housing were similar to mine. Would I agree to have lunch with them at the exclusive Granite Club? This was before it was proven to be a racist club, so I said yes.

The meal was as appealing as I had dreamed and my hosts listened to my radical views with rapt attention. It was only later that I realized they were not the least bit interested in my ideas; they were looking for a cash infusion to keep their failing company afloat. As I noted in my diary, I must have parked my brain when I parked my car because I agreed to invest my entire capital of $4,000 in their company. Much worse, I persuaded my sister and my father to invest $2,000 each.

On the basis of my signature alone, at a time when, as the old saying goes, I didn't have two nickels to rub together, a developer sold us 55 building lots in the old Dominion Nursery, near the De Havilland airport in north Toronto, where the company began to build. When a model house was ready, and a sales office opened, the houses sold like hotcakes, too fast for my comfort. My request to look at the books was rejected, as I was assured we were making $1,000 profit on each house sold.

When the brisk sales continued, I demanded to see the books and found that the company was just distributing the hard costs of the subcontractors, while excluding soft costs such as bank interest, legal costs, and so on. When all costs were taken into account we were actually losing about $1,000 per unit. Curran Hall Limited had exhausted its capital and was headed for bankruptcy.

With the help of another independent investor, Elwood Jackson, I was able to gain control and take responsibility for what remained of the company. My job was not one to be envied, but I was determined to do what I could to salvage the remnants, not just to rescue my investment, but also to recover my family's $4,000 outlay.

I thus embarked on what proved to be the most difficult 18 months of my life. I was a Member of Parliament at this time, and therefore had to be in Ottawa all week. I can honestly say that I never sacrificed my parliamentary duties while working to rescue Curran Hall. But weekends were a washout for family games and fun. I remember an extreme case when I carried the company books under my arm as we left home for a Christmas party. One good thing about these two exhausting responsibilities was learning business skills that were also applicable to my role in Parliament.

This was a start-up business with constant challenges. When I was at Curran Hall's building site I had to do whatever was to be done including unloading lumber. Some materials like cement were in desperately short supply so on one occasion I had to rent a truck to pick up a load from a Belleville company, where a fellow MP had sufficient influence to come to our rescue. On the way home I discovered that the truck was badly overloaded and the brakes were totally inadequate as I roared down a hill toward a one-lane bridge over the upper Don River. My luck held when I saw that no one was coming from the opposite side and I was able to regain control.

The only constant in the midst of all these problems was change. One of the original partners resigned when I took over the company. The other stayed on, but soon proved he was not sufficiently qualified for the job and had to be fired. It was the first time I had ever seen a grown man cry. Another crisis arose when our bookkeeper who had taught the subject at a Toronto school couldn't get a trial balance in three months. He became ill and resigned.

I had to learn bookkeeping virtually overnight and make the dozens of pages of corrections essential to balance the books. At that point good fortune struck when an Englishman, Geoffrey Hobsbawn, a Royal Air Force observer who had bailed out over Germany and been taken prisoner, responded to an advertisement I had put in the paper. Geoffrey was extraordinarily good at bookkeeping and kept first the company and then my personal records in order for more than 50 years.

We made a number of other key moves. The first was to increase the selling price of the remaining houses so that we made a profit of about $1,000 a unit. I persuaded my father to buy a few additional shares in the company to replace a small part of the capital that had been lost.

Frank Emery, an experienced builder, accepted an appointment as vice president in charge of operations. My brother-in-law, John Race, took the job as secretary in charge of quality control to ensure that every house was spotless when the purchasers moved in. These key men, plus a couple of good building superintendents proved to be a formidable group.

It was my responsibility to buy the raw land to subdivide in the hope of keeping lot prices as low as possible. We acquired the Watson farm at the intersection of Ellesmere Road and Warden Avenue, in Scarborough, and began the seemingly interminable task of overcoming every obstacle that myriad busy bureaucratic minds could erect. The subdividing process was a labyrinth to the uninitiated, and it was many months before we emerged with a subdivision agreement that officials felt worthy of consideration by the township's ubiquitous Reeve, Oliver Crockford, and his council. The final reward was a registration number, as rare as a slot machine jackpot!

There was no way that we could afford to develop the new subdivision with our meager resources, so we sold it as a block. This yielded a handsome profit, as building lots were in high demand. So at last, we were able to embark on a major project. This was a turning point because, until then, we had been buying serviced lots from others including sizeable blocks in Don Mills, E.P. Taylor's experimental satellite city.

We decided to embark on a huge 1,000-plus lot subdivision north of Lawrence Avenue East on both sides of Orton Park Road in Scarborough. There were miles of vacant farmland closer to the city, but development leap-frogged to the Highland Creek watershed because a new sewage disposal plant was being installed there. We named our project Curran Hall Park.

It was a large farm with a few lots backing onto a ravine. There were few trees on the part that had been farmed, but we preserved almost all of them to the point of designing a mirror image of one model in order to save a single, mature tree. You can imagine our dismay when an aerial photo of the subdivision appeared on the front page of the Toronto *Globe and Mail* to demonstrate the ruthless desecration (of trees) "when the bulldozers move in." The *Globe* subsequently apologized because someone had just written a story and then pulled a file photo that appeared to prove the point. If the story had been researched in conjunction with the photo it would have proved the opposite point.

By then we had hired a full-time architect, Edward Ross, B.Arch., MRAIC, who created a dozen unique house designs of sufficient variety to create a pleasant neighborhood environment. Models of each design were well underway before sewer and water mains were installed, a significant risk that is no longer permitted. I will never forget the sense of relief when the giant backhoe arrived and the sewer and water pipes started going into the ground.

Other memories include the mud and mess, and the catwalks we had to put down so that workers and potential customers could get in and out without sinking up to their knees in mire. I also recall the incredible sound of the European tradesmen singing opera at the top of their lungs as they plodded up the road at the end of a long day.

Fortunately, there were the purchasers coming and going, especially on weekends. No one denies that the pioneers had to put up with considerable hardship but I have yet to meet one buyer who regretted purchasing one of the $14,950 split-level homes that were being resold for as much as $750,000 in 2017.

The plan was registered and houses begun, but financing them and keeping the line moving was a Herculean task. Until I got into the business I had believed that the *Toronto Star* was correct in its view that the housing industry had failed ordinary people. By extension, only government could fill the void. In the school of hard knocks, however, I learned that the *Star* and I had been in error. It wasn't industry that had failed; it was governments at all levels.

Not only were officials unwilling to expedite the construction of modest housing, they threw every conceivable obstacle in the way. They were slow to approve projects and quick to raise specifications to Cadillac standards, while increasing costs through pre-payment of roads, sewers, water mains, sidewalks and eventually cash payments for each lot, as well. Instead of cutting into developers margins, as they had hoped, bureaucrats created such an artificial shortage of serviced land that prices and profits soared. One municipal politician who tried to help, the aforementioned Reeve O.E. Crockford of Scarborough, was chastised by Metro Chairman Fred G. Gardiner and told, "Stop Promoting Housing" because of the impact it would have on future education costs.

It was more or less the same in the country at large. Central Mortgage and Housing Corporation refused to insure mortgage loans on houses built on 40-foot lots, even though half the world's urban areas were built on less. It was blind bureaucracy, ignorance of the incredible economic and social damage flowing from mindless regulation. My tortuous experience in the building business was an intellectual eye-opener. It would be wonderful if there were comparable opportunities for any preacher, teacher, journalist or politician still wrapped in his or her academic cocoon.

When spring arrived and the weather moderated we soon achieved the kind of production schedule that I had dreamed of in my youth. We were able to build and complete four or five houses every day. It wasn't long before I began to look for another farm to develop in the hope that we could maintain the momentum.

Eventually I found a slightly smaller but adequate property on the east side of Midland Avenue, just south of Ellesmere Road in Scarborough. We named it Midland Park, which ultimately became a 626-unit showpiece of mid-century modern architecture. It took until 1959 to get the land subdivided and begin building.

In the early stages, due to mortgage money not being available, the cash flow was highly negative. On January 4th my vice president, Frank Emery, phoned to fill me in on how bad things were, bad enough that I didn't sleep a wink all night. We had asked the Toronto-Dominion Bank for additional "temporary accommodation" but were turned down. Not only that, they demanded a blanket mortgage on all our assets, including land. It was like a death sentence and I knew that if they got their way we would be bankrupt within weeks.

Luckily we had two companies with our raw land holdings in the name of Trepil Realty Ltd., while the bank loan was in favor of Curran Hall. I told the bank that I feared it was neither moral nor legal to pledge the assets of Trepil against the liabilities of Curran Hall, especially when the shareholders were not absolutely identical. Nevertheless, I agreed to get a legal opinion. Meanwhile I arranged a $100,000 second mortgage on the land, which put us in funds, although it didn't please the bank.

The lawyers looked at our situation and, for once, the normal speed of that profession was exactly right. By the time we got a written opinion confirming our view that it would be neither legal nor morally acceptable to pledge Trepil's assets, spring had come, houses were being completed and cash was flowing. The crisis was over and by July 2nd the second mortgage was paid off and our accounts were in good shape.

As a footnote, I learned later that, while attending a Canadian Bankers Association reception in Ottawa, Sam Paton, a senior Toronto-Dominion Bank official asked Finance Minister Walter Harris if he knew a fellow named Hellyer. When Harris admitted that he did, Paton added: "Well he's certainly learned the first lesson of banking." It was a lesson that made the difference between being comfortable or penniless in later years. The experience also made me sceptical of the Canadian banking system's willingness to support growth industries.

While financial independence is not to be sneezed at, the greatest satisfaction, by far, was watching the transformation from farmers' fields to attractive suburban communities. Not everyone is fortunate enough to be involved in a creative process where you can actually see and measure the results.

More than half-a-century later one of the homeowners in Midland Park, Lisa Duperreault and *Globe and Mail* housing columnist Dave LeBlanc, spearheaded a movement to have their subdivision designated as "heritage" in order to preserve its original character. Lisa describes it is as "a beautiful subdivision in the suburbs; one that incorporated each and every home and street into the topography. They (the developers) left many old growth trees intact and left the hills and valleys where they lie today."[1]

I had my first look at the finished product when my current wife Sandra and I did a 90-minute walking tour sponsored by Open Doors Toronto in May 2017. I had not been on the site since Phase II of the development was begun decades ago because I was fully occupied in accumulating the farmland for a much larger development in North York. I was really thrilled and very proud of the Midland Park that the majority of its residents want to preserve.

Our award-winning designs had been noticed by the public, so this was the encouragement I needed for another quantum jump in the scope of our operations. We put in an offer on the Henry Farm which was about 200 acres, and another offer for the acquisition of the adjacent 130 acres. In total it comprised the entire concession block between Highway 401 on the south and Sheppard Avenue on the north, from Leslie Street on the west to what is the Don Valley Parkway on the east. It was a gorgeous piece of real estate cascading down from an escarpment on the east to the Don River on the west, but it was well beyond our financial ability, so we formed a new company, Hendon Estates Limited, in a 50 percent partnership with George Wimpey Ltd., of London, England.

A most ingenious plan was prepared that would have seen the top third, above Don Mills Road, become a giant semi-circle of apartments with shops and commercial space on the ground floor. Inside the semi-circle we planned a village green of shops, theatres and medical services surrounded by a park in a more elaborate version of Toronto's City Hall profile. Regretfully official intransigence delayed planning on the grounds that "mixed uses" were not permitted. Land could be "residential" or "commercial" but not an intelligent blend of both. Partly due to the delay, and partly because I was gone before the actual building began, that part of the land was sold and the reality is far short of the vision we had.

Meanwhile I was always a little bit puzzled as to why George S. Henry, a former Tory premier of Ontario, would sell his farm to me, especially when an earlier sale to Cadillac Fairview had fallen through. It hardly seems possible now, but that company had been short of cash and its president, Ephraim Diamond, persuaded the old gentleman to let him off the hook by forfeiting the deposit. My curiosity was satisfied at a Royal York Hotel reception for Princess Margaret where I met Mr. Henry for the first time. After introducing myself I asked: "I have often wondered why you, a former Conservative premier, would sell your homestead to me, a former Liberal MP?"

"Well," he replied, "I checked you out thoroughly and I was convinced you would do a good job."

TIME OUT FOR ARUNDEL LODGE

A decision to acquire a small tourist resort was certainly not pre-meditated. When Ellen and I finally got to Arundel Lodge for a brief vacation in August 1958, we learned that the owners, Edith and George Paish, were planning to sell. The business wasn't profitable and Edith was getting tired of cooking. We understood their dilemma but it was devastating news because we were really in love with this unique place that we had first discovered in 1947. So, as I was not an MP at the time, I decided to use Curran Hall to buy it. This was not really a rational decision, although I had a vision of how the property might be developed. Still, it turned out to be a wonderful decision when measured by the ultimate intangible benefits for the Hellyer family and hundreds of others.

THE HENRY FARM

These were busy years in the building business. I had recruited John B. (Jock) Ross, to join the company as treasurer. He had been Defence Minister Ralph Campney's executive assistant when I became Ralph's parliamentary secretary in 1956.

Jock rounded out a strong management team that extended from the front office to field supervision and we had become innovators on many fronts. Curran Hall won regional design awards five years in a row, and our architect Ted Ross had gone to Ottawa to accept these on behalf of the company. We also won the National Builder of the Year Award in 1961.

In addition to architectural innovation we had introduced such things as a 30-day warranty, a 90-day money back guarantee and an employee pension plan which was completely novel to the house-building business. Our major project and number one priority at the time, however, was finalizing a plan for the Henry Farm.

Our big project finally got underway and became a huge success. The project pioneered several innovations, including putting all of the telephone, hydro and television lines underground. Our development company, Hendon Estates Ltd., sold the majority of the lots to several first-class builders, including George Wimpey Ltd. Curran Hall only built a few of the houses and they were more middle-class, with prices in the $30,000 to $35,000 range.

Home purchasers from all of the builders must have been more than satisfied because at the end of 25 years, they held a gala weekend to celebrate their subdivision. There were tours, keepsakes like commemorative cups, and an excellent book about the farm, its history and the development. There was a banquet dance on Saturday night and an ecumenical service on Sunday. The most unique feature was that the developers were invited to participate.

Proof of the enduring satisfaction was demonstrated on the fiftieth anniversary of the subdivision when a new book was published and events including a banquet were held, to which my brother-in-law John Race and I were invited. It was a pleasant evening that brought back happy memories of the team effort that had made it happen.

I resigned as CEO of Hendon Estates and Curran Hall Limited on December 31, 1962, just months before the election that made Lester B. (Mike) Pearson Prime Minister, and my appointment as Minister of National Defence.

The company treasurer, J.B. (Jock) Ross, succeeded me as CEO of Curran Hall. One of his first acts was to phone and ask me if I would like to take my "white elephant," i.e. Arundel Lodge, with me. He said he would let me have it for book value, which was a good deal that I was happy to accept. Ironically Jock, his wife Peggy and their four children became our best customers, renting one of the larger cabins for a month each summer.

Jock led Curran Hall successfully until early 1970, when he negotiated a deal with George Wimpey & Co. for its sale for more than $5 million. My father's share was just over $1 million. He had wanted to be a millionaire all of his life and had participated in a number of mining and other ventures without success. At last his dream finally came true with this most unlikely of investments.

My share was just over $2 million. For several years the press had been referring to me as a "millionaire builder." But that was hypothetical, as I barely had enough cash to meet my routine obligations. On March 9, 1970 however, I was in the chips at last. My long years of hard work and patience had paid off, both in knowledge and financially. What had appeared at the outset to be "mission impossible" turned out to be a blessing in disguise.

CHAPTER EIGHT

THE STILL, SMALL VOICE
THAT LED TO THE ROAD BACK

The loss of my seat in Parliament had been painful but I had much to be thankful for. My unease about the possible results of the election was sufficient that I had decided not to resign as president of Curran Hall Limited until the election results were known. It was one of my wisest decisions.

Another small benefit was that my colleagues decided to include me in their noontime bridge club and teach me how to play the game. I was raised in a strict Baptist home where playing cards was forbidden. All my life, until then, whenever I had been asked to make up a foursome I had to decline with thanks. It didn't take long before the daily hour of instruction from our very proper accountant, Geoffrey Hobsbawn, allowed me to master the rudiments of a most enjoyable pastime.

I was quite happy with this new routine, and politics began to fade into the background. A few months later, on February 1, 1958, Prime Minister John Diefenbaker asked the Governor General to dissolve Parliament to allow another general election to be held in March. I was determined not to run, if for no better reason than that in the intervening months the PM had "bought" just about every pressure group in the country by increasing old age pensions, widows' pensions and veterans' pensions. He handed out a new "goodie" almost every day thanks to the solid state of the treasury that we Liberals had left behind. As a consequence the government was extremely popular and I knew there wasn't any hope of getting elected. To make matters worse I was in bed with the mumps, which I had contracted from our youngest son David.

When Liberal leader Pearson heard that I would not be running he telephoned and started the pitch. "You owe it to the party," he said. "You owe it to your country," he added, when the first pitch didn't make a dent in my resolve. His long years of training in diplomacy allowed him to use every verbal trick in the book. I held out for almost half an hour, at which point he finally wore me down. I capitulated, phoned my ever-loyal secretary Marg Bulger and asked her to rally the political troops. Then I got up out of my bed and started to run for election, hard.

A funny thing happened. Our campaign organization was so sound that when we finished our canvassing we knew that we would get a couple thousand more votes than we had the last time, when we lost. We were under no illusions, however. Near the end of the campaign we organized a parade up and down the streets of the riding. As we slowed down for the intersections we could hear the children shouting "Yea Morton, boo Hellyer." Ellen turned to me and said: "Is there any doubt left in your mind?" "No, none," I replied.

The riddle was solved when the votes were counted. I did indeed pick up more than 2,000 additional votes compared to the year before. But the incumbent, Doug Morton, gained more than 4,000. The answer lay in the fact that the turnout of voters had increased from 70 percent to 80 percent from one election to the next. It was a decisive victory, both for my opponent and for the Prime Minister who won 208 out of 265 seats, one of the biggest sweeps in Canadian electoral history.

THE STILL, SMALL VOICE

After a couple of days, waiting for the bruises to heal, it was back to work. This was about the nearest I came to what could be called a comfortable and normal life in the course of my long career. Too comfortable, I suspect.

There had been times, almost from the date of my first election, when a "still, small voice" had said that my calling was the ministry, to be a minister of the cloth, not a minister in government. It didn't happen often, but it was persistent. My response was at least consistent. "Lord, you know that I flunked out of both French and Latin and I couldn't possibly cope with Greek and Hebrew." It was my standard reply, and I knew it by heart from using it so often. Now that I had more time on my hands, the message came through with increasing regularity, but the response remained unchanged.

Meanwhile, I had become friends with Arthur Poynter, a Baptist minister who was more interested in music than he was in preaching. He was the leader of a group called the Toronto Oratorio Society and I helped him incorporate an organization called the Christian Performing Arts to sponsor concerts. He dearly hoped to launch the production of an opera he entitled *The Birth of our Lord*, written in a style borrowing heavily from George Frideric Handel. His dream of staging an opera was never fulfilled but he did mount many lesser works including some of his own compositions.

On one occasion he organized a concert with a mass choir and orchestra in the old Varsity Stadium, with an attendance of about 12,000 souls. He asked me to sing a small solo part in one number in which I had to open unaccompanied with perfect pitch. Somehow my Guardian Angel (G/A for short) came to the rescue. I vowed, however, that was my "once," and I would never accept such a foolhardy assignment again.

Art's music was, by necessity, a hobby and he had to preach to keep bread on the table. Being involved with Art in musical productions was a good experience, but a far more important experience for me was due to our friendship. His charge was Dufferin Street Baptist Church, just a few blocks from my church, Westmoreland United. In July and August, when so many parishioners were absent on holidays, the two churches united for services first in one church and then the other. It was on one of these occasions in late August, when Art was preaching, that he said something that touched a tender nerve. I don't even remember exactly what he said, but I do remember going home and getting down on my knees and saying: "Lord, if you really want me to go into the ministry, I am willing. But you will really have to help me with the languages because you know I can't hack it on my own."

When I finally stood up I had what many religious people call "the peace that passeth understanding." You can't describe it, you can only feel it. The closest I can come to providing a sense of it is that you are totally at peace with the world and with everyone around you. It is a wonderful feeling. I realized what I had done. I had surrendered my life to God's direction whereas, previously, it had been my will that had prevailed. To capitulate was one thing, but there were practical consequences. When and where would I enroll in university? What preparation was required? There were myriad questions, but I was not dismayed because I knew that He was with me.

If I recall correctly, it was only about two weeks later that I heard another of Arthur's provocative sermons. The still, small voice spoke again, but this time the message was very different. "No, Paul, the ministry is not your calling. Your calling is politics, but first you had to submit your will to mine."

It was only a few days later that I got an excited telephone call from my close friend Keith Davey. "Have you heard the news?" he asked. "No," I responded, "what news?" "Edward Lockyer, the MP for Trinity riding, has just died of a heart attack while watching a World Series baseball game. You know what that means," he continued, "you will be able to seek re-election in the riding right next to your old one where you know a lot of people." I was flabbergasted as we chatted for a few minutes in a manner that really seemed quite inappropriate in the circumstances.

THE 1958 BY-ELECTION IN TRINITY RIDING

Winning the nomination in Trinity seemed like a snap because Dr. Stanley Haidasz, whom I had recruited to run there in 1957 and had been the only Liberal elected that year but was overtaken by the Diefenbaker sweep in 1958, gave me the green light when he said he preferred to concentrate on his medical practice. With no opposition to speak of, my team began to get signs and literature printed to gain time in what promised to be a mighty challenge.

At that point Liberal leader Pearson, who had a penchant for creating problems where none existed, phoned Stan to say that he would support whoever got the nomination. Stan thought the call meant that Pearson wanted him to run, so he changed his mind. Stan was invited to have lunch with Maj. Gen. (Ret.) Bruce Matthews, president of the Liberal Party of Canada, who set the record straight and got the train back on the track. This time the political system worked in my favor.

From that point on, everyone in the party was behind me. My friends backed me because they wanted to see me get back into the political arena. My enemies encouraged me because they were certain I would lose the election and that would be the final nail in my political coffin. So we were all united, although with very different motives.

There were a number of positive factors in my favor. The good parishioners at Westmoreland United Church, who had almost universally supported my opponent Doug Morton in the March general election, were now free to enthusiastically endorse me in the by-election. It seemed like a glorious opportunity to have their cake and eat it too. In addition, Ellen's parents lived in Trinity, and she knew many people in the riding. And, of course, we were able to draw on Liberal resources from one side of the city to the other.

The campaign got off to a slow start because it was the year for municipal elections in November. People would ask me if I was running for alderman or controller. They would look perplexed when I said, "neither." Once the municipal election was over, we picked up momentum quickly. Ellen and I knocked on doors together, an art that she was actually more familiar with than I was. The weather got so cold in December that when voters answered the door our teeth were chattering so much that it was difficult to find the words to make our pitch. I got the sense that we were picking up sympathy votes because people felt sorry for us standing in the freezing cold.

We put on what the Tories conceded was a textbook campaign. Every poll was canvassed not once, but twice. There were reserve workers slated for every poll on election day, in case someone didn't show up. We used all the tricks of the trade including, on the final Saturday before polling day, dressing workers in Santa Claus suits to give out flyers on each of the five main east-west thoroughfares. This was a clever move because people would sidle up to Santa, and whisper in his ear: "Tell Paul I will be supporting him this time." That was the kind of news we had been waiting for.

On election day, everything went according to the book. Ellen was in the committee room when, mid-afternoon, two Conservative heavy hitters, George Hees, Minister of Transport and "Fast" Eddie Goodman, one of the party's top strategists, came in to my committee room and said we were going to win, a "before the polls closed gesture" that I had never seen before, or since. They explained that they couldn't get their supporters out to vote. They were just sitting on their hands. I have no doubt they were convinced by my argument that with 17 supporters of the government in the Toronto area, there was no harm and possibly some benefit from having one Liberal on the opposition side to keep tabs on them.

When the polls closed, and the results began to come in Keith Davey exclaimed "my gawd, he's winning." It must have been a thrill for him because he had worked in two general elections, but this was his first winning campaign. I only won by 771 votes, but that didn't matter. I won, and my foot was back on the political ladder to the delight of my friends and the quiet dismay of my fair-weather friends. Despite the Gallup Poll showing the Conservative support at 60 percent to the Liberal's 30 percent, I had made a chink in the government's armor. The victory gave the Liberals their first sign of hope, and marked the beginning of the road back. This was acknowledged by Liberal heavyweight Jack Pickersgill when he autographed his book *The Road Back* for me: "Inscribed for Paul Hellyer who started us on the road back."

Triumphant Return to Ottawa

When I returned to Ottawa I was the hero of the moment. Within a few days I began to be recognized as the fifth Horseman of the Apocalypse along with the other Liberal Privy Councillors comprising Lester B. (Mike) Pearson, Paul Martin, Lionel Chevrier and Jack Pickersgill, who had been dubbed "The Four." It was easy to establish a niche in defense. The Diefenbaker government had approved the acquisition of the Bomarc anti-aircraft missile, a decision that we had been "generous" enough to leave to them in 1957. Unfortunately, however, when the Americans tested the Bomarc most of them fell into the Gulf of Mexico. So I would rise in my place in the House of Commons and ask the Minister of Defence, Maj. Gen. (Ret.) George Pearkes, why he would acquire such an unreliable weapon.

I am sure he became tired of me asking more or less the same question so many times, but in partisan politics one has to take advantage of every opportunity, and I certainly did. Pearson never did appoint me "defense critic" officially, it just happened by default. He began to get a significant volume of letters on the subject so his ever-loyal secretary, Mary Macdonald, would simply acknowledge them on his behalf and say that she was referring them to me for a more detailed reply. Soon, I was the defense critic (sometimes referred to as "shadow cabinet") *de facto*, even for the boss.

In 1961, I wrote a defense policy paper for the Liberal Party. Pearson adopted it as his own and decided to make it official policy when he spoke. It was a non-nuclear policy that he would reverse just prior to the 1963 general election.

Meanwhile he had named me as a delegate to the North Atlantic Treaty Organization (NATO) meeting in Paris, January 8–20, 1962. I came into contact there with senior officials, both military and civil, who were dismayed that the Diefenbaker government, after accepting nuclear roles for Canada's army and air force, was refusing to accept the nuclear warheads to arm the hardware. Our military liaison officer in Paris arranged a private session for me with General Lauris Norstad, Supreme Allied Commander in Europe (SACEUR) who, under the pretext that I was a privy councillor and former defense minister, gave me a "top secret" briefing.

In it Norstad showed me the maps of the Eastern front, and the specific targets that were assigned to the Canadian CF-104 strike aircraft in our No.1 Air Division. The aircraft were immobile, however, because they were unarmed. That same evening our Ambassador to NATO, George Ignatieff, told me privately how difficult it was for him to prevent the NATO Council from passing a resolution indicating that Canada was "in default" under the treaty. Even a gourmet dinner, a pub-crawl and the guttural sounds of a glorious French *chanteuse* couldn't erase the memory.

The information I received posed a dilemma for me. I had been the author of the Liberal non-nuclear policy because I was, and remained, firmly convinced that nuclear war would be totally insane, and the very best that such weapons can hope to do is to deter the use of similar weapons by others. On the other hand, if there was anything more useless than an armed Bomarc, it was an unarmed Bomarc. Likewise, an Honest John short-range army missile with sand as a warhead was worse than useless. The bottom line for me, however, was not the usefulness of the weapons, but Canada's reputation for fulfilling its treaty commitments. I decided that Canada should make good on its promises until such time that we could negotiate roles for our forces that were non-nuclear in nature and acquire the new hardware to accommodate them. In real terms, we were talking about several years, not months.

When I got back to Ottawa I wrote a memo to Pearson outlining my conclusions. I also briefed caucus, with the support of my colleague Judy LaMarsh, MP for Niagara Falls, who had enticed me to accompany her to East Berlin, against orders, when no one else was willing to go out on such a very long limb. Judy was a strong supporter of Canada fulfilling its commitments, even though she had not been privy to the secret information and was forced to rely on more general impressions. Together, we briefed senior party officials.

Nothing happened, which was par for the course at that time. Finally I wrote a speech on the subject to use at a Liberal meeting in Walkerton, Ontario. I knew that if I discussed it with Pearson in advance he would say no. Consequently I just wrote him a letter with which I enclosed a copy of the speech and slipped under his door not long before leaving for the event.

I suggested that he say I was expressing my own views rather than party policy.

The speech made headlines, as I expected. A genuine debate began. The Conservative government was deeply split on the issue and threatened to break up. General Norstad made an official visit to Ottawa and, in the course of a press conference, added fuel to the fire by mentioning Canada's unfulfilled commitments. I worked on John Gellner, defense columnist for *The Globe and Mail*, because I suspected he carried more weight with Pearson than I did. Others joined the fray, pro and con, and eventually, in early January 1963, Pearson made a speech reversing Liberal policy.

Not everyone was pleased. Mike's close friend and political adviser, Walter Gordon was furious, and threatened to resign, but was talked out of it. In Montréal, Pierre Trudeau, who had considered running as a Liberal, was outraged. He used his left-wing periodical *Cité libre* to malign the Liberal Party, and especially its leader L.B. Pearson, whom he described as the "Unfrocked Prince of Peace." Strong stuff for that time!

The vast majority of Liberals, however, and a majority of Canadians were delighted. I strongly suspect that a major part of the delight was due less to the issue itself than that at long last Pearson was portrayed as a leader who could make difficult decisions. This was in striking contrast with Diefenbaker who was dithering, torn as he was between Defence Minister Doug Harkness and the demands of his department on the one hand, and the contrary non-nuclear stance of Howard Green and the Department of External Affairs, on the other.

Pearson's strong stand led to the disintegration of the government and its defeat in the House. In the general election that followed, the Liberals won the most seats, enough to form a government, while the Diefenbaker Tories would find themselves in total disarray. The Liberal leader felt some obligation to me for setting up the issue that got him elected, as well as the very innovative and extremely successful rally that had consolidated his leadership at a time when his hold on the party had been very tenuous.

A RETROSPECT ON THE BUILD UP TO VICTORY IN 1963

In 1960 Pearson was widely regarded as politically ineffectual. So much so that Keith Davey, who later became national Liberal organizer and eventually a senator, sat in my car until 3:00 a.m. trying to decide whether we should make an effort to dislodge him as leader or go all-out in our efforts to help him. We concluded that he was the leader and we would do our best to elect him.

My by-election victory and the fiasco of the Diefenbaker government's first cancelling the Avro Arrow, the world's most advanced jet fighter, and then cutting up the existing planes with acetylene torches had helped. But there was still a long way to go. On November 2, 1959, I met with Walter Gordon, a prominent business consultant who had been reluctant to identify with any political party for obvious reasons, who had agreed to raise the money to pay off the party's debt.

The following morning I dashed off a four-page memo that outlined all of the major steps that seemed necessary to re-build the party. Many of the suggestions were taken up and Mike, as we called L.B. Pearson, got the ball rolling. In 1960 he decided to launch a risky double-barrelled policy initiative. The first would be an ostensibly non-partisan thinkers conference. This would be followed by a national convention where any new policy thrust would be sold to the party at large in a way that would make the rank-and-file think the ideas were theirs.

Mitchell Sharp, a former vice president of Brazilian Traction and later Deputy Minister of Trade and Commerce, was asked to preside at the Kingston thinker's conclave, and Mike asked me to organize the rally. I considered the Kingston conference to be a snap. There was a precedent for it and many academics anxious to get a platform for their views. The rally was different. There was no precedent, and it was considered highly unlikely that delegates could be persuaded to travel to Ottawa at their own expense in the absence of an exciting leadership contest.

I was reluctant to get involved for two reasons. My calendar was already overloaded with political and business commitments and the chances of failure were overwhelming. I consulted my good friend Jack Pickersgill for advice. I should have anticipated his candor. "You can't win," he said. "If you turn it down they will say the decision was based on lack of confidence in your own ability. If you accept, you run the risk of a near-certain disaster." His assessment echoed my own but I thought about it and decided to accept the challenge.

I recruited Hédard Robichaud as co-chair and a roster of high-powered committee chairmen. But even with their help and a lot of heavy lifting from Paul Lafond at the National Liberal Federation and Beryl Naylor, my Ottawa secretary, the job was all-encompassing and all-consuming. The results, however, justified the effort.

The great conclave of 2,500 delegates got under way on January 9, 1961, and as it progressed, it proved to be a smashing success. We introduced several innovations. Pre-registration was used to avoid congestion and to shorten queues on opening day. Simultaneous translation, English to French and French to English, was made available for the first time. A long-standing grievance was resolved through provision of transportation adjustments by which delegates from the central provinces would subsidize those who came at higher cost from greater distances. Then, finally, the use of a whole series of small policy groups made it possible to give everyone a sense of participation and the chance to be heard.

This technique had been used successfully in Kingston, but there was great uneasiness about transplanting it to a mass convention which tends to be unmanageable. It worked like a charm, however, and by the time a protracted policy session ended, party members had become personally involved with the new direction that was being set. Most important, the party attained a new sense of unity.

All that remained was a "blessing" from the former leader. Walter Gordon had been strongly opposed to involving Louis St. Laurent because of his age. But I overruled him because I thought my first political boss was both a great man and a good leader and therefore deserved the honor. Furthermore, he could do for Pearson what no one else could do.

After the closing dinner when Mr. St. Laurent effected a "laying on of hands" by moving a motion of confidence in Mike, the response was an uproarious six-minute standing ovation. It was punctuated by demonstrations as diverse as pigeons of peace fluttering to the rafters and a "rain" of western wheat. The ovation took so long that Mike had to slash equal time in order to be "out" before the TV cameras switched off. It was magnificent theater.

I was sitting beside the leader and kept passing him time cues. He proved to be a marvellous editor. He finished at 8:55 p.m., just as the flashing lights warned that he had less than a minute to wrap up, thus allowing the cameras to pan out on another standing ovation. We were home free. As soon as he sat down, Mike leaned over to say, "Paul, I will never be able to thank you enough for what you have done." They were kind words that reflected the general state of euphoria.

Mike was as good as his word, and gave me the prestigious defense portfolio, considered to be one of the top four, despite the pleadings of Walter Gordon on behalf of his brother-in-law, Charles M. (Bud) Drury, a wartime brigadier who had superior credentials to mine, at least on paper. Finance, which was the only portfolio I ever coveted, he had to give to Walter in recognition of the key role he had played in making him leader. I couldn't have asked for anything more.

CHAPTER NINE

THE PEARSON ERA: PART I

One of the first and most important jobs for any new minister is to assemble competent and congenial staff. Incompetence can get one into a pile of trouble, and if the staff can't work harmoniously, a great deal of effort is wasted on resolving internal battles. Marg Bulger had arrived from Toronto a week after the government was sworn in, so I was pleased to have a trustworthy and extremely capable private secretary.

I was assigned two first-class military secretaries, Lt.-Col. R.J.G. (Reg) Weeks and Commander J.M. (Marc) Favreau, who provided the liaison with the services.

My staff was effectively complete within days, except for the top job of executive assistant, essentially the chief of staff position. Despite my best effort, there seemed to be no obvious candidate. A few days later inspiration struck. I had been most impressed with the way RCAF Wing Commander Bill Lee had performed as Chief Canadian Public Relations Official for that year's NATO meeting, which had just been held in Ottawa for the first time. It suddenly dawned on me that I had one of the best men in the business in my own shop. Lee was an expert. He had topped his class at the United States Air Force Public Relations School.

I arranged a dinner during which Bill and I had a long and animated discussion about the Defence department and the difficulty of keeping the public adequately informed of any steps that might be taken to improve it. Before we parted I offered him the job and gave him 24 hours to think about it. After discussing the idea with his wife Charlotte (Chatty), and Air Marshall Hugh Campbell, Chief of the Air Staff, he agreed, subject to the stipulation that, because he was still in uniform, he be given the title of special assistant rather than executive assistant. That was immaterial to me, so we had a deal. My staff was now complete and a long, close, and happy relationship was born.

My good luck continued with the prime minister's choice of associate minister. He appointed Lucien Cardin, a young, bright and affable MP from Quebec. It would have been impossible to find anyone better or more congenial to work with.

It was a real pleasure for me to be part of a new Liberal administration charged with cleaning up the defense and foreign policy mess left by the Diefenbaker government. I also felt privileged to have a ringside seat to observe how prime minister Lester B. (Mike) Pearson would perform in office. He had been a reluctant politician who had sometimes appeared to be interested in the leadership of the Liberal Party, while at other times acted as if he couldn't care less.

When he won the Nobel Peace Prize for his part in stabilizing the Suez Crisis of 1956 his popularity surged ahead of the other main contenders for the Liberal Party leadership, including Paul Martin and Walter Harris, who would have been Louis St. Laurent's first choice. The die was cast when Pearson's close friend Walter Gordon, a well-known Toronto business consultant, seized the opportunity to persuade the front-runner by offering to raise the money necessary for a winning campaign and act as his manager. A few of us who knew Walter well suspected that he thought Mike would want to be his own *de facto* foreign minister, while leaving his Minister of Finance Walter Gordon to run the country.

This suspicion gained substance when the new prime minister decided that his first visit would be to the United Kingdom to discuss foreign affairs with his old friend Sir Alec Douglas-Home the British Foreign Secretary. Of course there would be a courtesy call on the U.K. prime minister but it was really Sir Alec that Pearson wanted to talk to. The PM decided to take me with him so that after brief formalities in London I could fly on to visit our troops on the continent. We left Malton Airport (later renamed Pearson International) on May 1, 1963.

My time in London was brief. I then continued on across the English Channel to spend time with our army and air force units which were part of the NATO shield in Europe. The conditions I observed filled me with dismay. Our Brigade Group had no modern equipment to provide either mobility or firepower. Its transport consisted of trucks rather than armored personnel carriers. The artillery was antiquated and even its few Honest John rocket launchers were useless because their warheads were filled with sand instead of an atomic device. Our Air Division was equally ineffective as it was not equipped with either conventional or atomic weapons.

When I returned to Ottawa I added these personal observations to the devastating written material already in my possession. The basic inefficiency of the three services was all-encompassing. Triplication of supply lines, storage and parts numbers led to some absurd situations. One service would sell surplus material as scrap at the same time that a sister service would be ordering the same item new. In one extreme case, a service sold equipment to Levy Auto Parts in Toronto and another bought it back at the full new price.

There was no cross referencing and this was especially ridiculous in cases such as that of the Mark NC-44 which was used by both the Royal Canadian Navy and the Royal Canadian Air Force. The two services used different parts numbers so if one service was short of parts for the torpedo there was no practical way to see if the other could meet the requirement from its inventory. Taxpayers' interests were seldom taken into account.

The Navy was also in considerable disarray. A commission of inquiry headed by Rear-Admiral E.R. Mainguy had reported this as early as 1949. He made many recommendations, but his main conclusion was that elaborate ceremonies should be drastically cut down, obsolete Royal Navy traditions should be abandoned, and the Royal Canadian Navy should cooperate more closely with the United States Navy. Little could have changed since that report was produced because, as recently as September 1963, *Maclean's* magazine had carried an article by retired Commodore James Plomer entitled "The Gold-braid Mind Is Destroying Our Navy." In it, Plomer paid tribute to the thoroughness of the Mainguy report and said: "On this document, this Magna Carta, an effective navy with high morale and enthusiasm could have been built. But it was not."[1] The article was a slashing attack on "the heart of the problem," which he defined as: "The self-perpetuating, self-electing group of admirals. Canadian admirals have come to believe in themselves as a social institution, a marching society, a kind of uniformed Tammany Hall ... Arrogantly, they believe that military law, the Naval Discipline Act, and pageantry are all that we need to make a modern navy ... In the year 1962, right up to the Cuban crisis, the state of readiness of the fleet was never the subject of formal discussion by the naval board. However, just before the Cuban crisis, the naval board did devote a whole morning to discussing a Tri-Service Handbook on Ceremonial and a new summer uniform for WRENS. I know. I was there."[2] Plomer was merciless.

Even more serious was the lack of integration at the top. During World War II the air force moved its overseas headquarters in London, England, out to the suburbs in order to get away from the army. The lack of communication led to some unnecessary tragedies such as the one related in the following account by Mr. Justice Keith of the Superior Court of Ontario.

"On the 14th August, 1944, when I was a senior Staff Officer in the 2nd Canadian Corps' Headquarters, I was an eye-witness to the devastation that was caused when a major air force attack intended to open the road to Falaise, was unleashed on the Third Canadian Infantry Division, including my own battalion, the Queen's Own Rifles, instead of the German defenders.

Although the aircraft were only a few thousand feet above us, there was no way the land force could communicate with the pilots, except by going through battalion, brigade, division, corps, army, army group to the war office in London, and thence back to the air force commander.

Idiocy prolonged the war by months."[3]

The problem of integration lay right at the top. The three services were operating as three separate fiefdoms. The Chiefs of Staff Committee was close to a total waste of time because each chief had direct access to the minister and none of their proposals, including equipment requirements, was coordinated with the other two services.

The straw that broke the camels back for me was when it became obvious that the three services were preparing for completely different kinds of wars. The air force was planning for a nuclear war lasting just a few days. The army plan was based on a long war with mobilization similar to World War II. The navy was somewhere in between, with a heavy emphasis on submarine warfare, which had played such an important role in their heritage.

To me the whole system was basically untenable so I resolved to prepare a White Paper listing the steps necessary to produce a rational unified system.

PRESIDENT KENNEDY IS ASSASSINATED

In November, the transitory nature of politics and of life itself was indelibly etched on the public consciousness. On November 19th, Toronto's mayor, Donald D. Summerville, died suddenly at the age of 48. I was the minister designated to represent the federal government at his funeral on November 22nd. We were of different political stripes, but he had served his city well, and I was honored to join civic leaders and colleagues at St. James Cathedral in Toronto in paying our last respects.

Midway through the service an ashen-faced Bill Lee came down the aisle, knelt down beside me and whispered, "President Kennedy has been shot. They don't know whether he will live or die." I couldn't believe it. Bill left the church but only a few minutes later he returned, knelt again and said "President Kennedy is dead." It all seemed so incredible. The leader of the free world shot down in his own country?

It was the only topic of conversation as we left the church for the committal service. Who could have perpetrated such a heinous crime? My mind flashed back to memories of the Kennedys, of their political rise and struggle, and of the times Ellen and I had been in their presence. The most exciting politician to come on stage in decades was gone, snuffed out in the prime of life. The whole civilized world mourned as our hearts went out to Jacqueline, Caroline, and little John, Jr.

Although the new U.S. President, Lyndon Johnson, was as different from his predecessor as night from day, the key players of his administration with whom we did business in the areas of foreign affairs and defense didn't change. Secretary of State Dean Rusk and Secretary of Defense Robert McNamara were an impressive team and, from my perspective, very easy to get along with.

The White Paper on Defense

After a great deal of thought and deliberation I began to write the White Paper in longhand in three sections. Most of it reflected my views of what needed to be done to eliminate as many of the existing anomalies as possible. The exception was the section on foreign policy which was largely cribbed from a report by Dr. Robert Sutherland, written for the chairman of the Chiefs of Staff Committee.

The drafts were widely circulated and many of the suggestions from readers were incorporated. I remember my Deputy Minister Elgin Armstrong requesting a private meeting one Saturday morning. His face was ashen white as he candidly advised that one section wasn't good enough. "Well," I responded, "in that case I will have to re-write it." He did me a great favor by telling me the truth, because the revised version was very much improved!

Eventually I had a document that was almost universally acceptable. The solutions went far beyond fine-tuning. They were fundamental to a new era when all significant military operations were combined operations. The new reality demanded elimination of the positions of Chief of the Naval Staff, Chief of the General Staff and Chief of the Air Staff with their replacement by a single Chief of Defence Staff with all of the powers previously exercised by the three.

Similarly, the Naval Board, the General Staff and the Air Staff were replaced by a single Defence Staff. This effectively eliminated the eternal bickering and internecine warfare over the allocation of funds and functions that had become endemic.

As a result of this streamlined command structure, staff meetings to organize United Nations operations, for example, which had previously lasted up to eight hours without agreement, were reduced to minutes, less than half an hour. Senior officers of each element knew exactly what was expected of them, and they did it.

The 267 committees that had previously recommended standard procedures and practices between services were abolished. Their recommendations could have saved taxpayers millions of dollars but were seldom if ever implemented because each service had a veto. The incredible frustration ended when the committees were replaced with staff studies that were binding on all elements. The improvements were so obvious that they were very well accepted by the service men and women themselves. They knew that public opinion demanded that something be done.

The initial reaction to the paper was splendid. It even received qualified support from Gordon Churchill and Harold Winch, the Opposition defense critics. One or two newspapers, including the *Toronto Star*, tempered their praise with reservations. Why, the *Star* asked, when I had rated thermonuclear war as the least probable eventuality, were some of the weapons systems that were proposed "wholly unsuitable" to insurrection and guerrilla conflicts.[4] The observation was valid to a point, but failed to recognize the spectrum of our responsibility, from deterrence to peacekeeping. Experience had shown that meeting diverse UN requirements, for example, was only possible if forces had a wide range of equipment.

Our troops in Europe, fulfilling our number one continuing commitment, needed tanks and heavy artillery. This kind of heavy equipment can easily be left at home when it is not needed, but there is no way it can be obtained in a hurry in the event of a major conflict. As for the continuing nuclear capability, this could not be renegotiated overnight, as some of the dreamers suggested. Whether we liked it or not, I replied to their questions, "We are committed for the present to what was decided in the past."[5]

Most editorial comment was overwhelmingly positive, as the following examples attest. In a two-page spread, the Canadian edition of *Time* magazine said, "At last, a sense of direction."[6] The *Montreal Star* observed:

"Mr. Hellyer could have drifted along, as many of his predecessors have done, with an out-dated *status quo*. Instead he has had the courage to uproot the vested interests for which the military establishment has always provided fertile soil. He has also had the imagination to see the form which that establishment should take in the context of Canada in this generation."[7]

Canadian Aviation magazine began: "Defence Minister Paul Hellyer's White Paper has been widely heralded as the most forward thinking defence document produced by any government for the past decade, and probably since World War II."[8] Finally, in a *Telegram* column entitled "Clear Thinking on Our Defence," Lubor J. Zink concluded: "Mr. Hellyer's realistic, non-partisan endeavour to create a lean, integrated force able to meet any exigency deserves the highest praise and full public support. Politicking aside, who can still say that there is hardly any difference between the past and present governments?"[9]

My popularity with the public soared. The respected *Maclean's* magazine named me as one of its "Outstanding Canadians of 1964, a politician who rose above politics to unify a nation's armed forces, a result long striven for here and abroad."[10] Twice I appeared on the cover of the U.S. *Armed Forces Journal*, supported by laudatory stories. Everywhere I went people would tell me what a good job I was doing, though I doubted that they had any real clue what it was. They were influenced by a positive press.

UNWELCOME DIVERSION

The subject of Walter Gordon's proposed Canada Pension Plan was one that I couldn't get out of my mind. I considered his plan unimaginative, because it addressed only the amount of retirement income, and then only in part, while ignoring the critically important areas of pension portability from job to job and early vesting rights in private plans, the gross inequities between citizens, and the economic impact of another pay-as-you-go program in which pensions would be paid from current taxes. This was how Walter was recommending his pension plan. To me, the proposal smacked more of political gimmickry than fundamental reform.

On the question of equity, vast numbers of people received only the Old Age Pension (OAP), while others who worked for the government, General Motors, or IBM, got both the OAP and their company pension. In some cases members of the forces had retired on a pension at the age of 45 or 50 and had found employment in the private sector. After 15 or 20 years in the new job, they would then be entitled to three pensions, all supported by deductions from taxable income. This was, I firmly believed, unfair and unjust, and in need of correction. The Canada Pension Plan proposed to perpetuate the inequity by adding another layer.

I objected strongly in Cabinet, and finally a mildly exasperated Prime Minister Pearson said, "If you don't like the plan, why don't you produce a better one?" to which I replied, "I would be delighted to." Then came the hooker, I was to be given only 10 days to do it.

Nevertheless, I took the PM at his word and busily began to sketch out an alternative plan with some help from Dr. R.W. James, a Defence Department economist. He put flesh on my ideas and together we completed the Herculean task on time. A Cabinet document was prepared for distribution.

My alternative plan was universal, funded, totally portable, fully vested from the first day, equitable, and adequate to meet the needs of all retirees. In effect it was something like a Registered Retirement Savings Plan for each individual Canadian. From the day each individual began his or her first job, that person's contributions, together with those of the employer, would go into their personalized fund as a tax-deductible investment trust. Self-employed persons would pay both employer and employee shares.

When Cabinet met on June 17th, I found that neither the PM nor Walter had taken time to read my alternative proposal, but I was given a good hearing. When I finished, you could have heard a pin drop. Finally, Judy LaMarsh broke the silence. She said a decision had to be taken that day to meet the 60 days of the beginning of the session. Some ministers said my plan merited further consideration and suggested that the resolution to be put on the Order Paper be drafted in such a way that it would embrace either plan.

As was the case with most Cabinet "discussions" of its kind, however, the die had been cast before we met. Pearson had neither the patience to consider genuine alternatives nor the ability to grasp the long-range significance of the issues. He dismissed all further discussion when he said, "the immediate object was to place on the Order Paper a resolution committing the government to do what it had promised to do in order to become a government. A real commitment had been made, which would not be met by the alternative proposal."[11]

Perhaps it was unfortunate that consideration of such an important issue overlapped with the "foofarah" over Walter Gordon's first budget, although I can't believe that it really made any difference. Too much pressure had resulted from the silly election promise to do so many things of major significance during the first 60 days in office. The result was simply that few decisions, if any, were thought out carefully enough. Certainly that was true of Walter's first budget, which shook the prime minister's faith in his finance minister, put the fate of the new minority government in jeopardy, and proved to be a major disaster. The budget proposals dragged on for months, until December. The government survived, and so did Walter. But the public's perception of us as a group of competent managers had been shattered. In the prime minister's words: "This was the end, however, the quick and almost catastrophic end of the honeymoon."[12]

REPRIEVE

The early months of 1964 were not easy for me. I had to cope with the rapidly developing separatist crisis in Quebec while trying to get the White Paper approved and published. Then there was the ever-present dilemma posed by the Canada Pension Plan. I had considered the question thoughtfully and arrived at the conclusion that I couldn't support another unfunded plan in addition to the Old Age Pension. It was too much at odds with the long-term interests of the baby-boom generation, who would have to pay the taxes for both. I decided to oppose the idea to the extent of my ability, and when I lost the battle, as seemed inevitable, resign.

The plan had not enjoyed the swift and easy passage its sponsors had hoped for. Its complexity had resulted in numerous redrafts, and provincial acquiescence was far from automatic. In fact, since Quebec had decided that it would prefer a funded plan of its own, the CPP could no longer be touted as a national plan.

On February 24th the PM indicated that the CPP would be ready within a couple of weeks. "It looks as if we plan to plow ahead, oh well!" I recorded wistfully and somewhat fatalistically in my diary. "It looks as if I have a few days' 'reprieve.'"[13]

It seemed a bit strange to be pushing ahead with the defense White Paper, knowing that I probably wouldn't be around to implement it. Still, I was never one to let what might happen tomorrow interfere with what has to be done today, so the show went on. Still, reality had to be faced, and I wanted the PM to know exactly where I stood on the CPP before the final decision was taken.

On April 9th I was granted my "long awaited interview with the Prime Minister. After a couple of awkward moments we had a good chat about the Canada Pension Plan. I outlined my objections on social and economic grounds. He undertook to check again the question of portability between the CPP and the Quebec Plan and let me know his findings on Tuesday. Regarding the White Paper, he agreed that the reaction was excellent. He said that some had thought it was a flaky proposal and some thought it would be suicidal. I wonder who."[14]

I had to visit the West Coast to address the troops and immediately on my return I went to the alcove in the parliamentary restaurant reserved for cabinet. When Mitchell Sharp arrived, he said, "There have been some dramatic developments over the weekend."[15] He explained that these included new demands for tax-sharing with the provinces and a plan to adopt a pension plan along the Quebec lines, which would permit the same benefits for all Canadians and portability from coast to coast. When the House met at two o'clock that afternoon, the PM made a brief explanation in reply to a question from John Diefenbaker, and I could hardly wait to get the story.

Later, when I saw him privately, Pearson said that the government had moved far enough in my direction that I should agree to stay. That seemed to be the case. The CPP was still a half-baked plan, but at least it would be funded in the short term, and an important element of universality had been restored. The immediate gains were enough to justify a stay of execution, a reprieve that would permit me to soldier on.

What had happened in the interim is difficult to piece together, but this much is known: Tom Kent and Maurice Sauvé went to Quebec City for a weekend meeting with the Quebec provincial government in a last ditch effort to try to reach a compromise. The meeting was arranged in great haste and maximum secrecy, so much secrecy, in fact, that no one bothered to advise Judy LaMarsh who, as Minister of Health and Welfare, was nominally in charge of the issue. That Sunday they received Premier Jean Lesage's assent and according to Judy "on their return, Kent met with the Prime Minister, Walter Gordon, Guy Favreau, and perhaps others. He made his report and the Prime Minister urged him on."[16]

When Judy learned that we were to make an accommodation with Quebec, she was livid. She didn't like the funding provision at all, not because she was opposed in principle, but because she felt she had been made a fool of. She had bought Walter's proposal hook, line and sinker and "had spent a solid year making speeches about our pay-as-you-go scheme."[17] In the end there were compromises on both sides, and cabinet accepted them. Judy capitulated on the grounds of universality. "There was no other way if there were to be a system of universal pensions across the whole of Canada. One for nine provinces was unthinkable and probably unworkable."[18] No one ever admitted that I had influenced the outcome. My only clue was that Walter Gordon didn't speak to me for three weeks following the reversal in policy.

Walter had warmed perceptibly by the time I saw him on May 6th, just after he got back from a trip to Vancouver. He said the prime minister was given great credit for his diplomacy and skill in working out the settlement with Quebec. Then he added: "That isn't exactly the way it happened. It was more like a game of poker when you have only one move left and it is an all-or-nothing decision. It doesn't always work out so well."[19]

Before actually walking the plank on this issue I had decided it would be prudent to get an independent opinion from someone whose judgment I trusted. So on April 2nd I had sent a copy of the proposed CPP, together with a copy of my alternative plan, to Graham Towers, former Governor of the Bank of Canada. I thought he had the best financial mind the country had yet produced. His reply wasn't received until after the government changed course, but his comments are well worth noting.

"I share your apprehension in regard to the Canada Pension Plan, even as amended. The inequities could be formidable ..." Mr. Towers showed unusual prescience. He continued: "Turning to your alternate plan, I think it is workable and much better for the country than the Canada Pension Plan."[20]

When it was all over Walter promised me that he would integrate the CPP with industrial pension plans. But he didn't follow through on this promise – so all of the old problems remained. It is a pity that the alternative plan wasn't adopted. It would have eliminated all of the angst and uncertainty suffered by former employees of Canadian companies such as Nortel and Sears Canada. Their money would have been safely invested in the registered financial institution of their choice and they would no longer have been dependent on the success – or failure – of their employer.

CHAPTER TEN

THE PEARSON ERA: PART II

A NATO MEETING IN PARIS

My experience as Minister of Defence was a fast learning curve in many ways. One conclusion I drew quickly was that many international meetings were little more than a forum to rehash old problems rather than to reach conclusions on which action could be based. Yet there was something compelling about doing your duties despite how they were perceived by others.

On December 9th Paul Martin Sr. and I took off for Paris to join the Americans and our other colleagues at the annual NATO council meeting. We crossed the ocean non-stop from Ottawa to Paris in one of the RCAF's long-range Yukon aircraft. Paul headed the delegation, which included his officials from External Affairs. I was accompanied by Air Chief Marshal Frank Miller, CCOS, and one of his aides, as well as Bill Lee, Lt.-Col. Reg Weeks, and Marg Bulger from my own office. In conformity with government policy, Nell Martin and Ellen were the only wives allowed, a rule that has been relaxed somewhat since then.

When ministers of several countries met, the discussion followed predictable lines. The United States felt it was carrying more than its fair share of the defense burden, and other countries, especially the European countries and Canada, should do more. Another perennial topic was the composition of nuclear forces and the control of nuclear weapons. Was it desirable to have a NATO nuclear force, so that the Americans would not appear to have exclusive responsibility in this field? If so, which nations should contribute?

Even more difficult was the thorny question of authorizing the use of nuclear weapons. What were the mechanics by which a decision for a nuclear strike would be taken, and was the process sufficiently realistic to prevent Europe from being overrun while the powers that be were still trying to agree?

Then there was the constant necessity for a build-up in conventional strength to raise the threshold at which nuclear weapons might be required. The agenda also included the question of assistance to poorer countries like Greece and Turkey, whose defense budgets were already stretched.

This was largely how the Paris discussions went, with only a few noteworthy deviations such as an American request that we widen NATO horizons on a global scale to encompass areas of conflict such as Vietnam, a request that fell on deaf ears. When the agenda which included the round of official receptions and dinners was concluded, it was time to go home. We hadn't seen anything of Paris except the fleeting glimpses we got through a car window. It all sounded so wonderfully glamorous to fly to Paris for a meeting, but it was just hard work and extremely tiring as well. One bright spot was the trip home. The work was all done, so everyone was relaxed and in a good mood, and some of us enjoyed a game of bridge.

It was the season for giving, and as luck would have it I had something for Governor General George Vanier's stocking, with no price tag attached. I promoted him, a valiant veteran of World War I who had lost a leg in battle, from Major-General to full General effective January 1, 1964. To give credit where it is due, the idea originated with Judy LaMarsh, who suggested it to me. She was very sensitive to that kind of special gesture, and I agreed wholeheartedly. It was strictly symbolic, because His Excellency was already Commander-in-Chief of the navy, the army, and the air force, but the parchment was a kind of tacit recognition of the sacrificial service the Governor General had rendered to his country throughout a long and distinguished career. He was as pleased as a child with a new toy, telling me it was the best Christmas present he had received that year.

MARITIME COMMAND

The next major item on the agenda was an intensive six-day immersion course into the functions of the navy and the RCAF's Maritime Air Command. On Sunday, January 19th, I flew from Ottawa to Bermuda where I transferred to a navy plane that took me to the aircraft carrier *Bonaventure*. It was like landing on a postage stamp in the middle of the ocean. I still remember the sense of relief when the hook on the plane caught the cable on the ship's deck and we came to a wrenching stop. The navy treated me and my staff royally. We had a wonderful dinner but during the night the weather changed and the ocean became very rough. Nearly all of my staff became ill. Nevertheless, it was pretty much business as usual.

In the morning I was scheduled for a jackstay crossing from the aircraft carrier to the destroyer escort *Restigouche* where the anti-submarine exercise "Gooey Duck" was well underway. A jackstay crossing happens when you transfer from one ship to another on a cable that has been strung between them while the ships are still moving. In this case the transfer across a thousand feet of ocean was difficult because the water was very rough and it required great skill to keep the two ships moving parallel to one another.

Eventually, all was set and I was snapped into a harness, but the final instruction, just as my feet left the heaving deck, was far from reassuring. "If anything goes wrong, for heaven's sake, let go. We will just circle around and pick you up." It was the kind of advice one reflects on deeply when suspended halfway between sky and sea.

Once on board the *Restigouche* I was particularly impressed with Commodore Welland, the officer in charge of operation "Gooey Duck." I was assured that it was a total success. Months later, after Welland had been promoted to Rear Admiral, one of his staff officers alleged that the Commodore had "cooked" the log in order to "impress the minister." I must admit I was surprised.

Before long I was back in Bermuda, and began the final flight to Halifax in a giant Argus submarine-hunter. We flew the entire route at 300 to 500 feet "off the deck," as they called it. The nearest comparable experience would be driving 800 miles on a very, very bumpy road. Once again, nearly all of our party were sick so it was a relief when we finally landed at Dartmouth naval base, across the harbor from Halifax.

THE CYPRUS CRISIS

On February 3, 1964, I noted: "The Cyprus thing, too, is boiling. It is almost certain that we will be asked for troops. Someone said that it would not be politic to send the Van Doos, (the popular abbreviation for the Royal Twenty-Second Regiment that was a French-speaking unit.) The GOC (General Officer Commanding) Quebec command disagrees, and so do I."[1]

For almost three weeks the question was front and center in the Commons, as the diplomatic dithering continued. In the end, it was Paul Martin who pulled the chestnuts from the fire. At the prime minister's suggestion, he had gone to New York to tell U.N. Secretary General U Thant that if Sweden would participate, he would announce Canada's decision to join a UN force in Cyprus. He found, to his dismay, that the possibility of Swedish cooperation was still in limbo, and the Secretary General was pessimistic about success. It was at this stage that Paul decided to phone some of his fellow foreign ministers directly, in an effort to break the deadlock. He succeeded. As he recalls in *A Very Public Life*, Vol. II, "The result of my phone calls was the establishment of the UN force in Cyprus. After everything had been arranged, I telephoned a rather surprised U Thant in New York to tell him the good news."[2] It was one of Paul Martin's finest hours.

I was called back to Ottawa from a speaking tour in Winnipeg. The Defence Department was ready. I hadn't taken the PM's earlier reservations too seriously, and a contingency plan for sending troops to Cyprus had been prepared. In this case the department deserved full marks for doing its job well, and we were in a position to act on a minute's notice.

Everything came together on March 13th when the PM asked for parliamentary approval. An emergency debate was held that evening with only a little procedural kicking and screaming from the Quebec *Créditistes*, who alleged that their parliamentary privileges were being abused. Meanwhile, we had our first contingent in the air and on its way by the time the debate began. It could easily have been recalled if Parliament had denied its approval, but at least we would gain a few critical hours if, as expected, Parliament concurred in the government's decision.

Everyone was impressed with Canada's quick response. In *Mike*, Vol. III, the PM recorded the U.S. reaction as follows:

"President Johnson was amazed and filled with admiration at our ability to act so quickly, and I think this may have changed his attitude toward Canada." He phoned me again the night we began our airlift to say: "You'll never know what this has meant, having those Canadians off to Cyprus and being there tomorrow: you'll never know what this may have prevented." Having praised us for our action, he concluded: "Now what can I do for you?" I replied: "Nothing at the moment, Mr. President." But I had some credit in the bank.[3]

Later, I talked to one well-known American-born economist who thought it may have been this "credit" that influenced the United States to sign the Autopact in 1965.

AN UNLIKELY STORY BUT TRUE

At the end of August I headed north to spend the final weekend of the summer season at Arundel Lodge, our "non-profit" tourist resort in Muskoka that I had acquired from Curran Hall. Early Saturday morning, Ellen took the car and headed for Ottawa to get the children ready for school. I was left all alone to close up on Sunday once the staff had left. I put on an old suit with badly frayed sleeves and loaded up our battered pick-up truck. By the time I cleaned out the refrigerator, there was nothing left but two slices of dry bread and one very small bottle of Muskoka Dry ginger ale.

Halfway to Ottawa I stopped for gas. As I pulled into the gas station I noticed a hitchhiker and decided to offer him a ride when I left. He was still there as I pulled out, and he cheerfully climbed aboard. I asked him if he had eaten lunch and he said no, so I offered him one of my two slices of dry bread and apologized for not sharing the ginger ale which I had already started.

After we finished eating I asked him where he was headed, and he said Petawawa. He was a soldier, he told me, although he was wearing civvies at the time. Then he asked me what I did and I said that I, too, worked for the Department of National Defence. He asked me where. "In Ottawa," I replied. "In the minister's office," I added, after further prodding. But what, specifically, did I do in the minister's office, he demanded, at which point I admitted that I was the minister. This caused a silence that lasted until we reached the fork in the road where I turned south and he went north to Petawawa. He thanked me for the ride and then, as an afterthought, he added a very hesitant, "Sir."

A few weeks later, in early November, Ellen and I visited Petawawa where we were guests at the 8th Canadian Hussars (Princess Louise's) Military Ball. I recounted the incident to the commandant, Maj.-Gen. R. Rowley, "Oh yes," he replied. "The story is all over camp about the nut who thought he was the minister of defence."

A NEW FLAG FOR CANADA

The year 1965 was memorable for many reasons. My Associate Minister Lucien Cardin was given a department of his own as Minister of Public Works. He deserved it, but he would be sorely missed in Defence because he had been most conscientious in dealing with the thousands of pieces of paper I had directed to him.

His replacement was Léo Cadieux, who was completely unknown to me. He was sworn in on February 15th, the day Canada's new flag was proclaimed after one of the most protracted and bitter debates on record. The subject of the new flag had been discussed for years but the final push began on May 19, 1964 after the prime minister's famous speech to the Canadian Legion when he had been booed by the veterans after suggesting that Canada should have its own flag.

The Royal Canadian Legion launched a campaign in opposition, so the prime minister decided we had to move ahead with the plan to choose a new flag. In May, cabinet approved a resolution adopting a design with three maple leaves and blue bars that became known as "The Pearson Pennant."

When the sixth report of the special parliamentary committee on a Canadian flag was presented to the House of Commons on Tuesday, October 29, 1964, it did not recommend the so-called Pearson Pennant. After 45 meetings, and *in camera* testimony from 12 expert witnesses, the committee eliminated all but two of the approximately 2,000 designs that had been presented to it.

At that stage the Tories decided to play a little trick. Confident that the Liberals would remain stubbornly faithful to the three-leaf design, the PCs decided to vote for the single-leaf version that subsequently became the Canadian flag. Imagine their surprise when the Liberals switched horses and backed the Tory choice. For the PM it was a typical, but in this case a very sensible, compromise. The debate on the motion for the House to concur in the committee report continued for weeks. Finally on December

14th, after 270 speeches, the government imposed closure, and the report was adopted with the Tories still opposed.

When February 15, 1965 came, there were few hitches. I drove to Parliament Hill with the Red Ensign flying for the last time from the staff on my car fender. At the ceremony, purely by chance, I stood near former Prime Minister John Diefenbaker, who had declined the opportunity to speak and who shed a few tears. The mood of the majority was movingly reported by *Ottawa Citizen* staff writer Jim Rae in his full-page article headed "Ten Thousand Cheer Raising a New Flag."

At cabinet the next day Jack Pickersgill said that "the inauguration of the national flag, including the Ottawa ceremony, had been a great triumph for the prime minister. The flag would do steadily more good for the country as the years passed."[4]

ANOTHER DIFFERENCE OF OPINION WITH WALTER GORDON

As early as December 1964 Walter Gordon sent the PM a memorandum urging an early spring election. Some polling had suggested the Liberal Party was in the lead. Walter continued the pressure in the spring. I was dead set against an election because there was no reason to justify it.

In addition to holding contrary views about the need for an early election Walter and I continued to differ on the best way to approach the development of social policy, this time on the subject of health insurance. I thought that we should ask for an in-depth study, beginning with the nature of the problem and progressing to alternative solutions, stating the advantages and disadvantages of each. It didn't seem either logical or sensible to assume that Canada would simply opt for some imitation of the British system, with all its imperfections, without so much as wondering if there was a better way.

When the subject was discussed in cabinet on July 16, 1965, in the context of determining a government position on health insurance for a federal-provincial conference, I put forward an alternative to medicare. After my experience with the Canada Pension Plan, I didn't prepare a cabinet document but simply made an oral presentation to see if I could elicit any interest. My formula was designed to satisfy all three of the criteria I had set out. Everyone would be allowed to go to the doctor and/or hospital of their choice, and each would be responsible for their own medical bills up to a limit of two percent of their gross income. They would be 100 percent insured for expenditures in excess of that amount. Those with $100,000 in annual income would pay their own bills up to $2,000. Those earning $30,000 would pay up to $600, while people with no income would pay nothing. No one would be subjected to financial hardship as a result of medical expenses because the burden would be proportionate to their ability to pay.

When I finished my presentation every cabinet minister who spoke, and most of them did, said it was a better, more efficient proposal than the one they had before them. There were no exceptions. Walter Gordon was the last to speak. He, too, said it was a better plan. "But," he added, "it wouldn't be politic." With those five words, rational debate ended, and the discussion of alternatives was over.

A FALL ELECTION

When cabinet met on September 1ˢᵗ, the results of a highly successful lobbying effort by Walter Gordon and Keith Davey were clearly evident. Previously, nearly the entire cabinet was opposed, but one by one the majority including Jack Pickersgill, had succumbed. To soften my opposition I had been shown Oliver Quale's polling results. I was unimpressed by what I read.

On September 24ᵗʰ Ellen and I left for England, where Ellen was scheduled to christen the second of our new "O" class submarines, HMCS *Onondaga*. Normally this would have been a seven-day affair. We were guests of the British government, which had purchased tickets for concerts at London's Royal Festival Hall and had planned an extensive and interesting program. Due to the Canadian election, however, the visit had to be what the military call a "fast turnaround." Ellen always referred to it as "the time I flew to England for lunch," which was a slight exaggeration, but only slight.

The election was called for November 8ᵗʰ, at a time when I had numerous commitments in addition to doing what I could in the election.

Election day was terrible, with rain teeming all day. Within minutes of the polls closing I knew I was okay. My campaign manager Ted Elliot and his super team had produced an overall majority for me. Nationally, however, the party didn't do so well. It was another minority. The prime minister was shattered and (according to Keith Davey who was there) almost resigned, but Mrs. Pearson talked him out of it.

On November 12ᵗʰ Walter Gordon resigned from cabinet. Keith (Davey) said that Walter submitted his resignation on the basis of his performance as Liberal Campaign Chairman, and it was ostensibly accepted on that basis. In truth, however, he was fired from the Finance portfolio. Mike offered him another portfolio, but he refused, as you might expect.[5] Walter was also offered the post of Canadian ambassador to Washington but said he "had no interest in such an appointment."[6] In retrospect, Walter's departure from the cabinet not only ended what he regarded as a "political partnership" with Pearson, but also their "long personal friendship."[7] The wound was so deep that, with the excuse of an ice storm, Walter wasn't present at Mike's funeral seven years later.

After the election the prime minister made it clear that he would not be seeking re-election. By 1966, after three years in the Defence portfolio, I was one of the most popular Liberals in Canada; therefore it was quite natural that friends and staff alike started talking about me taking a crack at the leadership when the PM stepped down. So, like several of my colleagues, I would take advantage of official trips to various cities to talk to local Liberals and find out what they were thinking. A number volunteered to support me when the time came.

The PM offered me a change in portfolio but I declined because I knew that my job at Defence was not finished. If I didn't unify the armed forces by means of legislation, nobody would. Other ministers including the venerable Brooke Claxton had begun the process. He unified the civilian side of the department and the military colleges but then gave up, when Prime Minister William Lyon Mackenzie King reneged on a promise to make him minister of external affairs if he finished the job.

I knew that unless the three services were legally one organization, someone would try to turn the clock back at some future date. Therefore I decided to unify them into one corporate entity. A collateral decision was to put everyone in the same uniform. This was not just to save money in forces too small to justify the administrative costs of three. It related to officers who would attend a meeting, count the uniforms, and complain if they were under-represented, even if the subject of the meeting had little to do with their element. The psychological warfare had to end in a single-minded desire to serve the best interests of their country in the fighting services. This was not a new idea sprung on the forces. My White Paper had made it very clear that "integration," as it was called, was the first step toward a single unified defense force for Canada.

Before tabling the unification bill in Parliament, however, I decided to meet with all of the senior officers of the three services and ask if anyone could give me a specific operational problem that would result from unification.

When we met, most of the "two stars" were supportive to varying degrees. It was sometimes difficult to determine who had an eye on future promotion and who were totally sincere, although in most cases I could guess. At least I found out what I wanted to know. There was no valid military objection to unification. The opposition was purely emotional. This I understood, although some of the comments were pretty superficial. It was so irrelevant that the secretary, Ron Sutherland, prepared two sets of minutes: one unexpurgated version, of which only three or four copies were made, and another totally innocuous version that stands as the official record. My own notes of the occasion show we were primarily concerned with buttons and badges. Important though these are, one is scraping the bottom of the barrel to include them in a serious discussion of whether it made more sense for land, sea and air forces to operate as a single unified team or in relative isolation.

The Unification Bill

From the moment that Bill C-243 was introduced in the House of Commons it was obvious that there would be total war along strictly partisan lines. The idea of a single service with a single uniform was the straw that broke the camel's back for many of the senior officers whose opinions had been muted until that point. Backed by veterans' organizations of all sorts, the battle was joined.

Of the two major objections I think the uniform was the biggest hurdle. It wasn't the principle as much as the color. I sensed as soon as I saw them that they were not as handsome as a naval officer's uniform, and this would be a problem. But the three "models" from the three services seemed so terribly proud of what they were wearing that I was reluctant to overrule what had been a staff decision. It was my biggest mistake as minister.

If I were to do it again, I would choose navy blue for the principal uniform, khaki for summer wear, as it had been common to all three services, and white for weddings and ceremonial occasions such as visiting foreign ports for the navy. But this is all hindsight and the color of a uniform doesn't influence the outcome in wartime.

All Hell Broke Loose

When Bill C-243 was referred to committee I allowed senior officers to speak their minds freely, more in the American tradition than in the British and Canadian where serving officers had always been required to keep any negative opinion to themselves.

The results were disastrous. Opinion was sharply divided between officers, but those who were opposed got headlines while those who supported the minister and the government would only get two or three column inches. The naysayers had a field day with the press and I got clobbered. The prime minister decided to pull the rug out from under me as he had a couple of other ministers, including Guy Favreau.

He decided to invite my wife Ellen and me to join him and Mrs. Pearson in his private railway car to Quebec City to attend the funeral of Governor General George Vanier. After a delicious dinner the two of us retired to his bedroom to chat.

The issue was whether to leave the key provisions of the Bill until the next session of Parliament, as the Conservatives were demanding, or pass the Bill before we adjourned for Expo 67. The Tory proposal would allow Bill C-243 to die on the vine, which meant that the whole process would need to begin again in a new session. The only way to save the Bill was to pass it before the current session ended.

When he asked for my opinion I simply said: "You are the boss and you can do whatever you like. But if you leave the Bill to the next session you will have to get a new minister to complete it."

"You are serious, aren't you?" he asked.

"Yes, Sir," I replied.

"Well I guess in that case we will have to make it one of two pieces of legislation to be dealt with in the current Session." And that, with a little prodding, was exactly the way it turned out.

TURMOIL IN THE MIDDLE EAST

Intelligence reports indicated that war was about to break out in the Middle East. Apparently this possibility had been discussed by cabinet during my absence in Western Canada, inspecting army cadets, so when I flew home and asked for permission to pull our troops out of the Gaza Strip it was agreed at once, without debate.

The evacuation of Canadian troops from the Gaza Strip began on Monday, May 29th. Six Hercules aircraft, the ones that the RCAF had been reluctant to buy, flew personnel from El Arish to Pisa, Italy, the UN staging base in Europe. The first 360 personnel were transferred to Yukon aircraft at Pisa for the trip home to Trenton, Ontario. The evacuation plan that was put into effect called for all Canadian troops in UNEF to be out of the United Arab Republic by sunset May 30th, the deadline imposed by Colonel Nasser after he learned from the UN Secretary General of the Canadian intention to withdraw. His indignant ultimatum was in response to our plan to pull out, rather than the reason for it, as was reported at the time.

On June 2nd, in an address to the World Federation of Canada, I admitted "that the compulsory withdrawal of the United Nations Emergency Force had been a 'setback' to the cause of world peacekeeping … the ideals of the United Nations Charter have been frustrated by the unwillingness of member states to accept the restraints on the exercise of national sovereignty implicit in such a system. This will remain the case until replaced by international trust. In the meantime, we must expect slow progress and not be too surprised when setbacks to the concept, such as the current one in the Middle East, do occur."[8]

On June 3rd I flew to St. Paul, Alberta, a bilingual community northeast of Edmonton. The brief visit proved to be both exciting and memorable. St. Paul boasted the largest number of Canadian Centennial projects (1967 marked Canada's 100th anniversary of Confederation) of any Canadian community, and I was showered with mementos ranging from imaginative computer printouts by school children to a cowhide bearing the signatures of the entire population. The *pièce de résistance* for me, however, was being able to preside at the dedication of the world's first Flying Saucer Landing

Pad, erected by the citizens of St. Paul. You can still find out more about it by searching the internet.

Dedicating the Landing Pad, in addition to the "sightings reports" which indicated that approximately 80% of all sightings reported by the public were natural phenomena, while the remaining 20% were literally unidentified flying objects (UFOs), were my only two connections to the extraterrestrial phenomena while I was Minister of National Defence.

The following week I visited Mobile Command Headquarters for another performance of the "Armed Forces Tattoo." None of the magic was lost when I saw it for a second time. The unique feature of the week, however, was the big naval review in Halifax, the most spectacular naval array ever assembled in Canadian waters. Forty warships from Canada and 12 from Commonwealth and foreign countries were reviewed by Governor General Roland Michener. As the big ships steamed past, I recall that two or three times, with a twinkle in his eye, the GG asked me when I was going to make him an admiral, presumably in accordance with the precedent set for General Vanier. I always assumed that he was kidding, although I was never completely certain.

When the festivities ended, the prime minister offered his nemesis, The Rt. Hon. John G. Diefenbaker, a lift back to Ottawa in a government plane. Later he told me that, en route, my name came into the conversation.

"I like that man Hellyer," the Leader of the Opposition told him.

"You're joking," replied the PM.

"Oh no," said the Dief. "I have a lot of time for him. He's my kind of guy."

"How can you say that," Pearson demanded, "when in the House of Commons you have been cutting him mercilessly into little pieces?"

"Ah yes," responded the old chief, "but that's politics."[9]

Friendship aside, the chief was probably not as pleased with a nice boost I got from the *Ottawa Citizen* the final Tuesday of Canada's 99th year. A brief editorial, entitled "Anti-unifiers Please Note," read as follows: "Armed Forces recruiting for the first five months of 1967 is up 73% over the same period of 1966. The month of May was the biggest recruiting month since 1962."[10] What had all that fuss about unification destroying morale been about?

Cabinet's morale was shaken on June 29th by a portent of things to come on another front. The PM advised us that arrangements for the visit of General de Gaulle were leading to a number of awkward situations and that plans were being made to minimize any serious friction. The Governor General would greet the French president on arrival, and would then turn him over to Premier Daniel Johnson of Quebec. He would be in the hands of Quebec authorities for the morning, and would then come back to the feds in the afternoon. There was some disagreement over the arrangements for the evening reception. Quebec wanted to host it, but the Canadian authorities were continuing to insist that it was the GG's prerogative, in keeping with the practice followed for other heads of state.

At the same meeting there was discussion of a constitutional Bill of Rights. Cabinet had a memo from Pierre Trudeau proposing that, at the July 5th meeting with the premiers, the possibility of a Bill of Rights be explored.[11] Late that afternoon the Queen and the Duke of Edinburgh arrived at Uplands Airport and excitement increased as the countdown to July 1st and the official Centennial birthday continued.

HAPPY BIRTHDAY CANADA

Saturday, July 1st, was a day to remember! For me it began in a most unexpected fashion. I was at my office early, taking advantage of a few quiet hours, when the phone rang. It was the irrepressible Premier of Newfoundland, Joey Smallwood, who seemed equally surprised and delighted that I was "on duty." Coming quickly to the point, he told me that fires in the Labrador forests were out of control and forest rangers could no longer cope. He asked me if I would send help from the armed forces? "Yes," I replied, and the conversation ended.

I called General Jean Allard, my new Chief of the Defence Staff, and within hours an advance party was in the air. By early morning there were soldiers on the ground, fighting the fires shoulder-to-shoulder with the rangers. The story ended happily a few smoke-filled, back-breaking days later when the fires began to abate. Joey credited the armed forces with saving the forest industry that was so critical to the economy of Newfoundland.

At Nepean Point, where the Centennial spectacle was to be held, we were seated directly behind the Pearsons and the royal party. The narrative in sound and light told the story of Canada from its early beginnings through to the day we were celebrating. Commenting on the Fathers of Confederation, a deep booming voice said: "I prefer Sir John A. Macdonald drunk to George Brown sober." With less than a second's interval Her Majesty turned to the prime minister saying: "We have a George Brown too, and he is seldom sober." It was a wistful comment about an English politician I came to admire for his many other endearing qualities.

When the performance ended, the fireworks began. An unbelievably dazzling display of pyrotechnics etched the gray stone Parliament Buildings and Peace Tower against the deep blue night. It was a thrilling spectacle that drew exclamations from the crowd, including some of us who are not known for expressions of emotion. Instead of subsiding with the flicker of the last barrage of rockets, the excitement actually intensified as we drove downtown and midnight approached. People waved and shouted, horns were blown incessantly, there was a general euphoria that resembled the celebrations at the end of a long war. The nationalistic binge was unlike anything I had seen before or am likely to see again.

Back to Business as Usual

The celebrations could not continue at that pitch, and soon it was back to work. On July 11th I flew to Newfoundland with my friend, Jack Pickersgill. In a brief interlude, pacing back and forth in front of his cottage, Jack confided that he planned to leave the government and accept a job as the first president of the Canadian Transport Commission, established by the legislation he had piloted through the House in 1966 and early 1967. My name, he said, was one of two he had mentioned to the Prime Minister as a suitable successor as Minister of Transport.

At noon on July 14th Ellen and I attended a luncheon Lionel Chevrier, our High Commissioner to London, held at the Montreal St. James's Club in honor of Lord Mountbatten. Our host seated me opposite the guest of honor, as we were well acquainted and had much of mutual interest to talk about. Inevitably unification became the main topic of conversation, and despite his publicly stated reservations about the uniform, Mountbatten was still very much in favor of the initiative. As we talked, the exchange became more and more animated until finally, in a burst of emotion and with that characteristic modesty for which he was noted, he slammed his fist on the table and said: "There are only two people who understand this; you over here and me over there." If only that declaration had been captured on film. It would have made a great endorsement.

General Charles de Gaulle Visits Canada

It was more than ironic that, in a year when relations between French and English-speaking Canadians appeared to reach an all-time high in the common celebration, trouble should come from abroad. The government had been nervous about General De Gaulle's visit and the persistent efforts by France and Quebec to bend protocol enough to establish a unique relationship between them. However, even given these warnings, no one was prepared for what did happen. De Gaulle's cry of "Vive le Quebec Libre" during his speech in Montreal seemed an obscene gesture in the midst of a celebration of Canada's 100 years as a federation. The prime minister and members of cabinet were appalled and shaken. Worse, they had to decide how to react to the General's outburst at a time when he had not yet visited Canada's capital and was still scheduled to do so.

I was in Saskatchewan at the time, which I consider a blessing as I was spared involvement in the protracted debate on how the Canadian government should respond. Apparently, after seemingly interminable argument, a watered-down press release was agreed upon. The invitation to visit Ottawa was not withdrawn, although there were some minor changes to the schedule, largely for security reasons. Nevertheless, mild as it was, the government's reaction could still be interpreted as a reprimand for a head of state.[12]

Cabinet must have been relieved when it met at 9:00 a.m. the following morning and Paul Martin reported that, in the middle of the night, the Canadian Ambassador to France, Jules Léger, had been informed by the Foreign Minister of France, Couve de Murville, that General de Gaulle had indicated he did not intend to come to Ottawa. Mr. Martin also said that he himself had spoken directly to the foreign minister, who had indicated that, in his judgment, pressing the matter with the General would not alter his decision, and the best course was to let him depart.[13]

The fallout from this incredible episode was not unlike that from an atomic explosion. It dissipated substantially over the years, but never completely disappeared. Argument raged as to whether the General acted deliberately or was merely carried away by the warmth and enthusiasm with which he had been greeted by the people of Quebec. In my view, based on the evidence, and influenced by my experience aboard the *S.S. France* and by subsequent events, it was a coldly calculated act. It was an escalation of French mischief, born in part of remorse for France's centuries of neglect of its former colony and in part of a dream of turning back the clock.

While I could not condone de Gaulle's impertinence, I was more understanding than many of my colleagues. I recalled the resentment he held against Anglophones in general as a result of the second-class treatment afforded him by Churchill and Roosevelt during the war. Inevitably some of this would have spilled over on the Canadian establishment, and the feeling was probably reinforced by the shabby way Canada treated France when it wanted to buy our uranium. We had imposed restrictions that had not applied to the United States and Britain, and which were unacceptable to the French for that reason. This must have been a festering sore. So, apart from the historic relationship with New France, meddling in Canada's internal affairs was one way of de Gaulle's getting even, with relish!

THE MILITARY VOTE

The week of August 6th, cabinet considered items of interest to the defence department. On August 8th I noted that it might be necessary to amend the Elections Act in order to integrate the armed forces vote with other returns on election night. This was to eliminate a long-standing grievance. Traditionally the service vote had been taken at the same time as the civilian vote, but by the time it was counted and reported from the four corners of the world, about a week would pass. In some cases candidates didn't know, until the service vote was released, whether they had been elected or not. Worse, from the standpoint of members of the forces, the delay meant their vote was singled out for national attention, which they did not like.

For years the chief electoral officer had insisted there was no solution to this vexatious anomaly. But as in numerous other cases where officials said something was impossible, once they were instructed to do it anyway, it did become possible. As far as the service vote was concerned, the impasse was resolved by the simple expedient of taking the vote in advance, so the results could be unobtrusively melded with national returns on election night.

When I got back to Ottawa, after spending some time with the army cadets at Camp Vernon, BC, I received a nice psychological boost from the *Ottawa Journal* in an article titled "Wants It as Quickly as Possible: Canada's NATO forces Stirred by New Uniform" by Maj.-Gen. F.F. Worthington, Special Journal Correspondent. "Worthy," who was Colonel-Commandant of the Royal Canadian Armoured Corps, had been invited overseas to present the annual trophy for the best tank gunnery among the NATO forces. He travelled in the new green uniform, the first Canadian to wear it in Europe.

As he wrote: "It was a curious sensation. I admit I felt somewhat like a little green man from Mars at times, but the reaction among all ranks was one of outright enthusiasm to get it. Perhaps even more surprising was the enthusiasm of our NATO allies. The Germans especially seemed keen on it. Now you Canadians will be recognizable – now you can look like yourselves and not like the British was the comment I heard over and over from Germans, Dutch and Belgian officers."[14]

A Change in Portfolio

Not long after that, Mike phoned to tell me that I would be moving from Defence to Transport. We didn't discuss the succession in Defence because I assumed Léo Cadieux would move up. I should have known that nothing can be taken for granted in politics and should not have been surprised when the grapevine telegraphed a whiff of uncertainty. My curiosity aroused, I phoned the PM Saturday morning, September 16th, to get the straight goods. I could scarcely believe my ears when he said he was going to appoint Léo "acting minister." Knowing Léo's strong feelings about the division of senior portfolios, between English and French speaking ministers, I was certain that this wouldn't be acceptable, and I said so. I also assured him that Léo was perfectly capable and probably better than anyone else, because he had been involved in the unification process and understood it. It was only logical that he should finish the job. After a few minutes he said, "Why don't I just call him and say I am going to appoint him." I agreed and said, "You're wonderful." To have done otherwise would have driven poor old Léo right up the wall, and rightly so.[15]

Sunday was sunny and warm, summer in September. I attended the Battle of Britain ceremony for the last time, and then went to Toronto for a meeting of my national campaign committee. It was a good meeting: Not as orderly as the last one, but worthwhile. The situation seemed to be improving in all provinces from Ontario west.

"I told the boys at the airport that this would likely be my last trip as MND. They seemed genuinely sorry. Group Captain Boland (Commanding Officer of Canadian Forces Base, Downsview) said I would be missed. He wished me well and said that he hoped I became leader of the country and that quite a few chaps at the base agreed."[16]

THE LEADERSHIP RACE

Transport offered a new challenge that I relished. I adjusted to the job like a duck to water. I traveled widely to gain first-hand knowledge of the personalities involved, which was important for problems that appeared to be intractable. At the same time I took advantage of the opportunities travel presented to talk to party officials and seek their support for the leadership contest that appeared to be increasingly imminent. The effort bore fruit and with the withdrawal from the race, albeit temporary, of my colleague Robert Winters, I was clearly a front runner. This was before Pierre Trudeau began his rocket-boosted ascent to stardom.

The possibility of Trudeau's entry made us all apprehensive. To begin, there was the Liberal tradition of alternating between English-speaking and French-speaking leaders that was bound to be an important factor. Pearson may have had this in mind when he tried very hard to persuade Jean Marchand to run; but Jean said no, partially due to his English, which was much better than he realized. In any event, Trudeau was Marchand's choice and soon became Pearson's quiet choice. The PM provided every support possible.

First, and most important, Pearson sent Pierre across Canada in a government plane to talk to premiers about the forthcoming Federal-Provincial Conference on the Constitution. Trudeau was considered an expert on the subject and a natural to brief premiers and be updated by them, in order to report to the PM. More important, from the standpoint of the leadership, he impressed some of them very favorably. His biggest coup came in Newfoundland, where he enchanted the premier, Joey Smallwood.

Smallwood had been firmly in Robert Winters' camp but when he withdrew, Joey's formidable power was up for grabs. He had told me that I was his second choice but changed his mind after Trudeau's visit. In the end, Smallwood wouldn't let anyone on the government plane for a free ride to the convention unless they promised to vote for Pierre. The result was a near solid block, with only a handful of dissenters having both the resources and the willpower to hold out in the face of Joey's wrath. A few, subsequently, paid dearly for their independence.

Another step that Pearson took was to promote Bryce Mackasey, MP from the Montréal Verdun riding to cabinet for the specific purpose of supporting Trudeau. He also backed my good friend Richard (Dick) Stanbury for the presidency of the party so that he would have to be neutral, rather than support me. It was further reported, on good authority, that Pearson's private secretary and confidante, Mary Macdonald, at a breakfast meeting of delegates from the PM's Algoma East riding, made it clear that they were expected to support Trudeau, which presumably they did.

In any event, on that fateful April 6, 1968, when the first ballot results were announced, Trudeau led by a wide margin with 752 votes, leaving me a distant second with 330, followed by Winters with 293 and Martin and Turner with 277 each. However, on the second ballot, Winters, a Maritimer, moved into the number two spot by a slim margin of eight ballots with the help of Maritime delegates who opted for their second choice when Nova Scotia's favorite son, Allan MacEachen, withdrew from the race. At that moment it was all over for both Winters and me. One wiseacre CBC reporter blamed me for Trudeau's victory by not moving to Winters immediately, rather than waiting until the fourth ballot. He was obviously not "in the know," as it were.

Toronto lawyer Bill Macdonald, who had written my speech, and his partner Joe Duffin, had done extensive polling on people's second, third and fourth choices as well as who they did not want as leader. There were more delegates who did not want Winters, presumably because he was too far right for the majority, than who did not want Trudeau. There were more people who did not want Trudeau than those who did not want me. So, if I had hung on to second place I would likely have won by a very slim margin.

Bill Lee, my closest advisor and I remembered about 16 ways that the eight-vote difference might, under other circumstances, have been overcome. One example involved Québec MP René Émard who was in my corner. He controlled three ridings which meant he could deliver 19 votes, including his own. Then Marchand called him to his office and read the riot act to him. It didn't matter who won the leadership – he, Jean Marchand, would be their chief lieutenant for Québec. He would personally guarantee that anyone who did not support Trudeau would get nothing for his constituency. Period. For a province that thrived on patronage, that would have been the kiss of death. René was crying when he came to my office to tell me that he had been forced to capitulate.

In the end, however, I was the author of my own misfortune. I had no one to blame but myself. I should have known better than to read my speech. After a few paragraphs I "lost" the audience, and never got them back. Martin Goldfarb, who cut his polling teeth at the convention *en route* to becoming a well-known pollster and consultant, claims that I lost 130 first ballot votes as a direct result of the speech. Most of them went to Joe Greene, who had made a Lincoln-style address that was fantastic by comparison. Many of my supporters who switched told me they planned to come back to me on the third ballot. But the way things worked out, that never happened. Winters became the runner-up, and Trudeau won.

It seemed like an extreme irony that as I cleaned out the top drawer of my desk, following my resignation from the Trudeau cabinet in 1969, I found a piece of yellow paper I had prepared "in case you decide to run for the leadership." It provided three bits of advice: the central location for supporters in order to gain maximum television exposure; the maximum size of signs they could hold that wouldn't annoy delegates sitting behind them; and third, and underlined three times, "Do not read your speech!" This merely confirmed that winning the leadership was not meant to be.

THE FINAL DAYS OF PEARSON

On April 9th, my wife Ellen and I took our family to Florida for a few days rest and relaxation with my parents, who had a small bungalow at Delray Beach on the east coast about an hour south of Palm Beach. Consequently, I was absent from cabinet when it met on the 10th to welcome and congratulate the victor and to make plans for the transfer of power, which was tentatively set for Monday, April 22nd, which would have been the fifth anniversary of the formation of Mr. Pearson's government in April 1963. The date was later moved forward two days for some unknown reason, which seemed rather a pity.

I returned to Ottawa on April 17th in time for a routine meeting of cabinet followed by lunch at the prime minister's residence at 24 Sussex Drive. Prime Minister Pearson was taking advantage of the few days' hiatus between administrations to dine one-on-one with each of the senior privy councillors who had been candidates for the leadership. This would have included Paul Martin Sr., Robert Winters and perhaps one or two others, although I don't know who might have been on his short list. That day it was my turn.

I was warmly greeted at the door by "Mac" MacDonald, who had been the sergeant in charge of my orderly room when I was Minister of National Defence and who later moved to Sussex Drive to be in charge of the hospitality section there. Mac took me through to where the prime minister was waiting. As I recall, we had a wee drop of sherry to mark the occasion, followed by a delicious lunch featuring a light fish of some sort. The conversation was as warm and good as the food Mac was serving. When it was time for coffee we moved to the library, a most pleasant oasis at the front of the house.

"You know," Mr. Pearson began, "that I was neutral in the leadership race." That did it. I can stand just about anything except to have someone lie directly in my face. "If that were true," I said, "why was the unification of the Canadian Armed Forces the only major accomplishment of your government that you neglected to mention in your farewell speech to the convention?" "I thought it was in," he began to sputter, "or at least it was in the draft." "And why, when my treasurer asked one of your closest friends, Toronto stockbroker William Harris, for a contribution to my campaign, he peremptorily said: 'No, not for the minister of transport!'"

Mike, the name by which Lester B. Pearson was known, and which I had used for years in informal circumstances, knew that he was cornered and there was no point in further pretence. "You always did let me know where I stood with you didn't you Paul?" It seemed like an odd thing for him to say; yet, I thought I had some sense of what he meant. Sometime later, when he drafted the third volume of his memoirs, he said that in retrospect he thought I would have made the best prime minister. Then he added "except for that way of his." "That way" included my irritating habit of telling him the truth when he was not particularly anxious to hear it.

There was just one more cabinet meeting before the change in regime. We met briefly on April 19th to clean up some routine business. Paul Martin was in the chair. As I watched his face closely, I felt sad for him. I knew that he was not a Trudeau admirer and that he felt better qualified for the top job, in much the same way he had felt about Lester B. Pearson some years earlier. Paul knew that the convention was his last chance at the brass ring and he had wanted so much to win.

The results must have been totally shattering, far more for him than it was for me. It was, for him, the end of the road after a very long and distinguished career in which he had accomplished so much in health care and diplomacy. There would be other opportunities and other honors, but none would have the same punch as active partisan politics. To witness my former seatmate's last hurrah and the end of the Pearson era that Friday morning was a lot like attending a wake.

CHAPTER 11

WORKING WITH
PIERRE ELLIOTT TRUDEAU

"I apologize for stealing your party," the newly elected leader of the Liberal Party of Canada said to me Tuesday morning, April 9, 1968, as he waved toward the amply comfortable chair in front of his desk in an invitation to be seated. "Not at all," I replied, "you won the convention fair and square within the existing rules."

Then we got down to business, which was to discuss a portfolio in his government. I knew that Finance, the only one I coveted, was going to Benny Benson, one of his strong supporters. So I said I would be happy to stay in Transport. Then I asked if he would also give me the responsibility for Central (now Canada) Mortgage and Housing Corporation (CMHC).

Trudeau then threw a bombshell into our discussion by saying he would like to appoint someone from my team to the cabinet. I recommended Bob Andras, my campaign manager, who was subsequently appointed minister without portfolio. The formalities over, I was dismissed to make way for the next candidate for cabinet.

The morning of April 18th we met at Government House to be sworn in, the PM first, then me, due to my seniority. To prove that no grass would be allowed to grow under our feet, a cabinet meeting was called for 2:30 p.m. that same afternoon. Most of the discussion revolved around whether or not to carry on as usual, or call an immediate election. It was the consensus that members of Parliament should be consulted, so a full caucus would be held before Parliament met the following Tuesday.

Meanwhile the PM must have made up his mind and eliminated all options except an immediate election. He introduced me and said he had appointed me "acting prime minister." He then said: "The acting prime minister will now explain why an immediate election would be a good thing." You could have knocked me over with a feather duster! I had no advance notice and was not really in the loop. I can't even remember whether I thought it was a good idea or not. I must have been fairly convincing however, because when I sat down the PM looked pleased and the troops sounded as if they were ready to do battle.

It proved to be the right decision because Trudeau won enough seats to form a majority government, and I had a majority in my own riding for the first time in my political career. It was a campaign unlike the others. The PM emphasized the need for a just society but there were no specific promises other than to set up a task force to study housing needs. This had been my idea when Trudeau asked me to write a housing policy for the campaign. I concluded that the subject was far too complicated to be expressed in one sentence suitable for campaign purposes. The alternative was to promise a widespread study, and this was agreed.

THE TASK FORCE ON HOUSING AND URBAN DEVELOPMENT

The creation of the Task Force on Housing and Urban Development was one of the few specific promises the prime minister had made during the course of the election. It was given a broad mandate because there was no single, simple solution to the housing crisis. The industry was hamstrung by numerous problems, including a desperate shortage of serviced building lots, too much regulation and an intermittent flow of mortgage financing.

On July 15, 1968, the Cabinet Committee on Communications and Works, Transportation and Urban Affairs authorized me to establish a Task Force on Housing comprised of not more than seven members to report to me within six months starting in September. This decision was confirmed by Cabinet on July 17, 1968. With approval given, I began assembling members of diverse talent to represent the various regions of our far-flung country. The prime minister nominated his trusted friend Pierre Dansereau to represent Quebec.

The press release indicated that I would serve as chairman of the task force, which was scheduled to commence nationwide public hearings in Ottawa, September 16-17, 1968.

William H. Neville of Ottawa was appointed executive secretary. The press release also announced that the task force would be assisted by Alfred E. Coll, executive director of CMHC, as the CMHC liaison officer, and by Lloyd Axworthy, my executive assistant (Housing), would write his doctoral thesis at Princeton University on the subject and who would later have a distinguished career in politics as Secretary of State for External Affairs. We were finally ready to take off and go.

At our first planning session we decided to take the Prime Minister's promise of participatory democracy seriously. We scheduled each day's work so that we listened to the experts and heard formal presentations from myriad interest groups at our morning and afternoon sessions. In the evenings we held town hall sessions where the people were given the opportunity to speak. And speak they did! But what they said, to our considerable amazement, was that they wanted single dwelling units, semi-detached or row housing, not apartment buildings. This was the opposite to what the experts were telling us during the day. It was a pattern that was to remain consistent from one coast to another. What a wonderful education we received.

When our task was completed our Executive Secretary, William Neville, wrote a high quality 80-page report in just a few days. He expertly outlined the problems we observed as they related to the federal, provincial, and municipal authorities. The provinces are primarily responsible for housing under the Constitution, but in the real world, solutions require a team effort on the part of all the players. Neville's nuanced report outlined what would be required from each jurisdiction, and it is still worth reading 50 years later.

Before the prime minister left for London, England, to attend the Commonwealth Conference, he invited me to have lunch one-on-one at his Sussex Drive residence. As his limousine pulled out of the parliamentary compound between the stone pillars onto Wellington Street, he slapped me on the knee and said how glad he was that the task force had completed its work and that I would be back in Ottawa full time. My wisdom, he said, was missed at cabinet. The greeting could not have been warmer.

We each had a glass of white wine to enhance the light lunch and I was a bit surprised when he added a splash of water to his. It was a practice I observed on several subsequent occasions. I can't remember for sure whether or not we discussed the housing report, but I do remember that I took more than my share of the time explaining my incomes policy, which was designed to eliminate the scourge of the tight money solution to inflation. He listened with rapt attention. When we finished he escorted me to the door where Lloyd Axworthy was waiting for me. "That boss of yours," the Prime Minister said to Lloyd, shaking his head as he spoke. I interpreted this to be a compliment as he had obviously been intrigued by my theory and been extremely cordial.

Before Pierre left for London he was less than enthusiastic about attending a Commonwealth Conference and wondered aloud if the organization had outlived its usefulness. He appeared to change his mind on that score as the conference unfolded. And while there were no reports of his contributing very much to the deliberations, he certainly captured the attention of the world press with his antics.

A photo of his famous pirouette behind the Queen's back just after she had passed by appeared on front pages of newspapers across continents. Later, after the conference, Pierre was spotted with German jet-setter Eva Rittingshausen and even Londoners got the Trudeau bug. Never in the history of Canadian politics had the world press covered a Canadian prime minister's personal life on such a scale. It was in stark contrast to the monotony of life in the Commons without him.

When Cabinet met on January 16, 1969, I was still in the chair. The first two items of business related to the Omnibus Criminal Law Bill and the Montreal International Airport and Peripheral Land Development plan. Then came the Task Force on Housing. The Minister of Forestry and Rural Development, Jean Marchand, enquired whether the report of the Task Force on Housing would be discussed in cabinet before being made public. I replied that it was expected the report would be made public in a couple of weeks and suggested that interested ministers might meet for dinner to consider it.

I explained that there would be two documents. First, there would be the "Task Force Report," which would be a public document. Second, I would make a submission to Cabinet recommending those items that fell within the federal jurisdiction that I thought should be implemented without delay. Cabinet, of course, would be free to accept or reject any particular recommendation. I pointed out that in acting as chairman of the task force I had been wearing two hats and that one was not binding on the other. My participation as a member of the group had been an interesting exercise in the field of political science and its value could be better assessed if judgment were suspended for several months.

Other ministers considered that the question of a minister signing a task force report that had not been approved by the cabinet affected the principle of collective responsibility, and I should discuss the matter with the prime minister.

Beware!

Late that afternoon my new deputy minister, O.G. (Gerry) Stoner, dropped by my office for a brief chat. He had learned via the grapevine that trouble was brewing and suggested that I should arrange to see the Prime Minister immediately upon his return to Ottawa the following day. By then it was too late to call him in London, so I sent him a message the next morning while he was mid-way across the Atlantic. In his reply he asked if I would be good enough to take Question Period, that unruly hour beginning at 2:30 p.m. when the prime minister and other ministers are bombarded with questions from the opposition side of the House, because he would like to get a little sleep, but he would see me immediately thereafter.

That is how the day played out. I left the House promptly following Question Period and headed to 24 Sussex Drive. Alas, I was too late. Someone had been there and talked to the Prime Minister before I arrived. He received me politely, but I could feel the chill. In the few minutes we were together there was absolutely no sign of the warmth that had been so obvious before his departure. It was as if summer had morphed into winter in a few short days. I was shaken by this turn of events, but with my perennial optimism I underestimated the depth of the wounds the PM's earlier visitor had inflicted on my political body *in absentia*. That earlier visitor had been Gordon Robertson, Clerk of the Privy Council.

On Monday morning I was extremely well organized because I had worked Sunday afternoon catching up on dictation, reading, and a myriad of decisions. I was therefore clear to spend a good two hours at CMHC trying to get them on side. I had given them advance copies of the report, but the reaction was very difficult to gauge. As I recorded in my diary: No overt opposition, but is there an iceberg? Time will tell. I made a plea for cooperation in the interests of all.

Cabinet met again Tuesday morning with the Prime Minister back in the chair. I was a few minutes late and arrived just as they were finishing House business. The final item, under the heading discussion was *me*.

All of a sudden the cabinet room was transformed into something like a courtroom. The Prime Minister was the judge. He also played the role of Crown prosecutor as a surrogate for the real one – Gordon Robertson. Gordon was not present in person, but his spirit was everywhere.

Members of cabinet were not listeners, as jurors would be. They sounded like a bunch of clucking hens. Don't sign the report; get the other six to sign it; can we amend it?; we don't have to publish it; we do have to publish it. In my six years in cabinet I had never seen anything like it.

For a while it was unclear what the "charge" was, but after penetrating the fog of uncertainly it appeared to be the fact that I had represented myself as chairman of the task force. Had none of my colleagues seen the press release? Had none of them ever watched television where I had been introduced as chair of the Task Force almost every night for four months?

The judge, also known as the prime minister, had asked his Minister of Justice, John Turner, to look up the precedents to see if there had ever been a case of a cabinet minister acting as chair of a task force. But was there any law against innovation or new experiments in political science? Some of us thought that was one of the prime minister's election promises.

There seemed to be an "inspired" opposition based on all sorts of technicalities that only became obvious as the debate continued. The PM said that the two of us would have further talks.

My description of the opposition was confirmed many years later when I read the cabinet minutes for that session. In my view they were technical gobbledygook set out like the case for the prosecution at a trial.

In the House of Commons later that day the PM leaned over and said he didn't think he would see the day when I would accuse him of being a traditionalist. Yet that was what I meant at cabinet during my quiet pitch when I said that he had suggested that we try new forms, new experiments for communications between governors and the governed. And yet when a new form was tried, which on the face of it seemed quite interesting and a good exercise in participatory democracy, it was running into trouble, four months too late.

On Wednesday morning I went to the airport to meet Quebec Minister Gaétan Lussier but he was 40 minutes late so I doubled back to present the PM with the "letter of transmittal" for the "Task Force Report." Then I spent the rest of the morning with the Quebec delegation who were still insisting that the new Montreal airport be built south of the city.

That afternoon, in the Commons, the PM handed me a revised "letter of transmittal." It was a masterpiece of quibbling. In any event, I decided that I had better bow the knee to Caesar if I wanted enough time to even reach the substance of the report itself.

Cabinet met again on Thursday morning as usual. The report from the cabinet committee came up for approval in the routine way and it looked for a moment as if it was going to be approved without debate. A weak inquiry from someone brought the response that the PM and I had agreed on a letter of transmittal the previous day. The PM said it was along the lines suggested by Jack Davis, and then volunteered to read it.

I knew that the type was already set, based on what I thought was an agreement with the PM the day before, and also the addition didn't make any sense, at least to me. Cabinet agreed. The Prime Minister then started to read a list of consequential amendments that should be made in the report. I could see on a slip of paper that there were half-a-dozen or more, obviously prepared by the Privy Council Office staff. They included eliminating all reference to my participation as a member of the task force. When I heard the list, I gasped!

I had an important decision to make, instantly. I said that during my years in political life I had often accommodated myself to the general good. In this case, however, I had already swallowed myself in accepting the letter of transmittal as re-written by the PM. What they were asking now was that I be a party to an attempt to try to change history after the fact. The "letter of transmittal" said, in effect, that I was a bad boy for appointing myself chairman of the task force, and I didn't mind this. To change the record now, however, and say that I had not acted as chairman, was like being asked to fudge the books. That would be dishonest!

In all my years in public life I had never lied publicly, and I wouldn't do so now. For four months I had represented myself as chairman of the task force and there was nothing I could do to change the facts.

It was finally agreed that I would leave the text alone, including the reference to me as chairman, and release the report as soon as possible. On the way out of cabinet, the PM turned to me, smiled, and said: "It was the reference to the 'exercise in political science' that we will never be able to forgive you for."

110

Getting cabinet approval to table the report was just the first hurdle to be cleared. There were more to come in what would appear, to me at least, as something approaching an Olympic challenge.

The press conference with task force members at my side was held at the Norlite Building at 4:00 p.m. It lasted about an hour and went well. There is always something to be thankful for. My colleagues and I were all greatly relieved when we adjourned to my office for drinks before dinner. The PM dropped by at 5:30 and stayed about half an hour. We had invited him to join us for dinner, but he had other plans. Before he left, he asked aloud what priority we thought housing should have. Then he gave his own answer by suggesting "twenty-fifth?" Needless to say, we were all shocked but none more so than Lloyd Axworthy, who was crushed by the broadside.

When we had recovered our composure we went for dinner at the famous New Zealand Room at the back of the Parliamentary Restaurant. If only walls could talk, what secrets that room would reveal. It was a very cordial event and many nice things were said about our common experiences reflecting general satisfaction with the exercise that we had been a part of.

The early days of February 1969 saw the Prime Minister and a few colleagues deeply involved in the Constitutional Conference. That provided a bit of a respite for me to spend time selling the housing program to the public at large. There were a series of radio and TV appearances, some very successful, others less so. On balance, however, the public was the easiest to convince. That, in my opinion, was because the "Task Force Report," based to a considerable extent on the Town Hall meetings, reflected what the public wanted and expected. Many politicians and officials, with their own axes to grind, were much less content.

Early in the month I flew to Vancouver to address the National Home Builders Association. It was a big meeting and very friendly because the builders strongly supported some of the recommendations designed to streamline procedures for the industry. At least I thought it was friendly until the president dropped a solid bronze trophy that he was in the process of presenting, directly on my head. I have often used this incident as an excuse for some of the errors I may have committed in subsequent years.

The President of CMHC, Herb Hignett, was with me at the convention. I knew, without being told, that he was strongly opposed to some of the Task Force recommendations and I strongly suspected that he was one of the principal stokers of the fiery furnace into which I had been cast. We flew back to Ottawa together and I could sense that he felt he had been beaten and that it was time to sign a truce and get on with the business of working together. What I didn't tell him was that I was already thinking in terms of packing it in.

On February 13th at the Cabinet Committee on Planning and Priorities we got our first primitive five-year projection of government revenues and expenditures. Simon Reisman, Secretary of the Treasury Board, said it was in response to my request of eight months earlier.

The briefing was a real shock treatment. From a position of balance in 1969 the government was headed for an $800 million deficit in 1970, which would be devastating! Ministers were horrified. Comments like "Sins of our Fathers" were heard. The PM asked why I hadn't made the suggestion two years ago, to which I replied that I *had* asked for a five-year projection almost every month for six years.

Tuesday, February 18th was set aside for an all-day meeting of the Cabinet Committee on Priorities and Planning with a full agenda including several items of primary interest to me, in particular, consideration of my submission to cabinet on housing. The paper comprised those items pulled from the "Task Force Report" that were primarily federal in nature, which I considered appropriate for early action. I pointed out that I had given a two-hour briefing to the housing committee and there was no reason to repeat everything. I made it clear that my submission was a personal document and although CMHC had been most cooperative in preparing it, some of their top management was less than enthusiastic. I suggested that the president, Mr. Hignett, state his case.

Hignett looked as if he had been shot. He spoke quite well, however. He said that the corporation was in substantial agreement with the proposal. One problem area was public housing, which he admitted we didn't know enough about, "and where some early mistakes had been made." In that admission he was stating the truth. Members of the Task Force had observed those mistakes on the ground, and one of the aims of the report was to prevent the corporation from repeating the same old mistakes. In fact the corporation had been bulldozing entire city blocks when not more than 20% of the buildings needed to be replaced. This had been at great cost to taxpayers and the consternation of well-established communities.

When the Cabinet Committee on Priorities and Planning met on March 13th, the Prime Minister deliberately put two items ahead of housing, which didn't come up until 6:00 p.m. At that late hour we were presented with a new paper on the social aspects of housing, and the "trial" began again.

Soon after I got back to my office, Ben Benson, Minister of Finance, called and said: "Relax, you will get it through." He went on to say that he didn't like today, that we were chewing each other up and that there was no team spirit. He had suggested to the PM that he should get four or five of us together before the cabinet blows up.

About five minutes later, Pierre phoned and said he didn't think he had handled the situation very well. I didn't disagree with him, but was pleasant. He felt we should get together socially. He suggested Monday night dinner and asked if it should be just the two of us, or if we should include Ben

Benson, Jean Marchand, etc. I said the larger group would be better and accepted for 8:00 p.m.

At 8:00 p.m. sharp I arrived at 24 Sussex Drive with lots of mixed emotions. The group comprised the PM, Ben Benson, Charles (Bud) Drury, Don MacDonald, Jean Marchand and me. It was a pleasant evening but we spent a lot more time debating defense and foreign policy, which was the PM's primary interest, than we did talking about housing. In fact, both subjects were very much on my mind and whereas the PM might have hoped that deepened friendship would be the principal achievement that evening, most of us really wanted to talk policy. The PM recognized that we had problems. The most significant and telling quote of the whole evening concerned Canada's participation in NATO. "I might have liked in the bottom of my soul to have come up with a decision to get out," the PM said. Wow! He wanted Canada to desert NATO?[1]

All that the dinner party confirmed was that the Prime Minister was neither a Liberal nor a liberal. I remembered when Mike Pearson had asked me in 1961 to organize the big rally for him, and we couldn't agree on a name. Pierre had refused to attend or participate in a meeting that was called either liberal or Liberal. In the end we did use the word Liberal but that was after many days of looking for an alternative.

THE POWER PLAY

It is important to understand what was really going on. To a very large extent, it was a power struggle between the bureaucrats and me. Some senior public servants don't like being told what to do. They treat the country or their province or municipality, as if they are the proprietors and treat politicians as transients who are expected to act as pleaders for more money and apologists when the bureaucrats foul up, as they often do.

The "Task Force Report" had, by inference, been critical of CMHC. The corporation had really messed up its public housing brief. We suggested a rethink. Millions of taxpayers' dollars were being wasted with more in the pipeline. It had to stop. The bottom line of our report was that, by listening to the people and considering their advice as well as that of the experts, we were offering taxpayers a bigger bang for their buck.

Two incidents support my thesis. At the time when the task force was being discussed my friend Ted Elliott, who had been in charge of sales at Curran Hall Ltd., flew from Toronto to Ottawa. He was seated between two senior bureaucrats who were exchanging views. My name came up, and one of them said, "He got away with it the last time. He won't get away with it this time."

Gordon Robertson was even more direct. After I left politics he addressed a class of students at Carleton University. My name came up and

Gordon said, "The trouble with Hellyer is that he thinks politicians are elected to come to Ottawa and make policy." If that is what Gordon thought he had me figured out correctly. But if politicians don't make policy, why bother holding elections?

NATO, A Bigger Issue

While the housing issue, or more precisely the Hellyer task force issue, was being hashed and rehashed in cabinet and several of its committees, the Prime Minister was attempting to commit what I and a few others considered to be a real crime. He was determined to bring Canada's troops home from Europe and undermine our solidarity with NATO, which had played a key role in maintaining peace in Europe during the Cold War between the West and the Soviet Union.

In a very real sense the Prime Minister was "on trial" too, but he was his own judge and his cabinet was the jury. He had been making his case beginning in the early days of his administration but when the Committee on Foreign Policy and Defence met on Friday March 7th, it was a real confrontation, and support for his policy was far from unanimous.

Cabinet met on Saturday, March 29, 1969, which was most unusual except in the case of a national emergency, but it was a clear indication of how important the subject was to the PM. The debate was very interesting. It was evident right from the beginning that the PM had not "given up" as he had indicated to Léo Cadieux a few weeks earlier and as he had indicated to me at dinner at 24 Sussex on the 17th. He was a most tenacious as well as clever fellow, and really doctrinaire. He said: "If we can reach a position honestly, okay. If we can't, or if we are split down the middle, we will bloody well start over again. We may be laughed at, but we will eventually achieve an acceptable result."[2] He obviously meant a result that was acceptable to him.

The "trial" continued on Sunday morning, a day of the week that was unprecedented in my experience. The anti-NATO people were much more militant and unbending. It was interesting to see some of the chaps getting off the fence and lining up with the Prime Minister. They were some of the more "left" types, but there was a perceptible change notwithstanding the argument that had favored remaining in NATO if Canada was to make any contribution to collective defense at all. At the end of the meeting the Prime Minister advised us that he was going to draft his view of the consensus for consideration on Tuesday night.[3]

On April 1st, April Fools Day, I had dinner with my old friend Richard (Dick) Stanbury, Al O'Brien from Liberal party headquarters and the legendary Ollie Quail. He was the phantom poll-taker that I had heard about for years but had never met. We had an interesting discussion about the

Constitution, race relations and other subjects. Dick said his wife Marg had just called to express her best wishes and to say that she had just heard on Toronto's CTV news outlet that I was about to resign. I suspect that I merely smiled and reminded them what day it was. (April Fools' Day.)

In fact, I had pretty well made up my mind about a month earlier to resign and had discussed it with Ellen. I realized that I couldn't state my primary reason for resigning because no one would have believed me. They would today if they had read *Citizen of the World: The Life of Pierre Elliott Trudeau, Volume One: 1919-1968*, in John English's official biography. English points out that Trudeau was a great admirer of Harold Laski, the widely known socialist intellectual, and persuaded him to supervise his thesis on the relationship of Communism and Christianity at the London School of Economics.[4]

It would have been against my principles to stay in Trudeau's government and criticize him from within. Fortunately, however, the absolutely rotten way I had been treated on the housing file was more than enough to justify my departure. So, I was quite comfortable using that as the issue. Trudeau's disinterest in the housing crisis was indeed a question of principle.

When I returned to my office and watched the gentle April snow falling I couldn't help but think it would probably be the last time I'd do so from this office, 515S Centre Block, House of Commons.

For the next three weeks I dutifully attended all the meetings of Cabinet, cabinet committees and caucus. My role, however, was more like that of the proverbial "fly on the wall" than that of a genuine participant. My next diary entry of any significance was April 23rd, which I had tentatively set as "the day."

That morning, the Cabinet Committee on Defence and Foreign Policy met to continue the PM's "trial." Of about 15 speakers, all but three supported NATO and Canada's military contribution in Europe. Then, the PM took them all on for size. It was a magnificent performance. He introduced the red herring of the role of the air division (in Europe) and avoided the central issues. With his masterful persuasion, however, he had most of them eating out of his hand. His power was formidable.[5]

My last day sitting with the PM, I took one long last look around the House of Commons, because it would never look the same to me again. During the day I wrote my letter of resignation. I reminded the prime minister of our discussion the first time we met after the convention, when I had told him that I had entered public life due to my interest in two subjects. The first was the necessity of achieving full employment for Canadians without the high inflation that I considered to be insidious, and the second was to facilitate the provision of decent housing for all Canadians. Now, I had concluded that the delays and frustrations in introducing amendments to the National Housing Act were deliberate on the part of the government and that this was not in the public interest.

It was a long, fairly tough letter that ended with my request that he recommend to His Excellency the Governor General that my resignation be accepted effective April 30, 1969. The letter made no mention of the real reason for my resignation.

At 9:50 a.m. on April 29th, I kept my scheduled appointment with the Prime Minister. We chatted for 40 minutes, amicably. Gerry Stoner (my deputy minister) had phoned to warn him. It was really difficult to know how sorry he was, if at all. He made a feeble attempt to get me to reconsider. We parted on good terms, although I sensed it was only on the surface. The countdown was nearly finished. It was an indescribable feeling.

Paul Martin came as an emissary to try to dissuade me. He told me I was still young and had a great future ahead (what a laugh). He lacked the force of conviction, however, because basically he agreed with me.

The press conference went quite well, I kept my cool and talked from the heart. Afterward there was some sense of relief to see it over. Tired, crushed, but relieved.

The following day it was my turn to play host to the Polish Minister of Marine. We met in room 601/602 just at the entrance to the Parliamentary Dining Room. I knew that it was my last official luncheon to host.

Midway through lunch I was advised that there was an urgent telephone call for me. I went to the foyer to take the call. It was Gordon Robertson. "Paul," he said, in his best no-nonsense tone, "the Prime Minister would like you to make your resignation effective today."

"Aw c'mon Gordon," I replied, "that isn't the Prime Minister, it's you."

"Well, all right," he confessed, "but we're concerned about your presence in the House in the meantime."

"I promise not to attend the House until after the 30th when my resignation takes effect," I assured him.

He wasn't too pleased but knew that I wasn't going to be cowed by him at that stage, so he hung up. Needless to say, I kept my word.

I was terribly embarrassed when Pit Lessard (MP) proposed a toast to "Our Minister of Transport" at my luncheon in honor of the Polish minister. I covered my eyes to avoid embarrassing my guests more than they were. All stood, including J.W. (Jack) Pickersgill (my predecessor as Minister of Transport), and cabinet colleagues Jim Richardson and Jack Davis.

In response, I referred to the late Chubby Power, Minister for Air during the Second World War years, who had been the last Liberal minister to resign on a point of principle. Power's classic rejoinder was, "It's just a short step from the private car to the upper berth."

I then faced the formidable task of clearing out three offices in five days, one of those days being a Sunday. Mercifully, I had the able assistance of my entire staff. A measure of the task was that when we had finished, including the office in Toronto, we sent 450 boxes full of files to the Public Archives (now Library and Archives Canada) and a couple of dozen more to my new parliamentary office. The latter was a pleasant little two-room suite on the north side of the building overlooking the Ottawa River, which had been home to Jim Richardson, my associate minister. Jim insisted on giving it up for me when the Liberal whip attempted to assign a nondescript little space under the stairs at the front of the building. My gratitude to Jim was profound.

At the end of the five days, when the task was complete, Ellen joined us for a little farewell party in the room I had occupied for six years. My staff all attended and there were toasts all 'round. Lloyd Axworthy presented Ellen and me with a lovely vase of blue Manitoba porcelain which I treasure to this day. Alas, all good things come to an end. So, amidst tears, we bade each other fond farewells, best wishes and Godspeed in the months and years to come. For me, at least, an important and exciting era of my life was over.

It was interesting to note that soon after my departure the government introduced legislation to implement most of my recommendations. An anonymous source told me it was to create the impression that I had just been impatient, and if I had kept going all would have been well. I have since concluded that the idea of having the responsible minister act as chair of a task force on urgent or complicated subjects is a marvellous idea. In my case it was inadvertent. But the principle is one that could save years of frustration and probably large sums of money by eliminating unnecessary delay.

The prime minister's "trial" on NATO continued after I had gone. It eventually ended with a "hung jury." Unanimity was never achieved and my successor as Minister of National Defence, Léo Cadieux, threatened to resign if the PM persisted.[6] The realization that another resignation so soon after mine would be very bad politics, no doubt helped a compromise be reached. Only half of our troops in Europe were withdrawn and this didn't create a ripple. So, in the language of a fairy tale, everyone lived happily ever after.

CHAPTER TWELVE

ACTION CANADA AND MY FLING WITH THE CONSERVATIVES

Just sitting in the House of Commons as an ordinary MP with no special responsibilities gave me the time to look for new outlets for my ideas and energy. I was not assigned to any parliamentary committee so I decided to try my hand at writing a book. This task, as some of you may know from personal experience, is easier to say than to do.

I was still popular with officials in the departments of External Affairs and National Defence who were more sympathetic to my views than those of the Prime Minister. Thus I was able to take advantage of their logistic support in arranging visits to 26 countries. In every case, I was able to interview top officials, usually including ministers of finance and central bank governors.

It was a wonderful post-graduate course in world affairs and I learned a great deal in every country, but especially, Japan and Russia.

A TASTE OF ACADEME

In between trips I enjoyed a taste of academic life. My friend Dr. James (Jim) Gillies, who had been a member of the Task Force on Housing and Urban Affairs, arranged for me to have an appointment as Distinguished Visitor in the Graduate Faculty of Urban Studies at York University. The course I taught was inter-disciplinary, so I had students with varied interests. They seemed to like my lectures because I talked about actual problems in the real world that I had gleaned from my experience in the housing and development business.

At the end of the academic year I was invited to the dean's banquet. I asked to be excused because I had to fly back to Ottawa and crib for a skin and scuba diving examination the next morning. The dean told me that of all the excuses he had ever been given, mine was the most unique.

An advantage of having more discretionary time than when I had been a minister was being able to share adventures with my family. My son Peter and I enrolled in a skin and scuba diving course at the Ottawa YMCA. We sailed through the early part of the course and passed our skin diving tests early in the new year. The scuba part was considerably more demanding. There is something quite intimidating about throwing your gear in the deep end of a pool and having to dive down and put it on, and then blow the water out of your mask before surfacing. But we both did it.

Only the written test remained, and it finally dawned on me that I hadn't written an examination in 20 years. I didn't really care about marks, but more was at stake. What would Peter think if I was to place near the bottom of the class?

When I got back to Ottawa I did my last-minute memory work and finally turned out the light. When sleep came I had a terrible nightmare. I was in a rabbit's burrow and although I could see a light at the end of the tunnel, I couldn't get out. I must admit that dawn and the advent of reality came as a blessed relief.

We wrote the examination and when we got our marks they were both in the 90s – to the best of my recollection Peter got 94 percent and I had 97 percent. Crisis over!

Action Canada

This is the story of an all-out effort to influence public opinion and attack the complacency of our rulers, who seemed to be ignoring the key issues affecting ordinary people. Several good friends joined me in putting together a formidable team of concerned citizens willing to write a manifesto, publish it, and promote it nationally.

Goals listed by the group as critical to the future of Canada included:

1. Immediate and fair tax cuts as part of a full employment program.

2. Immediate and mandatory wage and price guidelines to stop inflation and insure prosperity for all citizens. Mandatory guidelines can rescue the free enterprise system and keep it responsive to human needs.

3. Establish for Canada the highest environmental standards in the world.

4. The quality of housing must be increased to provide every Canadian warm, clean shelter as a matter of basic right.

5. Transportation systems essential to decent urban life must be designed and built to expand opportunities for happiness through choices in living, working, recreational and cultural environments.

6. Reduce in size and complexity the vast bureaucracy in order to restore a human dimension in government.

7. Decentralization of authority to allow greater democracy at all levels.

8. Tangible programs for increasing savings and providing capital for Canadian ownership of Canadian resources.

Initial press reaction was almost universally positive. The following two examples are representative of papers coast-to-coast.

In the *Toronto Star*, May 24, 1971. "ACTION CANADA sounds like some middle-of-the-road populism and, given the public's dissatisfaction with existing parties as well as Mr. Hellyer's formidable energy and abilities, it just might get off the ground."

In the *Vancouver Sun*, May 28, 1971. "Mr. Hellyer has jumped in to fill a vacuum caused by the federal government's failure to devise any kind of policy to deal with either inflation or unemployment... How strongly his movement may develop and what its impact may be are fascinating subjects for speculation, but, at least the government is on notice that a well respect-ed political figure is working hard to establish a rallying point for frustrated and discontented Canadians. And there must be millions of them baffled by the inaction of a government that commands an absolute majority in the Commons."

At the outset we put together an impressive group headed by my good friend Bill Bussiere, Ted Workman, owner of the Montreal Alouettes foot-ball team, and Don Armour, a recently retired air force major-general. We were off to a flying start and Bill, who was designated field organizer, and I, travelled back and forth across the country looking for key people and es-tablishing Action Councils that were pretty well autonomous. The nucleus of an organization soon took shape.

That is when I was given a once-in-a-lifetime opportunity of touring the Greek Islands with a star-studded galaxy of world famous celebrities assembled by Constantinos Doxiadis, the Greek architect who had estab-lished himself as a world leader in the field of ekistics, the science of human settlements. The participants included Buckminster Fuller, design scientist and engineer whose work I had become familiar with at Expo 67 – Canada's centenary celebration – where his geodesic dome was one of the outstand-ing attractions; Françoise Gilot-Salk, French artist-painter who had been Pablo Picasso's mistress; Lord Richard Llewelyn-Davies, U.K. architect planner; Margaret Mead, anthropologist; Jonas Salk, inventor of the Salk vaccine against poliomyelitis; Barbara Ward (Lady Jackson), U.K. econo-mist and member, Pontifical Commission on Justice and Peace; and finally, Dr. Doxiadis himself, whose ideas impressed me profoundly. The lure of exchanging views with such an august group overwhelmed me.

Ellen and I left Montréal on July 9, 1971 and arrived in Athens the fol-lowing morning. On Monday morning we boarded the *M/S Apollo* to begin a week of island hopping. Each day, in addition to a briefing on the history of the locale, the schedule included presentations by one of the participants, with questions and discussion, as well as lots of free time for personal conversation and exploration.

When it came my turn to present I talked about some of the things that the Task Force had learned about redevelopment. The federal government was not only permitting, but encouraging the razing of whole city blocks. Only about 20 percent of the buildings were sufficiently dilapidated to justify destruction and replacement.

The consequence of such scandalous waste, not to mention the disastrous consequences for well-established and happy communities, was an unsustainable policy that no one had taken the trouble to cost. It was a policy designed for consultants and contractors rather than people in need of housing. The first few projects cost about $400 per person in the municipality and when I multiplied this out for the major and minor cities where it was likely to apply, the total was $6 billion for the first round. Yet the government had only budgeted $25 million a year for the program which meant, at that rate, that it would take 240 years to complete the first wave. This was clearly as impractical as it was wasteful. I ended my talk with some suggestions that might improve the quality of life for many city dwellers.

At the cocktail hour that evening Buckminster Fuller sought me out to say: "I think you are the world's number one expert in your field." You will be relieved to know that I had the good common sense not to ask him what he thought my "field" was.

The tour was a marvellous short course in world affairs but it came at a cost. When we arrived home on July 30th I had to face an avalanche of accumulated work that needed urgent attention.

By the end of August, we had prepared a draft agreement of cooperation with the *Créditiste* Party of Québec, which was primarily interested in monetary reform, a subject close to my heart. As I recall, this was never signed because we went on to discuss the next stage, which was the actual amalgamation of *Créditistes*, the Progressive Conservative Party and Action Canada. At that stage, Action Canada was just a "movement." I met two or three times with Robert Stanfield, the former premier of Nova Scotia who had succeeded John Diefenbaker as leader of the PC Party. Stanfield showed some restrained interest but, I suspected, was a bit diffident. He probably thought that he could become prime minister on his own and was not convinced that we would be of significant help.

I wrote letters to both Réal Caouette and Stanfield stating that I thought the interests of the country were paramount and for that reason I undertook not to contest the leadership of the combined party if it were formed. This may have removed one obstacle but Stanfield's assessment of our political clout remained in doubt, so he opted to wait until after our national convention.

THE ACTION CANADA CONVENTION

We sent out a "call" to all Action Canada members inviting them to a convention to be held at the King Edward Sheraton Hotel in Toronto from October 1-3, 1971. Its agenda included electing a leader, a deputy leader, and establishing broad policy guidelines as well as seeking authority to align with an existing party or parties endorsing Action Canada's policies.

Two items of importance were dealt with in addition to leadership. The first related to local Action Councils sponsoring their own candidates in the next federal election. The motion was passed by a margin of more than two to one. The same endorsement was given to a motion authorizing Action Canada to ally itself with an existing national party or coalition of parties endorsing its principles if this would facilitate action in this respect.

In addition, the conclave approved the formal endorsement of individual candidates who supported its policies by an overwhelming four to one margin. The whole thrust was to get our policies adopted by any means possible without regard to party affiliation. The membership was actually more responsive to this approach than it was to the idea of creating another party through the Action Councils, although that approach was not dismissed out of hand. The endorsement of such a wide range of options changed Action Canada from its original status as a "movement" to one of "movement cum party." It was a subtle but nevertheless significant threshold.

The convention was closely monitored by both the Progressive Conservative and Social Credit parties. When the voting finally took place I was acclaimed as leader and George Skelton of Calgary, Alberta, was elected deputy.

When it was all over, those of us who were directly involved thought that it had been a very successful convention. Regrettably, the press was considerably less enthusiastic. Peter Desbarats, writing in the *Ottawa Journal*, penned the following summation.

"If they were trying to thoughtfully examine solutions to Canada's economic problems they succeeded, but if they were trying to start a political party with real clout, strong enough to force a national debate on Hellyer's ideas, they failed."[1]

That was about as good as it got. I never knew exactly what the Tory MPs reported to their leader, Robert Stanfield, but I always suspected that they downplayed our potential. In any event the post-convention reaction demanded that we review the options available. Our core group finally decided we should continue Action Canada as if it were a party, while keeping the idea of a coalition open.

AGENDA: A PLAN FOR ACTION

The idea of launching Action Canada had not even occurred to me when I wrote the book but the press didn't believe it. Therefore reviews were a mixed bag.

One of the more favourable reviews, that proves my point, appeared in the *Winnipeg Free Press* on November 6, 1971. The following are some excerpts:

"As the title indicates, this book is an account of the things to be done by the new group (Mr. Hellyer does not call it a party) founded by the author, and the reasons why. As such, it is an elaborate kind of political manifesto. There is no doubt that the author is an intensely humane man, deeply grieved about poverty, unemployment, and that anonymous swindle known as inflation.

"He has harsh things to say about economists, their orthodoxies and sacred cows, like gold as the monetary governor. For years, he says, gold has been phoney, but sustained by economic orthodoxy. We had the materials, the know-how and the men, along with the bitter need, but the orthodox economics stood in the way on our route to a better world ...

"Meanwhile we judge the book to be engagingly written, in a sensitive humane spirit, well produced, having only one serious literary error (which ought to have been caught by the editor). It is the kind of book which should be read by all who are interested in the present political scene."[2]

The most favourable comments came from Hugh Innes, reporting for Ryerson College Radio, who treated the book for what it was, an economic treatise, rather than a political manifesto. "The first 12 pages of the book are the best synthesis of what has happened in the last 200 years that I have read," he said. I considered that a great compliment coming from the son of the late Harold Innes and Mary Quail Innes, both icons of the University of Toronto. The younger Innes added that "the book was clear, readable, etc." This was music to my ears, but his finale was the sweetest note of all. "You are one of my heroes," he said in conclusion. My reaction was, "You have just made my day."

I became busily engaged in looking for good candidates for an election that was fast becoming imminent. The first one that was ready to run was Judy LaMarsh, who had been Minister of Health in the Pearson government. Unfortunately, she took off for South-East Asia just when we needed her. In her absence Dr. Nicholas Pohran was nominated and became our first official candidate.

There were some other "star" candidates recruited. Claude Wagner, the former Québec politician, agreed to run in a rural constituency and the exceedingly well-known star receiver for the Montreal Alouettes football team, Terry Evanshen, was set to go in Montreal. We managed to line up about 25 in all, which was probably as many as we could afford to finance.

Eventually, I began to have second thoughts about splitting the anti-Trudeau vote. John Cross, who had been one of the first people to suggest that a new party was needed, shocked me when he said that he "had decided to vote for that young man Hugh Segal." Hugh was the Tory candidate in the Ottawa riding where I lived. He didn't get elected but he did become Prime Minister Brian Mulroney's chief of staff, and later a senator. But the thought of John Cross doing a flip-flop really surprised me.

Then I learned that Gen. Bruce Mathews, my old friend and former president of the Liberal Federation of Canada, had abandoned ship. I recalled at once the words that had seemed so strong. "A new party by all means," he had said, "Max and I have decided." Max Meighen was another Toronto business tycoon, and a direct descendant of the Rt. Hon. Arthur Meighen, a former prime minister of Canada, who, for a time at least, had been totally fed up with both the Liberal and Progressive Conservative parties. Now, apparently, he too had changed his mind.

Then I remembered and re-read the extremely nice letter from David P. Smith, a Liberal friend who later served briefly in Trudeau's government, then as chief organizer in Ontario for Prime Minister Jean Chrétien and, finally, in the Canadian Senate. David set out the case more clearly and forcefully than I could have done.

David listed half-a-dozen reasons why I should make the move. Finally, he said, "You should join while Action Canada is still reasonably viable. Don't wait until it begins to fade visibly."

GOODBYE ACTION CANADA

The answer came through loud and clear in the spring of 1972. I agreed to meet British Columbia's Premier W.A.C. Bennett's chief fund-raiser for dinner in the plush Liberal red dining room of the old Ontario Club in Toronto. He had indicated an interest in helping to raise money for the election. My guest spent about two hours telling me how great I was, and how superior the Action Canada platform was to those of all other parties. Then, as we were about to part, he said: "But, I am going to support the PCs because I think that is the only hope of defeating the government."

There it was, that "but" word again, and from years of experience I knew exactly what that meant. Thousands of people who might have considered supporting us when the prospect of an election was more remote, were now coalescing behind the strongest opposition. If we continued, we would just be splitting the anti-government vote and providing comfort to the administration.

When I reported to the team we all realized that the decision had been made for us. We were unanimous in deciding to join the PCs and doing everything we could to help in spite of reservations about Stanfield and the party he led. We would have been less than true to ourselves if we had refused to marshal our limited resources in support of our primary objective, and where we might eventually find allies for some of the important policy objectives we had been fighting for.

MY FLING WITH THE CONSERVATIVES

Once the decision had been made, I moved quickly to the Progressive Conservative Party in a last-ditch effort to unseat the reigning Liberals. The deal was put together virtually overnight by two PC organizers – Paul Curly and Paul Kates. They were thrilled at the prospect and guaranteed that I would get the PC nomination in the Trinity riding without a serious contest. To the best of my knowledge, PC leader Robert Stanfield was unaware of the development until he read it in the press. His reaction, as anticipated, was positive.

In spite of my long association with the riding, and the fact that my opponent Aideen Nicholson was inexperienced, the election was close, too close for comfort. I only won by 183 votes, so an official recount was demanded to confirm my razor-thin victory.

When Stanfield formed his shadow cabinet he made me critic for Trade and Commerce, which was as close to Finance as I could expect. In the Canadian system, unlike the U.S. Congressional one, a government that has a minority can ask the governor general to dissolve Parliament and hold another election in the hope of getting a majority. So the opposition party has to be prepared in advance.

Stanfield asked Jim Gillies and me to come up with something new. This gave me the opportunity to promote my long-established incomes policy, designed to prevent big business and big labor from creating and perpetuating a ruinous wage-price spiral. Dalton Camp, one of the highest-ranking PC insiders and Stanfield advisor, had a poll taken that showed very widespread public support for a policy such as that, so he persuaded Stanfield to adopt it.

From that day on I was never consulted and Stanfield was not adequately briefed on the essential difference between wage and price controls, which are hopeless except for brief periods during times of war, for example, and mandatory guidelines to prevent monopoly power from distorting the system through highly inflationary wage and price increases. As a result Stanfield was totally unprepared for his first press conference after announcing the policy. He flubbed questions that touched raw nerves and left the battlefield wide open for Trudeau to slay the PC dragon with his famous one-liner "zap, you're frozen." That was the end for the Stanfield team.

In 1972, the names of the parties were not shown on the ballots, and quite a few electors were unaware that I had switched parties. In the 1974 election, for the first time, party labels were attached to ballots, and Aideen's entire campaign consisted of going from door-to-door and telling my Italian-Canadian supporters that "Mr. Hellyer is no longer a Liberal, you know." This did have a significant effect. Some of my long-term loyal supporters stuck with me but others, often with tears in their eyes, voted for the Liberal name. In addition, my old and erstwhile best friend, Keith

Davey, who was in charge of the Liberal campaign, went out of his way to defeat me.

This time I had neither a political nor business job to go to. I decided to bow out of politics and try my hand at journalism for a while. This was a decision that pleased Ellen immensely because, after the equivalent of a lifetime in politics, she had had enough, and really wanted a more relaxed pace than we had known for most of our years together.

CHAPTER THIRTEEN

TEN YEARS IN JOURNALISM

After losing the election in 1974 I had no job to go to as I had the last time I lost. So I decided to take a fling at journalism, got myself an office in the Ottawa Press Building and tried to find a newspaper that would publish a column by me.

My first choice was *The Globe and Mail*. Brigadier (Ret.) Richard Malone, who headed the chain that owned *The Globe*, didn't believe former politicians should be writing political columns. Next, the *Toronto Star* asked me to write a sample column. The editor liked it and offered me a job. I declined the offer because the *Star* had a reputation of expecting its columnists to follow the paper's editorial "party line." I treasured genuine freedom of speech so decided to look elsewhere.

A few days later, the Right Reverend Arthur Brown, an Anglican priest who was a personal friend and non-partisan political supporter, visited Arundel Lodge. He wrote a weekly religious column for the *Toronto Sun* which, I suspect, had been a minor concession the paper had made when it decided to publish a Sunday edition. I explained my situation, and he offered to introduce me to *Sun* publisher Douglas Creighton, who had become his friend. I was a bit reluctant, but Arthur was quite insistent, so I agreed to meet Creighton without, of course, mentioning that I already knew him and had an interest in the paper that remained a closely held secret.

When the time came for our appointment, the two of us were ushered into Creighton's office and Art introduced me to his friend Doug, who played his part with the skill of a real actor. Art gave me a big build-up, and then we all chatted about my wish to have an outlet for political commentary and the reasons for it. In due course Doug said he was convinced, and would like me to write two columns a week for the *Sun* and its syndicate. I agreed. Art was pleased with the role he had played and so was I. My work began at once, and my output appeared to be acceptable. After several months Creighton told me the column "was coming up roses," which was affirmation enough.

The Toronto Sun

Early in October 1971, I had received a call from my friend Peter Worthington, a reporter for the *Toronto Telegram*, and fellow "cold warrior" concerned about the prime minister and national politics. He reviewed the situation with the *Telegram* which planned to cease publication after a long battle to survive against competition from the *Toronto Star*, Canada's largest circulation daily. A small group of reporters headed by Douglas Creighton, Donald Hunt, and Peter himself had decided to try and launch a daily tabloid to fill the void.

They had canvassed all of the obvious people they thought might be interested in helping financially, but the response had been highly negative, with good reason. Quite a few North American daily papers were succumbing to competition and launching a new one was considered pure folly. Still, they hadn't given up and Toronto lawyer Eddie Goodman was canvassing some of his builder developer clients to see if he could assemble a group of investors. Would I be willing to talk to Goodman? Never one to say "no" until I had all the facts and could make a reasoned decision, I said yes.

Eddie filled me in on the progress that had been made, which was not great. He had a couple of modest subscriptions lined up and a few more in the discussion stage. I gave the matter considerable thought. From an investment standpoint it didn't make sense. No one, including the promoters, suggested that it was anything more than a wild gamble. My interest in the project was simple. I wanted more competition in the business. I knew from long experience that a politician was lucky to find one paper out of three that would give him or her an even break. If there were only two papers, and they were both negative about you at the same time, heaven help you.

Eddie phoned on Thanksgiving weekend and said that time was running out. I promised a decision within 24 hours. I phoned back Thanksgiving Day and said I would subscribe $100,000, and more if needed. "That means there will be a paper," he said. As soon as he hung up from talking to me he called Doug Creighton to give him the news and to say the project was a "go."

Years later in a birthday greeting Peter Worthington said: "There wouldn't have been a *Toronto Sun* without you."[1] I believe that is true but I can't prove it as Eddie Goodman is no longer around. But if the decision had not been made that day the fledgling paper would not have been in a position to publish the day after the *Telegram* folded without interruption, which many would argue was critical. The final edition of the historic *Toronto Telegram* was published on October 31, 1971 and the first edition of the saucy, irreverent *Toronto Sun* hit the streets the following day.

For a while the upstart tabloid hung on by its fingernails, but somehow each obstacle was overcome and the *Sun* eventually got its own streamlined presses, so it was no longer hostage to the vagaries of questionable machines.

By then the paper had become quite profitable and it was interesting to observe the attitude of the original investors. No longer just idealists willing to risk a little capital in a worthy cause, they viewed themselves as canny investors with a potential windfall to protect. There was a problem of liquidity, of course. The company was private and there was a shareholders' agreement that limited one's freedom of action. Therefore a decision was made to convert to a public company and that required a prospectus.

When the draft prospectus was circulated I was dismayed to find that my name was the only one listed. I was the only individual to hold more than 10 percent of the shares. It didn't matter that it was just a shade over 10 percent, rules are rules. So I contacted my sister Hazel Race, and asked if she would buy enough of my shares to bring the total below the magic guideline. She agreed, although she thought I was up to no good. I don't think she ever got over that feeling but she did profit handsomely when the company was finally sold.

For years my participation in the *Sun* was a closely guarded secret because I was still interested in politics and didn't want to be identified with the *Sun's* right-wing approach to the news. I never attended a board meeting, and only twice did I attend one of the lavish parties that Creighton held to build morale among his non-union crew and spur them on to ever-greater things, including establishing other *Suns* in several different cities across Canada.

I did not want to see the *Sun* sold to MacLean Hunter Publishing in 1982 because I agreed with Peter Worthington that the paper would never be the same again. The camaraderie began to fade and, ultimately, a union was certified. Creighton and his dream were gone. I had no reason to complain, however, because Toronto Sun Publishing proved to be the most astounding investment I ever made and provided me with the capital to pursue my projects in later years. For that, at least, I had to be eternally grateful.

The Conservative Convention

In the fall of 1975 the Progressive Conservative executive called a national leadership convention to be held in February 1976. I looked at the list of potential candidates and worried about two things. I was not sure that there was anyone who could defeat Trudeau, and second there was no one with federal cabinet experience.

Quite a few Conservative MPs held similar views. They were looking for a star candidate like Bill Davis from Ontario, or Peter Lougheed from Alberta, both of whom had extensive experience as premiers of their respective provinces. Another person high on their list was John Turner, former finance minister in the Trudeau government. Turner could easily have won the PC crown. Donald Mazankowski, MP for Vegreville and later deputy prime minister under Brian Mulroney, canvassed his colleagues and obtained a whole page of signatures of MPs pledged to support Turner if he entered the race.

I showed Turner the list and said I would support him if he ran. He was tempted, but after thinking it over for a few days he declined. That was my signal to begin testing the waters to see if I stood any chance at all.

I phoned Sean O'Sullivan, the youngest MP, and invited him to dinner. We agreed on a plan that would test the waters. The echoes we received were far from harmonious. We discovered, as we already knew, that many senior Tories were still very angry with me for the unification of the armed forces and in particular the change from the distinctive uniforms copied from the British. Then I was accused of being somewhat stiff and aloof.

Derk Kay, a prospective delegate from Prince Edward Island was brutally blunt: "If you rate the candidates on a scale of zero to 10, Hellyer starts below zero." Still he wound up being my campaign director for his province. Also, a number of former military officers, including several naval officers who had been most vocal in their criticism, decided to come aboard because, as several of them said, "at least he is a leader."

By late December, after several attempts to find someone better, the potential team began to shape up. O'Sullivan himself was the key. Not only did he recruit his large family, he had indirect access to many of former Prime Minister Diefenbaker's loyalists who were looking for someone to rally behind. Keith Martin, Diefenbaker's executive assistant, became a key player as did Don Matthews, party president, senior MPs such as Jake Epp from Manitoba, Elmer Mackay from Nova Scotia, Ontario's Walter Baker and most surprising of all, Ged Baldwin from Peace River, Alberta, who was probably Stanfield's closest confidante. His reason? He had concluded that I was the one most likely to defeat Trudeau.

Rob Lawrie, a Type A-plus lawyer became campaign director. Jake Epp was parliamentary campaign manager. Two well-trained Liberal organizers, Frank O'Dea and his partner Tom Culligan, co-founders of the Second Cup coffee chain, became invaluable organizers-at-large. Warren Ralph, my personal assistant and a close friend of both Sean and Keith Martin, was another key player. John Manley, who was articling with the Chief Justice at the time and many years later became a distinguished deputy prime minister of Canada, along with his cohort Marty Murphy were in charge of youth organization. Peter Hunter, a senior officer in the militia who was with Mc-Connell Advertising, was in charge of advertising. It was quite an impressive group even if it never did quite gel into the smooth-running machine that it was capable of being.

My campaign picked up steam as the days passed. My team insisted that I eliminate most of the substance from my speeches because, as Sean emphasized, a leadership race is more of a popularity contest than an idea contest. Still, I managed to include some of the issues that concerned me and it started to pay off. Hugh Segal, later Brian Mulroney's chief of staff and still later a senator, said: "We couldn't understand why he was doing so well until we sent some people to listen to him."

It was winter so John Manley and Marty Murphy came up with the idea of having a skating party at Montebello, halfway between Ottawa and Montreal. It was a nice afternoon, so Ellen and I put on our skates for a few rounds in the open-air arena. The press was there and took pictures of the event. Even when they had their film clips they didn't leave. They just hung around the sidelines for quite a while. Eventually someone asked them why they were still there. "We are waiting for him to fall," was the terse reply. Apparently, they thought they could duplicate a shot they had of Stanfield dropping a football, an image that stuck with him throughout his career. Ellen and I were both determined to prove that they were wasting their time, and we succeeded.

In the run-up to the convention it was critical to have the support of former PM John Diefenbaker. Sean had lunch with the old man and then wrote him a five-page letter explaining why he should support me and put the knife in Mulroney in the course of his convention speech. The plot worked. In the guise of an attack on Trudeau the old Chief reminded his audience that the PM had only been elected as an MP three years before he had achieved the highest office. "In the British tradition, those who have achieved prime ministership have had years of experience," he thundered. It was obvious that Mulroney was the target of the attack, which achieved the intended result and blew Mulroney out of contention.

My star was rising. At a luncheon on Friday I spoke from the heart, without notes. It was the way I communicated best and you could feel the momentum build through the course of the half-hour baring of my soul. There were quite a few uncommitted MPs present and many of them were caught up in the spirit of the occasion and moved to the Hellyer camp. In an irony of history, one of my themes was the need for party unity. In addition to the convention surge, Sean and Keith Martin had persuaded Diefenbaker to resolve a problem he had with Jack Horner, who had been loyal to the Chief when he needed him, by voting Horner on the first ballot and coming to me on the second. This had all been agreed and it meant that many Diefenbaker loyalists including Findlay MacDonald, the well-known broadcaster, were in my corner.

A measure of the overall impact came when my old right arm Bill Lee phoned his partner Bill Neville, a long-time Tory insider, to see who was going to win. "I don't know," Neville replied, "but that former boss of yours is doing extremely well."[2] There was a growing optimism in my camp which I shared.

That night Stanfield spoke and, like Dief, he too had the gloves off. It was a denunciation of those caucus members who he felt had been less than cooperative. For Wagner and me it seemed like an explicit denunciation as he warned against turning the party over to an outsider. His message also seemed to be that members of caucus should not be in the forefront when a new leader was chosen. That looked like a direct shot at me because I had the support of more MPs than any of the other candidates.

My team was spooked by Stanfield's innuendo, and convinced that the power brokers were out to skewer them again. I suspect that is true, because Ged Baldwin reported to me concerning a secret meeting held that night at which Stanfield, Camp and a few of their confidantes had decided to coalesce behind Joe Clark as the voting proceeded. Still, I am not sure that they would have succeeded if my team and I hadn't gone squirrelly and played into their hands.

I had taken three days off to return to Montebello to write my big speech and memorize it. I was acutely aware that reading my speech had cost me the Liberal convention eight years earlier, and I was determined not to make the same mistake twice. As fate would decide, my team phoned my former assistant Bill Lee, to ask if he had one bit of advice what would it be. "Make sure you see his speech," he replied.[3] So they waited until the night before it was to be delivered, when they had begun to panic.

My senior people got together at the Chateau Laurier Hotel. The group comprised Rob Lawrie, Don Matthews, Jack MacDonald, Jimmy Johnson, Jerry Davis and Sean. They were all in a high emotional strait with their ire directed at Stanfield. They concluded that my speech the next day had to be a hard-hitting counter-attack against Stanfield. They phoned to summon me to join them. I refused. One of the lessons I had learned in 1968 was not to get so overtired that you can't think straight.

Then the arm-twisting began. Rob Lawrie had read my speech and decided it wasn't "bombastic" enough, so he told me I had better get down there because they had a big investment in me. It sounded as though I was some kind of prize heifer. I continued to refuse and explained that it was too late, long past my bedtime. Finally Sean came on the line and explained: "There are some pretty serious concerns in this room. You'd better come here if only to calm your people."[4] I reluctantly agreed in what would be one of the biggest mistakes I would ever make.

When I joined the group in their late-night cauldron of desperation I grudgingly agreed to let Sean draft some notes and agreed that Jerry Davis and Jack MacDonald could do the same. Sean put his draft between our doors at 4:00 a.m. It was laced with good ideas but I knew at a glance that I would have to read it, and I was determined not to do that. Jack and Jerry showed up at our house about 7:00 a.m. with some index cards on which they had written all of the tough, aggressive one-liners they had dreamed up the night before. I knew instantly that their efforts were do-able without too much rehearsal.

Near the end of the stack of cards, there was one that made reference to "Red Tories" that rang a faint warning bell in my tired mind. "Are you sure that you want to leave that stuff in?" I asked. Their body language was affirmative, so I stuffed the cards in my pocket and headed for the convention center. I heard the others take direct shots at me as I became the number one whipping boy for the sins of not being a life-long Conservative and abandoning Action Canada. While criticism is never music to the ears, the fact that I was getting so much attention was clear evidence that the other candidates considered me to be a real threat.

This positive feeling was reinforced when it was my turn to speak and I worked my way to the platform past the area where the press were sitting. Several journalists wished me well, and one in particular, Carole Taylor, stood up, shook my hand and said "Good luck, Paul." All of this reflected the view that Trudeau had fallen out of favor and the press were ready to support a credible alternative.

My speech began well. The cue cards were my cup of tea. "Trudeau is taking us on a strange journey," I said, "and we don't want to go. I know all about Pierre Elliott Trudeau and he knows I know. I switched parties not to avoid the battle but to join it. There's much more at stake in this convention than banners and headlines. The issue is Canada itself." The momentum was building. The crowd was with me and I could feel it.

Soon I came to the fateful lines and read them with equal gusto. "The Red Tories were like the tail trying to swing the true-blue Conservative dog." The boos drowned out all the previous applause. Instead of being the candidate of unity, which had contributed mightily to my popularity the previous day, I became the candidate of division. I knew at once that I had blown my chances. I felt exactly like someone speeding along a highway only to have a big truck pull across the path when it was too late to swerve or change lanes. The damage was done, and my team knew that the game was over. Even my own paper, the *Toronto Sun* ran the following headline in the morning, "Hellyer blew it."

Saturday's first ballot count confirmed the worst. Wagner led with 388 votes, then Mulroney with 357, Clark 277, Horner 235, leaving me in fifth place with 231 votes. All of those people who had planned to come to me on the second ballot, including John Diefenbaker, never came. Support began to coalesce behind Joe Clark, the establishment's candidate, who became the winner and a credible leader.

Of all of my friends Sean was the most upset. He felt that his judgment had contributed to the chain of events that had seen us slide from contention to ignominy. He was deeply upset that some of his friends were attributing my "Red Tory" reference to him. He asked me to give him a letter absolving him of all responsibility, which I happily did. Some time later Jerry Davis, the real author of the fateful lines, sent me a letter accepting full responsibility.[5] He wanted me to have it in my records for the sake of anyone who might be interested or uncertain in years to come.

After the convention I tried to do what all decent candidates are expected to do by seeking a nomination to run for the PC party in the next general election. I looked at Norfolk-Haldimand riding, where I was born and raised, and then a riding in Toronto that would have been difficult to win. In both cases I had quite a bit of popular support but in both cases I was rudely rejected by members of the riding executive.

It was easy to forgive the Tories for their rude rejection, but it would be difficult to forget. As for Sean, I told him that we both knew that our campaign had been a dry run for an O'Sullivan leadership bid a few years down the pike. I did not know, at the time, that he had already decided to leave political life soon after in order to enter the priesthood.

BACK TO THE PRESS GALLERY

Returning to the Press Gallery the day after the convention was one of my most difficult days ever. It was a time of total humiliation but my colleagues were most gracious and seemed to sense that I had suffered enough without adding salt to an open wound.

Mine was not the *Sun's* most widely read column because I made no attempt to compete with the paper's more flamboyant writers. But when public polls were conducted there were comments such as: "Mr. Hellyer makes us think," which was satisfaction enough. In addition, I had the advantage of being able to attend political conventions on behalf of the paper and traveled twice with the prime minister, once to the G7 meeting in Paris in 1975, and the other time to the Commonwealth Heads of Government Meeting in Kingston, Jamaica.

I BLEW MY BIGGEST SCOOP

In the fall of 1976 I blew my biggest scoop. I decided to visit Montreal and check out the political situation provincially, including an interview with René Levesque. He willingly answered my questions for almost two hours. At the end, because he was late, I drove him downtown to his next appointment.

En route, we carried on our conversation. Of my family, my daughter Mary Elizabeth, who had studied at the University of Montreal, and was fluently bilingual, would be welcome in the new separatist state. Levesque knew Pierre Trudeau well and always thought of him as a "parlor pink." Then I asked him if he had any fear that following separation Montreal might cease to be the exciting and unique metropolis that it had become. He thought for a few seconds as tears formed in his eyes, and replied, "I hope not."

After completing my unofficial sample of voter intentions I drove back to Ottawa and wrote a column saying that the Parti Québecois would win the election that was expected the following month. My secretary, Margo Glaude, a Franco-Ontarian, read my piece and refused to type it. We had an uncharacteristic row, but she was adamant. There was no way she was going to aid and abet the separatists. Finally, I had to compromise. We agreed that I would say that it was my opinion that the Parti Québecois would do well. Opportunity lost!

WHAT IS TRUTH?

I wrote for the *Sun* and its syndicate for 10 years before deciding to leave. The immediate reason was a *contretemps* with Barbara Amiel, who had replaced Peter Worthington as editor. But actually I was getting anxious to write my memoirs and that was going to be a full-time occupation for some time, so I was ready to move on.

During the period that I wrote for the *Sun* I also wrote occasional articles for other non-competing papers and these tasks were enjoyable. In addition I worked in the electronic media from time to time, but my longest and best experience was being a panelist on a TV program called "What Is Truth?" that appeared weekly on CHCH Hamilton, and some other stations across the country. Our team comprised a moderator and four panelists, one of whom, Doug Hall, was a co-owner of the production company. We would tape four or eight programs at a time in order to save the expense of meeting weekly. Consequently, guests had to be known personalities of such universal interest that they wouldn't be *passé* by the time the episode was aired. These included stars in the world of politics, religion, science, medicine, diplomacy and other diverse categories.

On one occasion our guest was to be Pierre Berton, one of Canada's best-known journalists, authors and TV personalities. When it came time to tape his segment, he asked if we were a union crew. We had to admit that we were not. Pierre said that in that case he would not appear on our program. Our dilemma was not a simple one. If Pierre bowed out we would have to schedule a special taping to fill the void for the month. We had to negotiate to keep Pierre from walking out. Eventually, a proposition was made. If we would agree to become union members forthwith, before our next taping, he would relent, and be our guest. We made a collegial decision that we were willing to abide by his terms and the taping began.

By far the most remarkable experience of my years with "What Is Truth?" was our trip to Moscow. Somehow Ralph Kirtchen, our producer and co-owner of the show, had a special "in" with the Soviet government. He arranged a visit to the Russian capital in February 1977, to make a series of episodes that we thought would be of special interest to our Canadian viewers.

Our time in Moscow proved to be very productive and the Soviets must have been pleased with what we were doing as they held a banquet for us on our final night. It was quite an affair with the vodka flowing and the speeches warm and generous. When the main course was served, faces glowed at the sight of a huge 12-ounce filet. Canadian smiles were less broad after we noted the texture and realized that we were eating horsemeat. The next speaker was in full flight when someone entered the room and whispered in his ear. He excused himself, and when he returned a little later he radiated all the warmth of a Siberian night in February. A deep freeze had set in.

It was early the next morning, following a briefing by Canadian Embassy officials, that we learned what had happened. Our Minister of External Affairs, Don Jamieson, had expelled several Soviet diplomats after declaring them *persona non grata* for engaging in unacceptable activity. The Soviets were livid, and we were bearing the brunt of their displeasure. We packed our bags and prepared to depart.

We were placed in what they called a VIP holding area. There we cooled our heels for hours before flight time. We asked to be treated like the other passengers and be allowed to move to the gate area. "No," they insisted, we were VIPs and would be treated as such. About 10 minutes before flight time, one or two of our members were allowed to head for the gate, and about five minutes later, the others were permitted to leave. I was the only one left. I wondered if they were going to hold me and use me as a pawn in negotiations with the Canadian government. What a joke, I thought, Trudeau would just laugh out loud at such an idea.

With about two minutes to go before flight time I was "released." I literally ran down the corridor to the gate and bolted through as it slammed behind me. There were not even seconds to spare. The tension continued as I found my seat and prepared for take-off. The next few minutes seemed like an eternity as we taxied into position for take-off and finally became airborne. No one relaxed until the captain announced that we had left Soviet airspace, at which point a cheer could be heard from many of the passengers, including the Canadians.

About half-way home I noticed that the seam of the lapel of my winter coat was coming apart. I wasn't pleased, but considered it one of the least of my worries. As we approached Montreal, the one on the other side had also opened up. "Damn Bulloch Tailors," I said, loudly enough to be heard. I had worn the suits and coats of the Irish haberdasher for years and had never had any complaint. Then the light went on!

During intermission the night our hosts had treated us to a ballet at the Bolshoi, Soviet agents had taken my coat from under the seat and opened the seams of both lapels to look for microfilm, and there hadn't been time to properly sew them up before I returned for the second act. It must be terrible to be so paranoid. Every cloud has a silver lining, however. We had a number of interesting shows "in the can" that we were confident would be of real interest to our Canadian audience and we would also be able to claim that we were the first team to be allowed to film behind the Iron Curtain.

CHAPTER FOURTEEN

Farewell Ottawa – Hello Toronto

Around the turn of the decade Ellen and I began to think about moving back to Toronto. We had become empty nesters and there was no longer any compelling reason for us to remain in Ottawa. So, we began looking for a Toronto home.

We finally settled on a two-story suite in a high-rise building on the Toronto Harbour, with all of the rooms facing the water. A feature that was very important to me was a marvelous pool in the building where I could exercise regularly.

Dabbling in the Arts

It has been said that the arts are the soul of a nation, and that had long been my belief. Once a country has reached the stage where it can adequately feed and house its citizens it is inevitable that some of its most creative citizens will express themselves in one art form or another and soon a culture is born. My first interest was opera, to which I had been exposed as a young man on the farm where father always tuned in to the Saturday afternoon Texaco broadcasts of the Metropolitan Opera Company. As I matured, my tastes broadened to include ballet, the symphony, books, the visual arts and theater, both in my public and private life.

In 1970, Tory ringmaster Eddie Goodman phoned me in Ottawa and asked if I would join the board of the National Ballet of Canada. The Artistic Director, Celia Franca, was an extremely talented immigrant from the United Kingdom who took on the formidable task of developing a respectable ballet company in a city that had been something of a cultural backwater prior to World War II.

The contacts she made when she was a professional dancer in England enabled her to entice some of the world's best choreographers and dancers to work with her company, and to keep raising the bar for its increasingly professional rising stars. Her greatest coup was persuading Rudolph Nureyev to come to Toronto. He not only coaxed the standards to new limits, he created a major crisis in the process.

Nureyev designed a new production of the *The Sleeping Beauty*. Gorgeous on paper, the price tag exceeded even the wildest fears of the pessimists. The directors began to panic! At one point, it was even suggested that the company would have to declare bankruptcy. But the money was eventually raised, the company survived, and *The Sleeping Beauty* became one of the showpieces of the repertoire. Although I only served one term on the board when Ellen and I returned to Toronto we became faithful supporters and played our small part as the company grew and prospered.

THE CANADIAN OPERA COMPANY

Ed Mahoney, president of the Canadian Opera Company (COC) phoned me in the summer of 1983 asking if I would be willing to join the board. It would prove to be a wonderful experience that was often as frustrating as it was rewarding.

I was elected chair of the Facilities Committee. My principal task was to find adequate rehearsal facilities for the company. In this new role I was able to play a significant part in the acquisition of the Dalton Building on Front Street. It has become the home of the COC, providing both office space and the unique rehearsal space essential for opera.

A BALLET-OPERA HOUSE

Nothing succeeds like success, so when the Opera Centre, the Dalton Building headquarters of the COC, was complete, everyone began to turn their attention to the greater dream – an opera house for the joint use of the COC and the National Ballet. Toronto had been without an opera house for about a century, but the Sony Centre (originally the O'Keefe Centre) was built primarily as a music hall for productions such as *Camelot*, with which it had opened in 1960.

The two companies brought their corporate heads together, and ran a design competition that was won by Moshe Safdie, a world-famous Canadian architect, who was awarded a contract for designing the building. Eventually, a world-class design was ready to call tenders. But the timing corresponded with another recession and a change of government in Ontario. So the project was scrapped.

Subsequently, the management of the COC changed and Richard Bradshaw took over first as artistic director and later as general director. Richard kept the dream alive in the face of naysayers and scoffers. The National Ballet decided not to participate in the new project but Richard put together a team of dedicated believers who started to work on a new site for the COC only. They engaged Toronto architect Jack Diamond to prepare a new design to fit the new space. Wisely, in the circumstances, they set more modest goals in the absence of the generous federal and provincial funding that was no longer available. The first shovel went into the ground in the summer of 2003 and the Four Seasons Centre for the Performing Arts was completed just 38 months later, on-schedule and on-budget.

To launch its first season in the new house, Bradshaw produced Richard Wagner's *Ring Cycle*, considered the Mount Everest of grand opera. Tragically, he didn't live to see his second season in the new building He died suddenly and unexpectedly on August 15, 2007. His funeral in St. James Cathedral attracted a who's who of Toronto's arts elite with standing room only. This much-loved man, who lived long enough to complete "mission impossible," has been enshrined as one of the City of Toronto's genuine heroes.

RETURN TO THE LIBERAL PARTY (1981)

In 1981 I decided to return to my first political love, the Liberal Party of Canada. Not only had Trudeau mellowed considerably by then, I was convinced that it would not be too long before he stepped down as Liberal leader, an intuition that proved to be correct.

My reception was very mixed, as I should have expected. The young Liberals were open and welcoming, and invited me to speak at their convention. Some of their leaders, such as Alfred Apps and Stephen Lautens, seemed quite interested in the policies I was espousing. The more senior Liberals were polite, but less than enthusiastic. One exception was Norman MacLeod, president of the National Liberal Federation, who issued a press release saying that I was most welcome, earning him a permanent place on the roll of honor in my heart.

It occurred to me that when Trudeau retired the convention would provide a platform for selling my ideas. I had burned my bridges and knew that a serious run was impossible. But for a few weeks, public attention is concentrated on the candidates, and the television debates would be more powerful than millions of dollars in advertising.

With that goal in mind I consulted some of my old friends and supporters including Judge Colin Bennett, the politically astute Gordan Edick, my faithful former secretary Marg Bulger, along with others. I also sounded out the family, who were all adamantly opposed. Before I had reached a conclusion, and in the middle of a radio interview with the popular Lowell Green of Ottawa when I was promoting my latest book, the show was interrupted for a special bulletin. "The Prime Minister is going to announce his resignation later this afternoon."

Well! Wouldn't you know that he would pick February 29 (a leap year) in the middle of the worst snowstorm in years, with Parliament away and the press half asleep from boredom. Apparently, Trudeau had been "walking in the snow" the previous evening and had decided that it was time to make it official.

Within minutes, all hell broke loose. In addition to questions on all of the shows that were scheduled for the afternoon, half of the journalists I knew were calling to find out what I was going to do. I explained that I had not yet made up my mind in a matter of fact way, but sometimes the truth is hard for the press to accept.

When I got home, my closest friends did a thorough review of the situation. We agreed that there was no way we could get the 300 votes considered essential for a respectable showing for a leadership bid. I told them that I had been approached by senior officials from the York South-Weston riding who were very anxious to have me run there in an impending by-election. That was an alternative that we should consider.

At lunch I asked Ellen if she had been serious when she said that she would say "go" in York South-Weston if I agreed not to go to the convention floor. She replied "yes," and I told her it was a deal. Ellen told Mary Elizabeth the news, and the tension started to disappear at once. We even watched *Love Boat* together before turning in for the night.

YORK SOUTH-WESTON

I attended the National Liberal Convention in Ottawa but kept a low profile. When I was sure that John Turner was going to be the new leader I took time out to write my Sunday column. Once the big leadership show was over, the activity in York South-Weston increased dramatically. There were two powerful forces working against me: the Italian-Canadian community decided that this was a riding they could win for one of their own, so they marshaled their formidable organizational prowess in support of John Nunziata, who was my principal opponent. In addition, there were the Liberal brass who were hoping that they could eliminate me forever, so they postponed the nomination date long enough to give my opponent time to catch up. They got their wish. On Thursday, July 12th, Nunziata and I squared off at Runnymede Collegiate and it was clear from the moment we arrived that the game was over.

Meanwhile, the new Prime Minister, John Turner, decided to cancel a royal tour by Her Majesty Queen Elizabeth and call a general election, because the polls indicated he could win. Some of us thought it was a bad error in judgment. When the election was held on September 4th, it was a Tory sweep. Brian Mulroney won 211 seats and the powerful Liberals were reduced to a rump of 40.

THE MULRONEY ERA

The advent of a new Conservative government provided a respite from active politics. It took the neophyte prime minister quite a while to get his sea legs, but he ran a tight ship and jollied his crew to keep them loyally on station. There were a few years when I was primarily an observer rather than an activist, and this was wonderful for family relations. Ellen was given some much needed and well-deserved breathing space.

The months and years rolled by, and suddenly it was 1988 and the prospect of another federal general election seemed certain. The question of "free trade" had raised its ugly head. Mulroney, who had been adamantly opposed to it when he was running for the leadership of the Progressive Conservative Party, had done a 180-degree flip-flop. Now he was promoting it as a solution to Canada's future economic well-being.

Another Mulroney initiative had far-reaching consequences for Canada. When Pierre Trudeau had patriated the Canadian Constitution from Britain in 1982, Brian Mulroney had initially applauded Trudeau, but later he was overcome by the politics of expediency and took the position that Quebec had been robbed. He volunteered to make good on their demands, including an absolute veto on all future constitutional amendments.

The Meech Lake Accord, as it was called, required the consent of all provinces, and it appeared that Mulroney was going to achieve the impossible. But Pierre Trudeau was adamantly opposed. Not only had he spoken out against the Accord it was alleged that he persuaded his intimate associate Deborah Coyne to visit Clyde Wells, the premier of Newfoundland and Labrador, to make an impassioned plea that he scuttle the deal, which he did. Mulroney was devastated and never forgave Trudeau.

MULRONEY'S UNDOING

Mulroney wasn't too far into his second term when things started to go wrong, desperately wrong. The Finance Department talked him into introducing a Goods and Services Tax, and the Bank of Canada headed by John Crow, who was a dedicated follower of Milton Friedman, induced another dreadful recession in Canada.

I became so concerned that I wrote a long personal letter to Mulroney and explained how he had been sold down the river by officials and what he had to do to recover from a bad situation. I was not surprised that he stuck to the "official line." But the people of Canada were not fooled and the Conservative Party paid a heavy price for its acceptance of orthodoxy when the next election was held.

A BETTER ECONOMIC THEORY

Economic theory has been a lifelong interest of mine. There is a vastly better way of doing things but it is extremely difficult to get people to listen. I read about an Ottawa firm, Informetrica Inc., headed by a publicly-recognized American-born economist, Mike McCracken. His firm was specializing in economic simulation using a model based on state-of-the-art techniques. I arranged to have lunch with McCracken to see how much it would cost me to have my theories tested. He gave me an estimate that wasn't cheap, but still within my means, so we made a deal.

Mike assigned his second-in-command, Carl Sonnen, to the case. We spent some time agreeing on the parameters, the "base case," as they call it, in order to compare the existing to the "possible." On January 20, 1993, there was a message from Sonnen: "Have results so good that they are scary."

We did a little fine tuning in the following weeks but every scenario we tried produced significant improvement in unemployment, inflation rates and debt reduction. There were no negatives. McCracken and Sonnen were so impressed with the results that they took the unprecedented step of agreeing to a joint press conference on Parliament Hill to let the world in on our secret.[1]

We booked the parliamentary press room for 10:30 a.m. on Thursday, April 8th, but we were bumped by Hugh Segal, Mulroney's Chief of Staff, and then by two Liberal MPs. It was 11:30 a.m. by the time we did get on and there were only four reporters left in the room.

Good Friday, April 9th. Not a word! Nothing on radio, TV, or in the newspapers. It was just as though it didn't happen! I was devastated.

Saturday, April 10th. Nothing again! Not a word in either the *Financial Times* or the *Star*. I suppose it was just too much to expect. I felt dead inside.

In a way it was good to get back to work after a record three-day weekend. I had to prepare to meet Pierre Trudeau in Montreal on Wednesday.

I arrived at Trudeau's office promptly at noon. We went next door to the Hilton for lunch. I didn't repeat the analysis, as we had gone through that twice before. Instead, I told him a bit of my life history and then brought him up to date on the Informetrica report. (He thought Mike McCracken was a good guy.)

As the conversation continued, his attitude changed. He felt that now was the time the party should adopt the policy and make it the central issue in the election. The party should find a seat for me. He suggested I see three or four of the top insiders, not Chrétien, as he would spend the time talking about what he had done. Pierre was glad I came because it gave him hope for the party. "May God go with you," he said, in parting.

"Back in Toronto Ellen said she hoped it would work out as I wanted. Nice."[2]

I felt a lot better after seeing Trudeau. It was the first good thing that had happened to me in days. Ironically, I don't think I would have set up the appointment if I had known that the press conference was going to be such a disaster. I thought of cancelling, but decided it would be impossible to explain why, so I decided to go ahead and face the music. I never cease to wonder at the mystery of how the Lord works.[3]

With Trudeau's encouragement I had breakfast with my one-time best friend, Keith Davey, who listened politely to my dissertation but didn't really connect until I mentioned my time with Trudeau. Then he got interested. Other members of the "old guard" showed some interest but they were no longer the people who were running the party. Eventually it proved to be another dead end. Keith summed it up by saying, "A new generation of Liberals have decided that they do not want to go in that direction. They are on a roll and think they have it made without any need for help. But, thank Paul for his interest."[4]

THE NEW TORY LEADER – A LUCKY BREAK FOR THE LIBERALS

Sometimes a party gets lucky. When the Progressive Conservative Party held its leadership convention to replace the almost universally unpopular Brian Mulroney, they by-passed the young, charming and fluently bilingual Jean Charest in favor of the glamorous Kim Campbell, who was sworn in as Canada's first and, to date, only female prime minister on June 25, 1993.

She was an experienced politician and had a lot going for her, offset of course, by the record of Brian Mulroney, who had postponed an election for a year beyond the normal four-year term, in the vain hope that his political fortunes could be resuscitated. When that proved to be impossible, he turned the reins over to Kim Campbell.

She had little choice other than to call a general election. I canvassed for Doug Peters, someone I wanted to see in the House of Commons. My man won handily but, to everyone's surprise, it was the Reform candidate who came in second.

The final national count was Liberal 177, Bloc Québeçois 54, Reform 52, NDP 9, PC 2, Other 1.[5] The old political map of Canada had been torn to shreds. The Bloc, a new separatist party, led by Mulroney's old Quebec lieutenant, Lucien Bouchard, won the second-highest number of seats and became Her Majesty's Official Opposition. It was the Progressive Conservatives who were knocked out of the ring with a total of only two seats, unprecedented in Canadian political history. Not surprisingly PM Campbell resigned as party leader a few days later.

THE BEGINNING OF THE CHRÉTIEN ERA

I was ecstatic about the results of the October 1993 election. So, I wrote the new Prime Minister, Jean Chrétien, a letter of congratulation and wished him well. It read in part, as follows. "Now to the future. You have rekindled hope, and expectations are high – perhaps unreasonably so. But I know you will want to fulfill and even exceed those expectations if at all possible. It can be done if the economy is expertly managed."

The first response from the prime minister was a phone call on January 14, 1994. He was primarily interested in talking about the government's early achievements, as he called them. When we finally got around to the alleged purpose of his call, I was able to suggest that it was possible to have full employment and low inflation at the same time. "How could you do that?" he wanted to know. The answer was too complicated to explain over the telephone, I replied, but if we could arrange lunch I would explain. He agreed, gave me the name and number of his appointments secretary, and asked me to get a date from her. I tried, but she never returned my call.

"FUNNY MONEY" AND THE HIGH PRICE OF TOO MUCH TENSION

On January 24, 1994, as soon as I was sure that the door to my direct involvement in Ottawa was closed, I started to write *Funny Money*, which just means bank-created virtual money that has no tangible backing. It was the first time I had gone public on monetary theory and banking. Until then, my strategy had been to become minister of finance under a prime minister who trusted me implicitly or, failing that, become the party leader and prime minister in order to simply introduce the better system and show how effective it could be.

I decided that it would be a good idea to have my book published in the United States, because I knew that Canadians are more likely to pay attention to anything coming from south of the border. I asked my good friend from "the Fellowship," Kent Hotaling, if he could find a U.S. agent for me. Kent referred me to a chap named Doug Holliday. By summer, I had a draft ready to send to the publisher that Holliday had lined up. The response was positive and resulted in an agreement in principle to publish the book. Then, a problem arose.

I wanted it out in the fall of 1994 but the publisher, being realistic, said no. My perennial impatience prevailed, and I decided to self-publish. That was one of the biggest mistakes I ever made.

It may have been the strain of self-publishing *Funny Money* or it may have been the cumulative tension of constantly swimming against the current that resulted in a heart attack on January 11, 1995. I had felt the pain of angina from time to time for quite a while, but it never lasted much more than the three or four minutes limit that the doctors tell you is the danger point to be on the lookout for.

That morning was different. I had gone to the office very early and it wasn't too long before the trouble began. Five minutes went by with no relief. Soon 10 minutes had passed. I phoned Ellen to tell her I was unwell and intended to call a taxi to take me to the hospital. The taxi line was busy, however, and a still, small voice told me to call 911 instead. In what seemed like no time flat the paramedics were there. Two robust females strapped me on a stretcher and had no trouble carrying my 205 pounds, but they were admittedly nervous going down the steep front steps that were covered with snow and ice.

I pleaded to be taken to Toronto General Hospital (TGH), which was renowned for its cardiac department. After checking my vital signs and ensuring that the General was "open" for new patients, TGH became our destination.

When we arrived at the hospital the wisdom of calling 911 immediately became apparent. Almost instantly two doctors were at my side checking me and giving me a new wonder drug to dissolve the blood clot before it was too late. The care and attention that I received from that moment on for the nine days until I was allowed to go home was absolutely superb. I was deeply grateful for the skill and compassion of all the health care workers, and also glad that they didn't have to ask me for a credit card on the way in. When I was discharged, Ellen provided the same kind of wonderful care and nursed me from a wobbly patient to full health again.

On February 27, 1995, Finance Minister Paul Martin delivered the fateful budget that might have given me another heart attack, but which simply energized me to carry on the fight against Friedmanism and economic madness for as long as my strength allowed.

Au Revoir, Dear Friends

If there was one lasting result from my first brush with serious illness it was a new consciousness of my mortality, and of my total dependence on my Lord and maker from one day to the next. It was a sobering realization, and one that was reinforced by the loss of my two closest friends. Most of my life I had only had one, or occasionally two at most, really close friends in whom I could confide with confidence.

From the days of my first election I had two close political friends. In Ottawa, it was Colin Bennett, MP for Grey North who left active politics in 1957; in Toronto, it was Keith Davey, a local broadcaster who became Executive Director of the Liberal Party of Canada, a confidante and supporter through many years until the 1968 Liberal Convention. He effectively wrote me off as a friend in 1972 when I joined the Conservatives even though, knowing how I felt, he had advised me to do just that.

The void left by Keith's separation was filled by two men, Sean O'Sullivan, a youthful Progressive Conservative MP, and William (Bill) Bussiere, a political neutral who stood beside me in matters both political and spiritual. Sean was elected at the tender age of 20 years old and became my mentor and guide through the PC Leadership Convention in 1974. Soon after that he decided to leave political life and enter the priesthood in 1977. Ellen and I were privileged to attend his ordination by G. Emmett Cardinal Carter on October 3, 1981.

Sean wrote a book entitled *Both My Houses* in which he tells his life story and also some embarrassingly nice things about me. He had not been a priest very long before he was stricken with leukemia and despite the best efforts of the medical profession, no cure could be found. There was a short period when his faith was sorely tested as he traversed the "Why me?" stretch of his journey. We discussed the struggle at more than one of our frequent luncheons where we laughingly said that we took each other's confessions. Actually, that was closer to truth than fiction.

Ellen and I often discussed why such a young man with so much promise would have to suffer a fatal disease. "Why couldn't it be one of us?" she would say. It is one of the great unknowns of life where answers escape us. Eventually his ravaged body could take it no longer and Sean succumbed to a heart attack. He died in March 1989, when he was 37.

With Sean "promoted to glory," as my Salvationist friends describe it, Bill Bussiere became my only remaining intimate friend and confidante. We were together a long time. He had left a good job in the financial industry in Montreal to help me with Action Canada in 1971. Later, when that folded, he had taken on responsibility for the work of the Fellowship on Parliament Hill and in other parts of Canada. In this position he was politically neutral as he ministered to MPs of all faiths and diverse political persuasions. All his friends seemed to understand, however, even though he was "everybody's best friend," that if I embarked on some political enterprise he would assist to the extent possible without compromising his work.

We became inseparable on all counts. Our wives, Ellen and Sandra, were also good friends and worked together at the Ottawa branch of the Canadian National Institute for the Blind. We became a foursome who worked together, prayed together, traveled together and took holidays together. It was a wonderful blessing for all of us until it was terminated suddenly in September 1994 when Bill suffered a massive heart attack and died on the way to the hospital.

As sad as it was, it was not totally unexpected. Heart problems ran in Bill's family and he had suffered an attack in June 1972, two years after he had come to work for me. In the intervening years, Dr. Wilbert Keon, the renowned Ottawa Heart Institute surgeon, had implanted by-pass arteries on more than one occasion. Now, at last, his heart had given out.

Sandra phoned to ask me to give the eulogy at the funeral, which I was happy to accept, even though I knew how difficult it would be. Fortunately, Ellen and my daughter, Mary Elizabeth, collaborated with me in a joint effort. Henri Nouwen, the well-known priest philosopher who had given up his post at Harvard in order to work with the mentally challenged at L'Arche, Toronto, was asked to do the homily. As it turned out, his homily was more of a eulogy, so there were two eulogies, a fact that reflected the tremendous impact Bill had had on so many lives.

Perhaps the greatest triumph of the funeral was the fact that all believers were invited to participate in the Eucharist. The parish priest explained that Bill had never turned anyone away from his table, and it was his wish that no one be turned away on this occasion. It was Bill's last statement about the kind of Christianity he believed in and practiced in his daily life.

Bill's passing was a grievous blow to Sandra, who was left with three daughters, Linda, Lori and Wanda. The girls were all married by then, one consolation being that he had walked each one of them down the aisle. Still, his death was an unfathomable loss to his myriad friends, and it left a giant void in my psyche that has never been filled.

CHAPTER FIFTEEN

THE CANADIAN ACTION PARTY

If Bill Bussiere had lived, he might have tried to talk me out of attempting to launch a new party based on our mutual experience with Action Canada more than two decades earlier. True, the circumstances were different, but the amount of tension, frustration, long hours, and the incredible odds against success were similar. But he wasn't there to counsel me, so slowly but surely, I began to convince myself that voters would endorse an idea that could produce almost magical benefits if they were only widely known.

I was involved with several organizations that were incompatible with active involvement in partisan politics. Consequently, I felt obliged to make sure that each one would be passed on into capable hands. The first was the chairmanship of the Canadian Foundation on Compulsive Gambling, the brainchild of Tibor Barsony, a former gambler who had lost everything and wanted to spread the news that gambling can be addictive and lead to a dead end. My good friend Rix Rogers, general secretary and CEO of the National Council of YMCA's of Canada agreed to take over.

Next on the list was Prison Fellowship Canada (PFC), which I had helped found. I persuaded Chuck Colson, founding chairman of Prison Fellowship International, to attend a fundraising dinner on March 29, 1996 at which we raised a significant amount of money, enough to keep PFC solvent for a while. It is still thriving as I write.

In May I chaired the Ontario Prayer Breakfast (OPB) for the last time. I had succeeded Claude Simmons, a titan of business and a man with a profound faith. At a private luncheon on September 30, 1996 with Rix Rogers, a fellow member of the OPB steering committee, I shared the information that Toronto businessman Peter Bouffard was prepared to accept the reins of that great organization, which is still flourishing today.

At that same luncheon, I talked openly with Rix about my future plans that, by then, were pretty well formulated in my mind. Rix was really gung ho about the idea. I found this very reassuring because he was as level-headed as he was nice. Part of the plan was to hire Don Champagne, a member of our Thursday morning group, to act as my chief of staff in the new party. Don was a lawyer who desperately wanted to leave the practice of law for personal reasons, so his desire and my need were complementary. It didn't take too long to make a deal with Don, who showed up on Saturday, November 2nd to measure his new office just two doors from mine.

One of the immediate hurdles was to assemble a team of well-known people to provide the kind of credibility that any new organization must have to succeed. No one wants to be first. Show them a list of names, including some they recognize, and they are "in." I decided to start on a short list of "stars" in the hope of convincing one or two to lead the others.

I started with Dr. James Fraser Mustard, CC, founding president of the Canadian Institute for Advanced Research. He had read my book and understood it. He wasn't interested in being a candidate but said he would consider talking to some of his friends.

My friend Bishop Arthur Brown was next on the list. With a twinkle in his eye he said that I was making mischief. He repeated his long-held belief that I am a prophet and, like all prophets, have paid the price. He was, of course, concerned about Ellen but agreed to help on that front. Arthur wondered about a Pugwash-type conference, or something such as that, but I explained that we had to make up our minds whether we were interested in talk or action.

The next star on my list was Maj. Gen. (Ret.) Lewis MacKenzie, former commander of UN troops during the Bosnian civil war of 1992. He was interested in learning about it, but confided that in the event of entering active politics he had a moral commitment to run for another party.

Still "reaching for the top" in potential candidates, I had lunch the following Tuesday with the aforementioned Art Brown and Archbishop Ted Scott, another Canadian folk hero. It was interesting and very friendly. The Archbishop had an agreement with his wife not to take on anything new. Still, he said he would talk to her and get back to me by the end of the week.

For weeks I had been working feverishly to get the groundwork laid. This marathon included getting a cartoon booklet prepared that would explain the monetary evolution in simple and succinct fashion.

One other hurdle was the discovery that there was already a registered federal party, the Canada Party, committed to monetary reform. Our aims and objectives were very similar and its president, Ian Woods, and leader Claire Foss, were both princes of political dedication. So, I asked them not to run candidates in the next election and cooperate with us in a coalition effort. Despite formidable constitutional and other obstacles, a deal was ultimately struck. The workdays kept getting longer, however, and the tension mounted as we braved the overload. It became a moot point whether or not we could meet the launch deadline.

On Sunday, January 12th Ellen and I went to the Metropolitan United Church. It was so cold we had to leave our coats on throughout the entire service. The sermon – 'New Beginnings' – was uncanny. Stephen Benrose

Fetter talked about the butterflies in your stomach when starting something new. He couldn't have described my situation better if he had known what I was going through.

The following Thursday was the big launch day. When we arrived there was only one camera crew. Later, others arrived. In the end, there was quite a good attendance (except CBC and CTV National). Rix introduced me and I said my piece, first in English and then an abbreviated version in French, ending with a plea that the press would not trivialize the ideas. Mercifully, my nerves held for the press conference itself. I was terribly relieved when it was over, and grateful.

The show was on the road and we received quite a few calls from people who were interested in getting involved, members of the Reform, National, Conservative, and Libertarian parties, but it was to be an uphill battle on all fronts. The press reaction was mixed. The print media was less than flattering with a few notable exceptions, including a column by Thomas Walkom in the *Toronto Star* – the one reporter who actually understood monetary theory. The electronic media were much more cooperative and a few downright laudatory. But we lacked the clout that would have come with a star-studded cast.

Getting organized was a big problem. I hired Brad Chapman, a long-time political junkie, to help recruit the 50 candidates minimum to have the party name on the ballot. Don and I had helped by mailing more than two million cartoon booklets that explained our policy, and how to get in touch. The reaction was so positive that we couldn't cope with the response. David Weston, another experienced campaigner, who I hired to organize in British Columbia, proved to be extraordinarily successful and was key to our finally reaching the qualifying number.

I decided to run in Etobicoke-Lakeshore because I thought it was easily accessible by highway. My good friend Warren Ralph took responsibility for finding an office and hiring Patricia Anderson, a former colleague at the Board of Trade, to manage my campaign for me. When I was in the riding knocking on doors I was received politely, but without the enthusiasm that signals a winning situation.

On election night Don and I watched the results come in and ultimately went to the committee room where there were about a dozen forlorn looking people including Marg Bulger, Irene Hobsbawn and Terry Prout. We watched until almost midnight, I made a little speech, and that was that. The rout was total.

I had been relaxed before the election because I knew we were going to get clobbered. I probably hoped for a few more than the 769 votes that I received personally, but three weeks before polling day I was fully aware that I had miscalculated terribly. The old adage about building a better mousetrap and people will come flocking to your door simply isn't true in the realm of ideas, at least when the subject is money and banking.

In early 1998 party president Rix Rogers became ill with the dreaded melanoma. On April 16th Don and I went to visit him in the hospital. As we left we agreed that the end was near. Rix died the next day, a prince of a man, a believer who practiced what he believed and a rare individual in every respect.

Filling his shoes was no mean task. In fact, we went six weeks without a president until June 24th, when Connie Fogal, a Vancouver lawyer who had been one of our star candidates in the election, agreed to take the job. We could not have made a better choice and she served her party well.

When fall came, I warned my staff that I sensed the possibility of an election, a full year ahead of the normal four-year cycle. We therefore started once again to look for potential candidates. A few of our 1997 candidates were able and willing to run again, so the final count was 70, an improvement on our first attempt. I ran in my own riding because it was so convenient.

When the election came, thousands of people who had sworn they would not vote for Chrétien again changed their minds because they preferred him to the far-right alternative Stockwell Day, who the prime minister successfully portrayed as the bad guy. His political street smarts had saved the day for Chrétien and gained another convincing majority. I received 1,466 votes, about double what I had obtained before, but still barely enough for some sort of respectability.

I hadn't really wanted to fight another election as leader of the Canadian Action Party (CAP), but we did our best against insurmountable odds, and lived to fight another day – or consider another strategy. It was the latter that preoccupied my mind as the year wound to a close.

One Big Party

To make a very long story short, I was authorized to make overtures to other parties and individuals. I met with several former Progressive Conservative MPs and members of the Green Party. The former indicated some interest so we began formal negotiations that we hoped would lead to the formation of a big, new, progressive, pro-Canada party comprised of the NDP, CAP, the bulk of the progressives from the Progressive Conservative Party and some dissident Liberals who were looking for a new home.

At one point, immediately after the NDP had been reduced to a rump in the province of Newfoundland and Labrador, it appeared that our scheme was being taken seriously. Our hopes were short-lived, however, because negotiations with the NDP seemed interminable due to the foot-dragging of the more reactionary elements, and eventually the brief window of opportunity was lost.

Stephen Harper, the new leader of the Alliance, made a deal with Peter McKay, the new leader of the Progressive Conservative Party, to merge the two into a new Conservative Party. Once that happened any dream of forming one big new progressive party was gone, because it depended on significant support from the old Progressive Conservative Party. Without that, the scheme would never have worked as planned. Another good idea died on the vine.

As usual, it turned out to be a blessing in disguise because during the course of the negotiations Ellen had taken suddenly ill.

ELLEN HAS A SERIOUS SETBACK

On Monday, October 1, 2001, when I returned home from a late lunch and looked for Ellen I finally found her in the upstairs bathroom, both hands on the counter, leaning against the wall. I said she should lie down but when she moved she fell flat on her face and hit her head on the table. I had to pick her up like a sack of wheat to get her to the bed. I said I was going to call an ambulance, but she was adamant, as she always was. Before long, she lost consciousness and I called 911, and she was taken to St. Michael's Hospital.

The service from the medics, the Toronto Fire Department, and the medical team from St. Mike's was phenomenal. When I was able to see her, Ellen was in bad shape. Her eyes wouldn't focus. Her face was partly paralyzed with one side of her mouth drooping. It was pitiful for me to see, as a doctor kept working on her, asking her questions that are routine for patients suffering from a stroke.

About 9:00 p.m. two radiologists came along to discuss the options. They could do a procedure like an angiogram to try to find the clot and then insert a needle to try to dissolve it. But there was a risk, it could cause bleeding in the brain.

The neurologist said she was satisfied with Ellen's progress, nature was doing the healing. She did not think heroics, dangerous ones, were required. Eventually everyone agreed, and the decision was taken. Ellen was made comfortable, I kissed her goodnight, and went home to have a bowl of cereal before bed.

On Friday, the floor doctor said that Ellen could go home Saturday morning. The timing was perfect for me. When we got home I made grilled tomato and cheese sandwiches for lunch, and she told me they were delicious. Sunday, after reviewing some of her mail, Ellen came through to the kitchen and said: "I guess I really did have a stroke." The reality had finally become apparent to her. This had been her worst nightmare because she had a family history of strokes and there had been some pretty sad cases. She had escaped lightly, and was recovering quickly. I made her a delicious dinner so when son Peter phoned to enquire how she was getting along she replied: "The room service is excellent."

MY ASSOCIATION WITH CAP COMES TO AN END

The party had held a convention in September 2003, at which it had unanimously approved a resolution to merge with the NDP as a first step in the formation of one big, progressive pro-Canada party. Walter Pitman, president of Ryerson University, who was our keynote speaker, had given a marvelous address in full support of the One Big Party (OBP) proposal.

When I spoke, I made it clear that if the OBP idea didn't fly, I would resign as leader. It was not an idle threat. On January 30th, CAP put out a short press release announcing my decision to leave partisan political life after 55 years of service to my country. Consequently, a convention would be held on March 21-23, 2004, to elect a successor. The press reaction was zilch.

On the opening day of the convention I was honored with a farewell banquet. When Ellen and I arrived just shortly after 6:00 p.m. the hall was already almost full.

Eventually every seat was occupied by friends, relatives and former colleagues with whom I had served in one capacity or another. It was really heart-warming to see so many wonderful people, some of them for the first time in years or decades.

My speech lasted a total of 45 minutes, sort of my last kick at the cat, so to speak. I had spent some considerable time preparing it, and that always makes a difference. At the appropriate moment I paid tribute to Ellen for the indescribable contribution she had made over the years, one that no words of mine could adequately recount. I stopped in mid-flight, stepped down off the stage, went to the spot where she was sitting at the first table, handed her a single red rose and kissed her. It was a long overdue recognition. I finished with a flourish that ended with a spontaneously gracious and extended standing ovation. I don't think the evening could have been better.

When we got home, Ellen said: "It was really a very good speech you know," adding that it might have been a little bit long at the end. I took her endorsement as the supreme compliment. She also said she wouldn't have wanted to miss it, especially with the flowers she was presented.

At the convention the following morning, I chaired the election (by acclamation) of Connie Fogal as leader. I was pleased by the outcome and surprised at the unanimity. Proof that she was the right choice was the fact she kept the party alive and flourishing for a number of years against seemingly insurmountable odds until it finally fell on hard times and ceased to exist.

Concerning CAP, you may wonder if I would do it all over again if I had the chance. The answer is a resounding no. The price was far too high for the results achieved. I completely overestimated the interest of the public and the press in subjects that affect them mightily, but are too complex for them to understand and in which they have no interest in taking the time to learn about.

THE SADDEST FIVE WEEKS OF MY LIFE

I enjoyed a general sense of euphoria to be free from partisan politics after 55 years in and out of the vocation. A tremendous burden had been lifted from my shoulders. Ellen and I began looking ahead. At long last we would have more time to do things together.

One commitment that we always looked forward to was the planting weekend at Arundel Lodge, when we prettied up the place in anticipation of the summer season. Little did we dream that this would be Ellen's last. We always went home on Tuesday to avoid the holiday traffic. But this time, May 25, 2004, Ellen said she wasn't feeling well, and skipped breakfast. Then she asked if I would put the food in the cooler for her, which I did for the first time in my life.

The trip home to Toronto was more or less routine, but I had to unpack everything and put the food away. We had no idea what was wrong, but whatever it was it took away Ellen's appetite. By Friday, I thought, I don't know how I am going to keep this poor girl alive if she doesn't eat anything. By Sunday, I was convinced that it was a losing battle and that she must go to a hospital despite her absolutely fierce resistance.

Ellen's illness came at an extremely busy time for me. We were in the middle of a federal election and although I was no longer a member of CAP, I had agreed that the campaign could be run from my office. In addition, the lease expired on June 30th, and there were decades of accumulated stuff to dispose of.

Meanwhile, Ellen remained adamant about not going to the hospital, giving the excuse that she had an appointment with Dr. Brenda McDowell, her medicine angel, two days later. I think we both used that fact as an excuse to procrastinate until our 59th wedding anniversary the following day, when I gave her a couple of books and a refill of her Shalimar perfume bottle, which pleased her. But our "toast" consisted of eggnog for her and a drink for me. Later she remarked, "Some anniversary."

Wednesday morning I phoned 911 and she was soon on her way again to St. Michael's Hospital. The doctors did all the routine tests and noticed her distended tummy. She was moved to an isolation room and asked a thousand questions. They then advised that they would be taking a sample of fluid from her stomach, but it could be the middle of the night and I might just as well go home, so I did.

Thursday proved to be the saddest day of my life. When I arrived at the hospital in the morning Ellen had been moved for tests. When I got back in the afternoon she was not on IV, so I asked the nurse to re-instate it. She replied that she couldn't because it was not on the chart. I demanded to see a doctor. A long time later, after saying the doctor was off the premises, she advised that they had paged the chief physician, Dr. Peter Kopplin, and he had authorized the IV be restored. I wondered if the doctors knew something I didn't and had pulled the plug.

My state of mind wasn't improved when I returned after dinner and Ellen was hallucinating. Meanwhile, the IV wasn't working and I refused to leave until it was, which was at about 10:15 p.m. When I got home I couldn't sleep and by morning I was a total wreck, acting as if I were the one without a mind. Later when I arrived at emergency she was fully cogent and wanted to go home. Just as I told her that was the plan the doctor appeared and advised that they had found white blood cells in the fluid but didn't know if they were benign or cancerous.

On Monday the doctor arrived and said he wanted to talk about cancer. Ellen said if it was about cancer she didn't want to hear about it. He said the cells were cancer of unknown origin, and asked if we had any questions. After the doctor left, I put my face against hers. Ellen whispered, "We have been together for a long time." "Yes," I whispered back, "but it won't be the same without you," as the tears started rolling down my face onto hers.

Tuesday morning both Dr. Dhalla and Dr. Kapplin came to chat. They had made an appointment with an oncologist, and suggested chemotherapy, but Ellen and I said that was not her wish, a prospect we had discussed many times. We agreed that I would take her home at about 4:00 p.m., enough time to recruit my daughter-in-law Kathy to assist.

Ellen did not want to die in the hospital. Her desire was to be at home, surrounded by family and their love as she left this world. My two daughters-in-law Catherine and Kathy were really wonderful, and achieving her wish would have been impossible without them. Then my daughter Mary Elizabeth, who had lived in England for many years, came home to help as well. The two of us were primarily in charge until the last few days, when we had to get help from the Ontario government home care plan.

Dr. McDowell dropped by with a bouquet of freesia, Ellen's favorite flower, and left a prescription for morphine, a pain killer that became increasingly essential. Monday, June 28th was election day. When I went in to see Ellen she wasn't moving. It was very difficult to give her medication that she was now desperate to take, as the pain had been intensifying. I voted at noon, but was so busy I didn't even watch the election results except for five minutes, just long enough to know there would be a Liberal minority. Ironically, two days before the election, Ellen asked who had won. She really did have a deep-seated interest in politics.

The next morning, I got up at 5:30 a.m. because I had to be at the office at 7:45 a.m. to meet the movers. Ellen was having difficulty breathing when I went in to give her the morphine drops. When I returned after breakfast I knew at once that she was gone. I broke down completely. Even though I knew her passing was inevitable, the pain in losing my closest companion for so many years was almost unbearable.

To make matters worse, with the necessity of moving out of my office and the details of all that happens when one dies we were not able to schedule the memorial service until July 7th. My family came to the rescue in myriad ways, and they were fantastically helpful. I would have been totally lost without them. Meanwhile Ellen was cremated, as was her wish.

It was holiday time so two senior ministers were not available for the service. Fortunately, Rob Knighton from our little Lakeview Church in Muskoka came to the rescue. I also asked Reverend Doctor John Gladstone, Pastor Emeritus at Yorkminster Park Baptist Church to participate. It was his last public service before he died. Ellen would have been pleased because they were two of her very favorite people.

She vastly underestimated her popularity. Her friends turned out en masse, as did our mutual friends and relatives. It was a great tribute to her, as were the wonderful words that were said about her by John Gladstone, Rob Knighton, and George Waters, who represented members of the Seniors Bible Class that I had taught years earlier, and whose members had benefited so much from Ellen's care and compassion.

Later, the family met at the condo for a lovely dinner catered by our friend Peggy Turcot. There, the reminiscing continued.

What a change it was to wake up in the morning and not feel dutybound to get up and get going. I stayed in bed until 8:00 a.m. After breakfast, I sorted the mail and then had a swim that was desperately overdue. Later, Mary Elizabeth and I packed and headed for Arundel, the first time without Ellen. It was the end of an era.

CHAPTER SIXTEEN

A NEW AND VERY DIFFERENT ERA

The days and weeks following Ellen's death were extremely difficult. I was busy settling Ellen's estate, deciding what to do with her clothes and jewelry, while trying to adjust to a small one-person office, and do all of my own work. My biggest problem, however, was the loneliness. It wasn't just going home to an empty condo and having to make my own dinner, it was getting dressed and heading off to church, the ballet or an opera and wondering, in the two latter cases, who I could find to go with me and use the extra ticket.

After a few agonizing months I phoned my daughter Mary Elizabeth who lives in London, England and asked her if she would be willing to come home to Toronto and be my escort for the ballet and opera. She wanted to remain in London, so I started to think about other alternatives. Although my two sons Peter and David and their wives and families were very sensitive and considerate about including me in their special events, for which I am eternally grateful, it was not the same as having someone with whom to share my hopes, aspirations, and my life.

It therefore wasn't too long before I began to think of re-marriage. But the thought of dating, followed by courtship, appealed to me about as much as a cold shower in winter. The name of Sandra Bussiere, widow of Bill who had been my best friend, came to mind. When Bill died in 1994, our close friendship with Sandra continued. She spent time with us at Arundel Lodge every summer, and whenever she came to Toronto to visit her daughter Wanda, Ellen and I would invariably invite her to dinner. It was on one of those occasions when Ellen asked her some questions about her welfare that she had admitted that she was ready for a new relationship.

I saw Sandra several times in the Fall of 2005 when she came to Toronto to see her daughter and occasionally asked her to have dinner with me at one of the local restaurants. Sandra is a very spiritual person so this was a ready-made bond, in addition to the 35 years of acquaintance when she and Bill, Ellen and I had worked, prayed and travelled together as couples. We seemed to be a perfect match.

One night in late November, I invited her to dinner and then back to the condo for coffee. I asked her if she thought she would ever re-marry and she reassured me that she had not changed her mind. So I asked her if she would marry me after an appropriate time had passed. She was genuinely surprised, but after thinking about it for a few minutes, she said yes, on the spot. When I kissed her goodnight, I realized that it was our first kiss, except for a polite peck on the cheek. We must have set some kind of a record for spontaneous marriage proposals.

We set the wedding date for October 1, 2005 and were married by our mutual friend Rev. Jim Lee, the pastor of Carleton Memorial United Church, who had also been Sandra's partner in the work of the Fellowship on Parliament Hill. Her best friend, Joy Heft, was Sandra's matron-of-honor and my brother-in-law, John Race, stood up with me. The reception was held across the Ottawa River in the *Salon des Voyageur*, the cafeteria in the Canadian Museum of Civilization. My long-time friend Doug Zimmerman, who had brought his orchestra from Toronto, delighted everyone, as he went from table to table asking for their requests.

It was a beautiful sunny day, unusual for October, and a number of the guests stood out on the lawn by the Ottawa River enjoying the classic view of the Parliament Buildings where Sandra and I had spent so much time with our previous partners. Our choice of venue for the reception was a nostalgic connection to the past.

It was well past our bedtime when the dancing ended and the last of our guests departed. We had booked a room right across the street so we could get up at 4:30 a.m. to catch our flight to Cancun, Mexico. We were both very tired, and it wasn't until we got on board the plane that we could finally relax.

Even though the Ottawa weather had been unusually nice it was wonderful to disembark and feel the tropical warmth en route to our hotel where we could hardly wait to dash into the water for our first swim in the ocean.

We had a wonderful week of swimming, sightseeing the countryside, especially the Mayan ruins where we let our imaginations run loose on what that great ancient civilization had really been like, and how it had differed from ours. The whole area was a photographer's paradise. Evenings involved gourmet dinners and our most memorable was when a great saxophone player came by to entertain us. We spontaneously left our table and went down to the beach to dance in our bare feet on the sand.

When our truly wonderful seven-day honeymoon ended we flew back to Toronto and a new beginning as a married couple. We just got back in time, as a couple of days later a tropical storm hit Cancun, wrecked the hotel where we had stayed, and washed away the beach we had enjoyed so much.

A New Reality

In late 2002, I began to receive mail from a complete stranger named Pierre Juneau, a young bilingual chap who lived in Ottawa, who had become interested in unidentified flying objects (UFOs). He didn't state his objective but I sensed he was looking for someone whose name was well known to help publicize a subject that wasn't discussed in the popular press. In response, I told him that I was too busy to read what he was sending me. Pierre acknowledged my problem and simply suggested that I put his material on a shelf somewhere and keep it for a "rainy day," that proverbial lull in activity that seldom ever comes.

Most of the documents he sent me were related to the UFO phenomenon, which was not high on my priority list. Then he sent me *The Day After Roswell*, by Colonel Philip J. Corso (Ret.), which looked like an excellent read for my summer vacation.

In February 2005, I received a call from Pierre almost pleading with me to take two hours off to watch a *Prime Time Live* special broadcast put together by Peter Jennings, a producer for the ABC network. I agreed and watched every minute of it. Former airline pilots, retired United States Air Force (USAF) pilots, air traffic controllers and policemen all stated unequivocally that they had seen UFOs. I thought to myself that they all appeared legitimate and seemed to be telling the truth.

That summer, I took *The Day After Roswell* to Arundel Lodge with me when I went on vacation. I found the story told by the former U.S. army intelligence officer to be totally compelling, especially because he had been a member of President Eisenhower's National Security Council and, later, head of the Foreign Technology Desk at the U.S. Army's Research and Development Department. I concluded that it was not the kind of book that anyone could fake. There were too many real names and real places that I recognized from my days as minister of defense.

Corso confirmed beyond any shadow of doubt the long-circulated rumor that on or about July 4, 1947, a UFO had crashed not far from Roswell, New Mexico. The colonel was not at the crash site, but subsequently saw one of the alien bodies while it was being transported for autopsy. (We now know there were two crashes that same day in July and I actually have a document in my files that shows the precise coordinates of the two wrecks. But for many years, most of us were only aware of one crash.)

Even more convincing was the colonel's involvement 10 years later when he found himself in charge of the army's Foreign Technology Division of Research and Development. In this top-secret job, his boss Lt. Gen. Arthur Trudeau turned over the filing cabinet full of scrap collected at the Roswell crash site. Corso was given a mandate to sort it and then feed it to U.S. industry for the benefit of the military. This was done without any reference to the source of the materials, but the carefully-screened recipients, who were experts in their respective fields, would recognize at once that what they were given was technologically decades or centuries ahead of our own.

As I sat entranced by these exciting revelations my nephew Philip came by and asked me what I was reading. When I told him he said he was incredulous and highly sceptical. My response was that he was entitled to his opinion, it was still a free country, more or less. Philip went home and a couple of days later phoned to say that he had called a retired USAF general of his acquaintance to ask him about Corso's book. "Every word is true, and more," the general had told him. That was enough to convince Philip, who wanted to know where he could get his hands on a copy of the book.

It was also the confirmation I needed to change my mind about an invitation I had received from Victor Viggiani and Mike Bird, two of Canada's more active ufologists (a ufologist is one who specializes in the study of UFOs and the extraterrestrial phenomena) to address their Exopolitics Toronto Symposium on September 25, 2005. I suspect that the invitation was a last-minute affair. Victor and his friend Richard Syrett had a late-night show on CFRB radio, in Toronto. One night, as the show ended, the phone rang. Victor said it was their policy not to answer phone calls but that night they did. It was Jim Duchesne, who had been a member of the Seniors Bible Class I once taught.

Jim asked why they didn't interview me. As Victor admits, they were not sure that I was still alive. But as a result of one of these "inexplicable coincidences" they tracked me down and sent me an invitation to speak at their symposium. I had intended to decline with thanks, because it was not my subject and I had nothing to say. One of my many sins is procrastination, however, so I hadn't responded before leaving for a brief holiday.

My reluctance changed abruptly when I finished reading Corso's book and contemplated the enormous policy implications of the extraterrestrial presence and technology. I had concluded there were issues of earth-shattering consequences that were not being discussed or debated because the official policy of the U.S. government was that UFOs did not exist. As a lifelong policy "wonk," I knew that someone had to speak out.

Before going public, however, I thought that it would be prudent to hear the confirmation from the retired USAF general personally. I had met him at an aviation exhibition so I asked Philip for his phone number and to give him a "heads up" that I would like to talk to him. When I called, he didn't even give me a chance to say, "Hello, how are you?" He said, "Every word is true, and more." We then spent the next 20 minutes discussing the "and more" to the extent that he could without revealing classified material. He told me that there had been a face-to-face discussion between the celestial visitors and U.S. officials. With that assurance I was ready to say my piece.

There was one major complication, however. The symposium was being held exactly one week before I was to be married. So, I had to ask Sandra if she had any objection. I assured her that it would be a "one-off" affair, but that I thought what I was proposing to say should be in the public domain. If I recall correctly, she was a bit reluctant, and she would have been more so if she had realized what would happen to my well-intentioned promise. However, neither of us were blessed with a crystal ball, and I got the green light from her to proceed.

Consequently, on September 25th, at the very end of the program, most of which I had missed due to preparation of what I intended to say, I took my place at the podium and told that assembly that "UFOs are as real as the airplanes flying overhead," and that "the time has come to lift the veil of secrecy and let the truth emerge so there can be a real and informed debate about one of the most important issues facing our planet. Forgive me for stating the obvious, but it is quite impossible to have that kind of informed debate about a problem that doesn't officially exist."

With this speech, I had just earned the dubious distinction of becoming the first person of cabinet rank from what was then the G8 group of countries to say unequivocally that UFOs are real, we are not alone in the cosmos, and we had better get used to it and make any adjustments necessary to benefit from what I call the "broader reality." My short speech was not too different, in a way, than the hundreds I had made before. In another more profound way, I had set my feet on an unfamiliar road leading to the cosmos, a road that I had been quite comfortable not to know about.

THE BROADER REALITY

The press reaction exceeded my expectations, especially in the United States. An interview on Fox News TV stands out. The conversation seemed civil enough until the end when the final question was, "Have you actually seen a UFO?" I had to admit that I had not, to which he replied, "Then you don't know what you are talking about." If I had been faced with the same question again I would have said, "No, but I haven't seen the Taj Mahal either, yet I know it exists."

As a result of the publicity, I began to receive documents of all kinds, some classified and others unclassified, that contained a vast amount of interesting and useful information from people who were familiar with the subject. Many of them, perhaps a couple of dozen, sent me copies of books they had written, and in those early days I read every one of them.

In November, I received a message from Paola Harris, a well-established ufologist advising that she was flying from Rome to interview me. Paola had been on the program for the September 25th symposium along with veteran ufologists, Stephen Bassett, Richard Dolan, and Stanley Friedman, but became ill and missed my debut. The wonderful interview in my office was one of my best ever and still may be seen on occasion after circulating online in several countries in three or four languages.

Paola gave me a copy of *Connecting the Dots*, one of her books that contained a lengthy interview with Monsignor Corrado Balducci who had a regular program on Vatican radio and TV. In response to Paola's questions, the Monsignor made it very clear that while he was not an official spokesman for the Vatican, the Holy Father John Paul II had seen and heard his broadcasts and there had never been any negative reaction. It was clear that the Pope was well aware of life on other planets, according to Balducci.

As a result of taking a categorical position on the existence of UFOs, there were many people who wanted to brief me. One of the best known was Dr. Steven Greer, who had given up a lucrative medical practice because he was deeply concerned about the secrecy surrounding the subject of extraterrestrial life. When Dr. Greer visited Toronto in May 2006 we had lunch at a waterfront café about a 10-minute walk from our condo.

In the course of a three-hour briefing, I was brought up to speed on a number of subjects he had researched from about 400 former military officers, scientists, civil aviation experts, policemen and pilots who had been willing to talk on the record about the important subjects the U.S. government had been hiding from citizens for half a century or more.

Not only was I struck by the depth and diversity of the testimony assembled by Dr. Greer for his "Disclosure Project," I was alarmed by statements from witnesses who confirmed my suspicions of American military plans, including the militarization of space that I consider extremely dangerous and not in the best interests of either the United States or the world.

Even more alarming was Dr. Greer's assertion that government leaders are unaware of what is going on in their own country, and that the real power lies in the hands of a "shadow government," the composition of which is unknown. As the late U.S. Senator Daniel K. Inouye of Hawaii described it: "There exists a shadowy government with its own air force, its own navy, its own fundraising mechanism, and the ability to pursue its own ideas of the national interest, free from all checks and balances, and free from the law itself."[1] This is an incredibly important summary with which I totally agree.

The following month, in June 2006, I delivered the keynote address at the Extraterrestrial Civilization & World Peace Conference at Kona, Hawaii, at the invitation of Dr. Michael Salla, head of the Exopolitics Institute and his wife Angelika Whitecliffe, co-organizer of the conference, that provided me the opportunity to listen to a number of speakers, all of whom knew more about the subject than I did. My role was to expand on my concerns about the military and political implications of visitors from other planets, aspects of the new broader reality that were well within my comfort zone.

A very pleasant episode that occurred at the conference was a chance meeting with Capt. Robert Salas, USAF Ret., and his wife Marilyn, who agreed to join Sandra, Mike Bird, and me for dinner. The captain told us his story, which bordered on science fiction but was real, only too real. In summary, on March 16, 1967, when he was 60 feet underground as part of the 490th strategic missile squad, a guard reported something that Robert identified as a UFO, a shiny metal disc, right outside of the front gate. The bottom line was that seven or eight of the missiles were rendered inoperable. Despite an extensive investigation, the cause was never determined but the whole incident was kept secret. You can read about it in Bob's excellent book *Faded Giant*, or on the internet.

Before Sandra and I left Kona for home, Michael gave me a copy of his exceptional book *Exopolitics*. In it he explains how the U.S. government lost control of the ET file, and how Nelson Rockefeller, as advisor to President Eisenhower, reorganized the control mechanisms for back-engineering UFO technology and essentially placed them in the hands of the military-industrial complex. Brigadier General Stephen Lovekin, a military officer who served directly under Eisenhower, confirmed, as one of Dr. Greer's disclosure witnesses, that it was the realization by Eisenhower that he had been sold down the river that led him to use the occasion of his farewell address as president to warn the American people to beware of the military-industrial complex. Regrettably, his warning fell on deaf ears.

The Canadian Connection

Wherever I went in those early days someone would ask me if I was familiar with Wilbert Smith or knew about the Shag Harbour incident. I admitted that I was unfamiliar with both.

I subsequently learned that on the night of October 4, 1967, just days after I had left the Defence Department, officers of the Royal Canadian Mounted Police and six civilians witnessed what turned out to be the best documented UFO sighting in Canadian history. It occurred at Shag Harbour, located at the southern tip of Nova Scotia, about 256 kilometers from Halifax.

There are several good books on the subject and a friend from Halifax, Graham Simms, sent me a copy of a book he and Chris Styles had written entitled *Impact to Contact: The Shag Harbour Incident*, which I read with unparalleled interest. It is the world's only officially documented UFO crash. In it, we learn that when UFOs appear to crash in the water they do not disintegrate. They can navigate underwater. This book is a real eye-opener![2]

Wilbert Smith turned out to be a former employee of the Department of Transport, who wrote a top-secret memo dated November 21, 1950, in which he noted that information from Washington had revealed that: the matter was more highly classified than the H-bomb; flying saucers exist; their *modus operandi* is unknown, but concentrated effort is being made by a small group headed by Dr. Vannevar Bush; and the entire matter is considered by U.S. authorities to be of tremendous significance.[3]

Smith was responsible for the establishment of Project Magnet in 1951 and spent many years deeply immersed in the UFO and ET phenomenon.

A whole book could be written about Smith, but there is only room here for one paragraph from one of his speeches.

"We may summarize the entire flying saucer picture as follows: We have arrived at a time in our development when we make a final choice between right and wrong. The people from elsewhere are much concerned about the choice which we will make, partly because it will have its repercussions on them and partly because they are our blood brothers and are truly concerned with our welfare. There is a cosmic law about interfering in the affairs of others, so they are not allowed to help us directly even though they could easily do so. We must make our own choice of our own free will. Present trends indicate a series of events which may require the help of these people and they stand by ready and willing to render that help. In fact, they have already helped us a great deal, along lines that do not interfere with our freedom of choice. In time, when certain events have transpired, and we are so oriented that we can accept these people from elsewhere, they will meet us freely on the common ground of mutual understanding and trust, and we will be able to learn from them and bring about the Golden Age all men everywhere desire deep within their hearts."[4]

The challenge we face is how to learn from them and to move forward to work in harmony for a better world.

CHAPTER 17

SUPPLEMENTARY EVIDENCE

I had absolutely no doubt about UFOs being real when I first said so publicly on September 25, 2005, therefore I wasn't looking for additional evidence, but I got it anyway. Not only was I inundated with documents and books, the majority of which were interesting and informative, but there was also personal contact and e-mails, hundreds of them, from all over North and South America and several other countries. I've not stopped receiving them, and by now they number in the thousands, sufficient to fill several books with eye-witness accounts. But limited space demands that I only include a few select examples here.

One such account was a chap, Leo Pearce, who lived in our building. He wanted to share an experience he and a girlfriend had years earlier when they were driving from Port Hope to Cobourg, two small towns about two hours east of Toronto, when they saw a big object the size of a football field hovering directly over them. It was a dual saucer, inverted, with portholes both top and bottom. It had a glowing blue flame around the outside but the sound was not that of motors, it was more like generators, a humming sound. "I watched it for about 15 minutes, then all of a sudden it started to glow on the outside and then accelerated over the lake (Ontario) and just disappeared … there was nothing in the papers!"[1]

Next, a Canadian World War II veteran tracked me down to relate his wartime and post-war experiences. Flight Lieutenant, (Captain) RCAF Stan Fulham of Winnipeg, Manitoba, told me of seeing what the airmen called Foo fighters, small orbs that dogged both Allied and German planes during the war. More recently, one night in the early 1960s when Fulham worked as a fighter controller for NORAD, he had monitored UFOs on radar and scrambled fighter aircraft to investigate the alien spacecraft. "As soon as our jets were airborne the UFOs streaked away at phenomenal speeds approaching three thousand miles per hour. The discs reappeared and hovered over the ocean near Vancouver, British Columbia. When our fighters caught up with them … they streaked away and disappeared over the Pacific."

Fulham reported that thousands of people had seen both the UFOs and the RCAF fighters and quite a few called the control tower to give their version of events. "Early the next morning the Base Commander called and advised me of the media interest. 'However' he cautioned, 'since nothing unusual took place last night, I suggest that we have nothing to discuss with the media.' I understood. This was the standard response to the public and the media in NORAD under the secret United States-Canada Communications Agreement signed in 1956 relating to the control and reporting of UFO sightings."[2]

At that point I hadn't talked to anyone who had seen a UFO close-up. My long-time friend and former Canadian Forces Information Officer, Ray Stone, advised me that one of his friends, Nicholas Evanoff, had. The following is a condensed version of his story as received by Ray via e-mail. Evanoff was a Canadian Emergency Preparedness Officer who, while visiting a U.S. government organization (CIA headquarters in Langley, Virginia), was asked if he would like to see a real UFO because it would be useful in the event of an incident (UFO crash) in Canada. "Of course," he said, and after signing a non-disclosure agreement he was flown to somewhere in Arizona or Nevada [Area 51]. (Area 51 is the huge, top-secret base where the U.S. has back-engineered ET technology.)

To quote Evanoff: "Then we went into a humungous hangar and there was a damaged UFO. When it crashed it had eight aliens on board and six of them died on impact, and the pilot and co-pilot survived for a couple of days. The USAF doctors didn't know how to treat them because they were from another planet and they died. I didn't see the bodies but I was shown some photographs of them and they were similar to us humans but thinner, had a head and arms and legs and a torso with five digits on their hands and feet. On board was a nuker for cooking food and a supply of water along with two bathrooms. The manuals were in hieroglyphics but no one could read them ..."[3] He couldn't tell anyone, including his wife.

I wanted to get the full story from Nick personally so Ray set up an interview for a Sunday afternoon in October 2007. Before the day came Ray advised that if I wanted to talk to Nick, who had Lou Gehrig's disease, before he died, I had better telephone him at once, which I did, on October 7th. He confirmed the story in detail and also told me about a UFO landing near Winnipeg, Manitoba, that had not been publicized. A few days later he passed on to his reward.

A VISIT TO THE MIDDLE EAST

As early as the Spring of 2006 I felt guided to write a book about world affairs and some of the issues facing humankind, including the situation in the Middle East, global warming and, of course, some of the issues raised by the extraterrestrial presence and influence. I felt that a visit to the Middle East was essential to have better first-hand knowledge to add to my extensive reading on the subject.

My wife Sandra thought it would be nice to travel with another couple and suggested our wonderful friends Kent and Kay Hotaling from Oregon, who had moved to Canada for a few years to help launch the Prayer Breakfast movement here. They were delighted to join us, so we agreed to meet in Tel Aviv because we were traveling by different routes. Sandra and I decided to stop over in London, which would allow me to have lunch with Nick Pope, the UFO desk officer for the United Kingdom Ministry of Defence, who had contacted me by e-mail.

Nick was limited in what he could say, but we agreed that the percentage of UFO sightings that were natural phenomena and those that were genuine UFOs was roughly the same in both countries. Before we parted Nick gave me two UFO files that had somehow gotten into the public domain and were subsequently unclassified, including the well-known Bentwaters Forest case that he thought I might like to investigate.

We then took off for the Middle East and an incredible visit to Israel, the Palestinian-occupied territories, Lebanon, Jordan, and a short respite in Cairo, Egypt. By the time we left for home we had learned so much in such a short time that it was difficult to digest, and one of our fears was how we could share our knowledge without undue incredulity from friends who hadn't been privileged to see what we had seen. A full report of our incredible journey and the conclusions we reached can be found in my book *Light at the End of the Tunnel: A Survival Plan for the Human Species.*

My Spiritual Journey

From the time I made a decision to surrender the direction of my life to God in 1957 I witnessed a serious of miracles, some that I designate as mini-miracles, and others of major significance. My unexpected return to the House of Commons so soon after being defeated in the 1958 general election was a big step along the road for my political career, as was my later appointment as Minister of National Defence when the odds were definitely not in my favor. During those hectic political years my relationship with the Creator grew slowly, but in later years when I had more time for reflection, the bond grew stronger and deeper.

We began to communicate telepathically, and often I was given small but greatly appreciated favors, such as which route to take when I was driving and whether or not it was necessary to take an umbrella. I learned to express my appreciation not just three times a day at mealtime, but very often in response to countless blessings. The Source, as many ET species call the Creator, was a constant help as I wrote my last two books, and is responsible for me accepting the challenge inherent in this one.

THE RENDLESHAM FOREST CASE

After our visit to the Middle East Sandra and I decided that we would attend the National Prayer Breakfast (NPB) in Washington in February 2007. When Sandra was married to Bill, they would go every year as leaders of the Canadian delegation. For quite a few years the Washington NPB was on my agenda as well, and on more than one occasion I would schedule a meeting with Defense Secretary Robert McNamara so that the two events would correspond and I could offer MPs the opportunity to travel with me. But more recently, neither of us had attended, so we thought it would be a good year to renew acquaintance with our many friends.

I had another reason for attending that year. I had contacted Colonel Charles Halt, the deputy commander of the two U.S. bases involved in the Rendlesham Forest incident to ask if he would meet with me. At first, he said that he didn't talk about such matters, but when I told him that Nick Pope had recommended me, he changed his mind. On February 2, 2007 I met the colonel for lunch at the gated community about one hour's drive south of Washington where he was employed.

After lunch we talked for two hours and he allowed me to tape the entire conversation, which consisted of about 95 percent of his story, interrupted only by the occasional question. I had the interview transcribed and used nearly all of it in my book because it was a classic case. Here is part of his story.

When the routine night patrol of the forest area between the two bases first reported a sighting the news was received with disbelief and ridicule. A similar sighting Christmas night in 1980 ended differently. When the two non-commissioned officers (NCOs) reported a glow in the woods, Halt told his boss who was presiding at the Christmas dinner, "We've got to put this thing to rest." "I've got to make all the presentations in a few minutes," the commanding officer replied, "Why don't you go?" Halt headed out with his "I'm going to put an end to this nonsense once and for all" stance, but what he saw later that night changed his life forever.

Although it was never admitted, Bentwaters and Woodbridge, known as the twin base complex, had a nuclear capability and Halt realized later that the visitors were interested in the storage area. The follow-up involved all the usual denial, missing documents and other nonsense common to similar events. The only reason that this one became public was because a report had to be submitted to the British authorities and they inadvertently leaked it to the press. My book *Light at the End of the Tunnel* covered the whole story as the Colonel (he had been promoted to full colonel before retirement) told it. Years later he wrote his own book, *The Halt Perspective*, which included photographs and diagrams to illustrate the story.

All of the interesting and knowledgeable people I met, the wide variety of books I read and conferences I attended, equipped me to accept quite a few speaker engagements. The following is but one example.

The Society for Exploration Conference, Boulder, Colorado, June 2008

I have received many invitations to speak at diverse conferences but this particular one was special. The attendees comprised cutting-edge scientists, and politicians were not usually invited. My invitation was arranged by Dr. Courtney Brown, Director of the Farsight Institute, a world renowned center for "Remote Viewing." I will return to this fascinating subject later in this book.

My presentation to the scientists was quite routine and included mention of some of the technology Colonel Philip Corso claimed to have shipped to U.S. industrial giants without disclosing its origin. The list included, among other things, image intensifiers, which ultimately became night vision, fiber optics, supertenacity fibers, advanced lasers, molecular alignment metallic alloys, integrated circuits and microminiaturization of logic boards.[4]

I remember in the question period a school teacher said, "I thought all of those things were invented in the U.S. What will I tell my students?" My response, as I recall, was "Why don't you just tell them the truth?"

One special point concerning this event was that I realized my "debunker," Colonel John Hamilton who must have been assigned to discredit me, was there. For a while he followed me around wherever I went. At first, when I said UFOs were real, he would say, "There is no such thing." When the crowd started laughing at his brazen denial, he was forced to change his tune. He would say, "Well, as a matter of fact they do exist, but the United States government is not the least bit interested in them," a case of replacing one big lie with an even bigger one.

The episode that made this event memorable was Col. Hamilton's belligerent insistence that I give him the name of the general who told me that UFOs were real and that the Roswell crash actually happened. He said it was my duty to disclose the information. Hamilton made it clear that if he could identify the man he, the colonel, would beat him up as he had never been beaten up before. The official intimidation knew no bounds!

The 5ᵀᴴ Annual UFO Crash Conference

This event held in Las Vegas, Nevada, in November 2007 was sponsored by Ryan Wood and his father Dr. Robert Wood. I decided to sign up to make sure I was current before writing the first book in what has become a trilogy discussing the major problems facing our world, including the necessity of adjusting to the broader reality of life beyond Earth. I knew the conference would be a veritable gold mine of opportunity to meet and rub shoulders with many of the most knowledgeable people on the continent.

Before I left for Nevada Ryan Wood sent me a copy of his book *Majic Eyes Only*, which told the stories of 78 UFO crashes over a period of a century, beginning in 1897. Wood admitted that the evidence in some cases was stronger than in others, but if even half of them were adequately authenticated, which would be on the conservative side, there had been a large number of crashes.

Equally important Ryan's book contained allegedly authentic documents concerning the Top Secret/Majic Eyes Only, or MJ-12 as they were popularly known. This was the small, select group established by President Truman and given almost dictatorial powers to monitor and exercise control over the whole spectrum of the extraterrestrial presence and the exploration of their technology. One section at the end of the book purported to show the extraordinary lengths that were to be taken to keep the public in the dark including misinformation, disinformation and ridicule.[5]

The conference not only met my expectations, but exceeded them. I was able to renew acquaintances with well-known ufologists and to meet new ones with a wide spectrum of expertise. One rare treat was to meet and have lunch with Linda Moulton Howe, author of *Glimpses of Other Realities*, Emmy Award winning TV producer, and acknowledged to be one of the world's most thorough and successful investigators in the area.

Another bonus was a private briefing on Area 28 that Ryan arranged for his father and me. It was presented by retired intelligence officers who had worked there. What they could say was limited but it was fascinating to see a Google satellite picture of huge trucks driving across the desert and then disappearing into an opening in the sand. We were not told what was done there but we surmised it might be weapons development. Since that day I have never heard Area 28 mentioned by speakers rattling off other Areas such as 51, S4, and so on.

The major coup as far as my breadth of understanding necessary for my book, however, was the opportunity to interview at great length, two abductees, or "experiencers" as some people prefer to call them, named Travis Walton and Jim Sparks. Travis, who had been the subject of a movie, Paramount's *Fire in the Sky*, lived in Arizona not too far from Las Vegas, so I persuaded him to come to the conference and let me interview him until I was absolutely satisfied that his story was the truth. You can read all about it in his book *Fire in the Sky*, and skip the movie with the same name that was negative propaganda.

Jim Sparks had the distinction of being one of the best-informed "experiencers" anywhere. He had been abducted dozens of times, eventually becoming comfortable in the ETs presence, and had the distinction of having been conscious throughout most of his encounters, whereas the majority of abductees only recall significant details under some form of hypnosis.

Jim, who also passed my litmus test of truthfulness with flying colors, says the ETs have a message for us that should make headlines in every newspaper and magazine in every language in the world. "We are hell bent on the destruction of our planet as a hospitable place to live or visit." Jim's book is *The Keepers: An Alien Message for the Human Race.*[6]

Fast Forward to 2013

My book *Light at the End of the Tunnel: A Survival Plan for the Human Species* was completed and published. It generated new interest in what I had to say and led to many invitations to speak.

One invitation that I couldn't resist was from my dear friend and mentor Paola Harris to give the keynote address at her spring UFO Symposium in Florida. The only problem was that she wanted my talk to be exclusively related to UFOs, ETs and related matters, which was not my forte. I am not a ufologist and never will be. I am a politician, economic maverick, and a social engineer of sorts.

Desperate for some kind of inspiration I swung my chair around to look at my library. There, staring me in the face, was a book entitled *The Secret History of Extraterrestrials* by Len Kasten. I don't know how it got there, because I didn't buy it, and Len claims that he didn't send it to me, but there it was. I leafed through it quickly and found references to Project Serpo, a top-secret exchange between the U.S. and the Ebens from planet Serpo, 38 light years from Earth. That was new information and perfect for the occasion. Paola was delighted and claimed that it was one of my best presentations.

The full story can be found in Kasten's later book *Secret Journey to Planet Serpo: A True Story of Interplanetary Travel.*

Citizen Hearing on Disclosure

A few days later, I was on my way to Washington to be one of 40 witnesses at Steve Bassett's week-long hearing on the necessity to reveal the truth about UFOs. He had rounded up six former congressmen and women and one former U.S. senator, all of whom were sceptics and completely in the dark about UFOs and ETs. They acted as a mock Congressional Committee, and administered oaths to each of us as we spoke.

The all-day hearings lasted five days and one by one the former legislators were convinced, with just one former congressman holding out until the last day. One of the former congresswomen said it was the Brentwater Forest case that finally convinced her, because it was so well documented.

I was the last speaker on Friday afternoon. Most of the others had spoken twice so I was given 20 minutes as opposed to the 10 that others had been given. I had prepared a brief paper, but by Thursday I realized it wasn't worth reading. It was just more of the same. So I just made a few notes, and marked a few key paragraphs in my book that I had with me.

I began by giving the chair, who was the holdout, a short list of origins for several species, because we could no longer refer to them as "they" when the species were all different and had different agendas. In addition to Zeta Reticuli, I mentioned the Pleiades, Orion, Andromeda and Altair star systems, where different species come from, which seemed to satisfy him.

Then I shifted gear totally and started explaining who was actually running the U.S. – the Cabal – and what their agenda was. They were the ones responsible for the secrecy that had to end. I explained the composition of the Cabal and its plan for an unelected, unaccountable World government. It was not a good presentation, halting and disjointed, so I was happy to have it finished.

A few days later someone called to say that my presentation was getting the most "hits" on the internet. Strangely, it was taken down after a day or two without explanation. Meanwhile, several copies were made, and the total number of hits kept climbing to more than five million, which proves the widespread interest in the subject matter of the Cabal discussed in the next chapter.

CHAPTER EIGHTEEN

THE CABAL

The Cabal is a very large and amorphous body that cannot be defined with precision. It has no charter or articles of association. There is no written document that would prove its existence. Yet I, and numerous other writers and commentators, have attached the Cabal label to this group because we believe it is real, based on its influence over U.S. and world governance over a period of more than half a century. In my case, I have concluded that it represents one of the greatest, if not the greatest, assembly of collective power in the history of the world.

To begin, I will list some of the components of the group and later explain the roles that each has played or is playing in the overall scheme of things.

The first organization, and one invariably mentioned by conspiracy theorists, is the Bavarian Illuminati. For those of you who, like me, have never heard of the organization, Wikipedia's brief summary provides this description.

"The Illuminati is a name given to several groups both real and fictitious. Historically, the name usually refers to the Bavarian Illuminati, an Enlightenment-era secret society founded on May 1, 1776. The society's goals were to oppose superstition, obscurantism, religious influence over public life, and abuses of state power."

That sounds noble enough, but secret societies sometimes change their objectives, as I will point out in reference to the Bilderbergers. I suspect the Bavarian Illuminati exercises some considerable influence, perhaps through individuals in the banking fraternity and control of some media outlets.

Next on my list are what I have dubbed the three sisters: the Council on Foreign Relations, the Bilderbergers, and the Trilateral Commission. I have commented on each of them in my two earlier books, so I will limit the descriptions here to very brief summaries.

The Council on Foreign Relations (CFR or Council) is the oldest of the three organizations. Although it was active in the 1920s, it only came into a position of great influence with the outbreak of World War II. As early as October 1940, years before Germany surrendered to the Allied armies, the Council's Economic and Financial Group drafted a memorandum outlining a comprehensive policy, "to set forth the political, military, territorial and economic requirements of the United States and its potential leadership of the non-German world area including the United Kingdom itself as well as the Western hemisphere and Far East."[1]

The Bilderbergers name comes from the group's first meeting place, the Hotel de Bilderberg of Oosterbeck, Holland, in May 1954. The brainchild of Dr. Joseph Retinger, a top aide to General Wladyslaw Sikorski, head of the Polish government in exile in London, the meeting was chaired by Prince Bernhard of Holland. He and Paul Rykens of Unilever, drew up the original list of participants: two from each country, with representations from business, banking, politics, and academia.

The list included a fair balance of conservative and liberal views that were not too far left as perceived by the Prince and the steering committee chaired by him. The group was pragmatic enough to ensure that their views would carry weight regardless of who formed the government of the day. The group started out with ideas for a federal union of neighboring European countries in which states would "relinquish part of their sovereignty."[2] Over the years, however, it developed into a highly secret society dedicated to a New World Order including an unelected, unaccountable totalitarian government.

The Trilateral Commission (TC) is the youngest of the three major groups pushing globalization and a New World Order. Founded in July 1973, its roots can be traced to Zbigniew Brzezinski, a professor at Columbia University at that time. He organized the Tripartite Studies at the Brookings Institute in recognition of Japan's increasing power and influence on the world stage. These studies helped convince David Rockefeller that trilateralism could be a useful instrument in building a community of interest among North America, Western Europe, and Japan. Therefore, he presented the proposal to the Bilderberg annual meeting in 1972 where it received an enthusiastic response, the endorsement Rockefeller needed to follow up and make the dream a reality.

Although the TC is the most open, it is elitist and anti-democratic. A1975 report entitled "The Crisis of Democracy: Report on the Governability of Democracies to the Trilateral Commission," states: "The vulnerability of democratic government in the United States comes not primarily from external threats, though such threats are real, not from internal subversion from the left or right, although both possibilities could exist, but rather from internal dynamics of democracy itself in a highly educated, mobilized and participant society."[3] Astonishing! The principal danger to democratic government is democracy. That is a concept that you have to dig deep to come up with.

THE PYRAMID OF POWER

The apex of the Cabal is the banking cartel. Its member banks have persuaded governments to let them create money out of thin air first, by simply making an entry in a book and then, after computers became widely used, through a simple computer entry. The Bank of England was chartered in 1694 to provide King William with the cash he needed to pursue his war with France. The King rewarded the bankers by allowing them to lend the same money twice, once to him and once to their friends, and collect interest from both at the same time. Now, a little more than 300 years later, these same bankers have persuaded the politicians to allow them to lend the same money to 20 different borrowers and collect interest from each. (Actually, the banks don't lend money, because they have no money to lend. They just lend their credit.) The bottom line is that they have a monopoly on the creation of "money" and the people who are the real owners of that right have been left out in the cold.

This subject is the most urgent facing humankind because bank-created money is debt that has to be repaid with interest, and the whole world is drowning in debt. I will return to this subject in a later chapter. Meanwhile, the following fable illustrates the problem clearly.

The Camel's Nose in the Tent

One cold night, as an Arab sat in his tent, a camel gently thrust his nose under the flap and looked in. "Master," he said, "let me put my nose in your tent. It's cold and stormy out here." "By all means," said the Arab, "and welcome," as he turned over and went to sleep.

A little later, the Arab awoke to find that the camel had not only put his nose in the tent but his head and neck also. The camel, who had been turning his head from side to side, said, "I will take but little more room if I place my forelegs within the tent. It is difficult standing out here." "Yes, you may put your forelegs within," said the Arab, moving a little to make room, for the tent was small.

Finally, the camel said, "May I not stand wholly inside? I keep the tent open by standing as I do." "Yes, yes," said the Arab. "Come wholly inside. Perhaps it will be better for both of us." So the camel crowded in. The Arab, with difficulty in the crowded quarters, again went to sleep. When he woke up the next time, he was outside in the cold and the camel had the tent to himself.[4]

The Oil Cartel

I rate the oil cartel as runner-up to the banks in power and influence. It doesn't have the absolute power that the money-manufacturing industry enjoys, but its influence in creating doubt about the reality of global warming may have even greater negative effects on the human species if it supports and encourages our addiction to an oil economy. The science is irrefutable; all one has to do is check the trends in ocean water temperatures, air temperatures, and the alarming rate of shrinking glaciers and polar ice cover. But despite the evidence, the reaction is much talk and little action.

This in spite of the fact that a solution exists and is well known by the rich elite. Decades ago, Dr. Michael Wolfe, a member of the MJ12 special studies group and appointed to its leading agency, the Alphacom Team, said, "Satellite government scientists have successfully created zero-point energy and cold fusion. There needs to be a smooth transition into these new sciences. Otherwise the world economy could be wrecked."[5]

That opinion was expressed more than two decades ago. Today I would say that a super-fast transition to zero-point energy is the only hope of saving the planet as a hospitable human habitat and is by far the best way to produce a permanent robust economy for people who are unemployed or underemployed. For your information, zero-point energy is the energy that exists everywhere in the cosmos, and it is free and inexhaustible once the capital cost of harnessing it has been provided.

This subject is likely to be new to the majority of readers, so I will return to it again later in the context of global warming.

THE TRANSNATIONAL CORPORATIONS

Number three on the totem pole of power and influence are the transnational corporations. I give credit to Dr. David Korten and his prophetic book, *When Corporations Rule the World*, for first informing me of the trend that the Cabal established to accelerate the concentration of wealth under their control. There have been studies showing the alarming nature of "The Club," which is one way of describing the phenomenon. Through the practice of interlocking directorships and their incestuous banking connections, the combined Chief Executive Officers (CEOs) have acquired the characteristics of a steam roller in pressuring governments and regulatory agencies to allow them to circumvent anti-competition laws. Worse, nearly all "trade" agreements give them greater power and privilege in foreign countries than that which is enjoyed by the citizens of those countries.

INTELLIGENCE AGENCIES AND ARMED FORCES

In a sense, the intelligence agencies and armed forces are in categories of their own, but they are all working components of the Cabal, which includes certain segments of many intelligence agencies. How many are deeply involved is difficult to gauge, but some of the more obvious ones include the CIA, the FBI, the National Security Agency, and, most certainly, the British MI6 and the Israeli Mossad. This is deeply worrisome because none of these agencies are without skeletons in their closets related to questionable activities.

Of the armed forces, the navy and air force are more actively involved than the army. The navy was involved in the retrieval of a crashed ET craft in 1941 in the Pacific Ocean west of San Diego; dead Zeta Reticulans, also known as the "Greys," were found inside. The U.S. navy has held a leadership position in UFO matters ever since.[6]

The air force, of course, has been fully involved since the Roswell crash in July 1947. And a powerful new force has recently been added with Space Command, a power to be reckoned with.

These are the elements of the Cabal that are also known as the "shadow government" or "the alternate government." This is the power that the late U.S. Senator Inouye referred to, "with its own Air Force, its own Navy, its own fundraising mechanism, and the ability to pursue its own ideas of the national interest, and free from all checks and balances, and free from the law itself."[7]

The Cabal is also the same group that President Bill Clinton was referring to when senior White House press correspondent Sarah McClendon asked him why he didn't reveal more about the ET phenomenon. His reply: "Sarah, there is a government within the government, and I don't control it."[8]

Shivers ran up and down my spine when I heard that. Imagine, the president of the most powerful country on Earth, and Commander-in-Chief of its armed forces, with his finger on the atomic button, is unaware of the projects and plans of the troops he theoretically commands. Regrettably, President Clinton's admission is fact, not fantasy. The Cabal, directed by the "Three Sisters" has been the ultimate power in the U.S. for decades, without checks and balances, and operating outside the law.

A Post-World War II Opportunity

As the Second World War drew to an end, both the British and the Americans were concerned about the fate of the Nazi scientists. They recognized that German technology was more advanced than their own in some areas and became concerned that the scientists responsible for the advances might fall into the wrong hands. Therefore, the Americans decided on an all-out effort to recruit the German specialists before they disappeared. The plan became known as "Operation Paperclip" and the first three paragraphs from Wikipedia are quoted below.

The Nazi Connection

"Operation Paperclip was the Office of Strategic Services (OSS) program used to recruit scientists of Nazi Germany for employment by the United States in the aftermath of World War II (1939-45). It was conducted by the Joint Intelligence Objectives Agency (JIOA), and in the context of the burgeoning Cold War (1945-91). One purpose of Operation Paperclip was to deny German scientific expertise and knowledge to the U.S.S.R.,[9] the U.K.,[10] and the newly-divided East and West Germanies themselves.

"Although the JIOA's recruitment of German scientists began after the Allied victory in Europe on May 8, 1945, U.S. President Harry Truman did not formally order the execution of Operation Paperclip until August of that year. Truman's order expressly excluded anyone found 'to have been a member of the Nazi Party, and more than a nominal participant in its activities, or an active supporter of Nazi militarism.' However, those restrictions would have rendered ineligible most of the leading scientists the JIOA had identified for recruitment, among them rocket scientists Werner von Braun, Kurt H. Debus and Arthur Rudolph, and the physician Hubertus Strughold, each earlier classified as a 'menace to the security of Allied Forces.'"

"To circumvent President Truman's anti-Nazi order and the Allied Potsdam and Yalta agreements, the JIOA worked independently to create false employment and political biographies for the scientists. The JIOA also expunged from the public record the scientists' Nazi Party memberships and regime affiliations. Once 'bleached' of their Nazism, the scientists were granted security clearances by the U.S. government to work in the United States. Paperclip, the project's operational name, derived from the paperclips used to attach the scientist's new political personae to their 'U.S. Government Scientist' JIOA personnel files."

These Nazi scientists were assigned key roles in the development of missiles, weapons and anti-gravity flying machines (flying saucers), as well as in intelligence organizations. Their power and influence could be identified almost at once. They moved the most sensitive and secret developments to Nevada and Arizona, far away from the prying eyes of U.S. officials and politicians. They labelled them "Special Projects" and limited the knowledge of their existence and their state of development to those individuals who absolutely had to know, and there were no exceptions, including presidents of the United States.

Consequently, when President Eisenhower asked what the scientists were doing in what was called Area 51, they refused to tell him. Eisenhower was furious! In total exasperation he threatened to send in the army from Colorado if they didn't cooperate. It was soon agreed that he could send in some of his personal friends from the CIA (the numbers reported are as low as two, and as high as four, which I suspect was the actual number) and they would be allowed to look around the site (the existence of which wasn't officially recognized until only a year or so ago). Eisenhower's envoys reported that the most urgent project was back-engineering the UFO that had been recovered from the Roswell crash site. To the best of my knowledge, no U.S. president has been allowed to visit and inspect the site.

This story was verified by Richard Nolan, an experienced and highly respected ufologist, who was allowed to interview one of the four participants who decided, on his death bed, that the story should be put on the record. The video was shown at the week-long Citizens Hearing on Disclosure at the Washington Press Club in June 2013.

Readers who have not had the advantage of studying this clandestine top-secret world beyond science fiction may be wondering why you are not in the loop, why you haven't been informed by the press? The short answer is that the Cabal, more specifically the Bilderbergers, control the English-language press worldwide.

The following quote from Daniel Estulin's absolutely amazing book, *The True Story of the Bilderberg Group*, lets you in on the secret. The words are those of the late David Rockefeller, the only top member of the Cabal I have named because in his memoirs he proudly admits what the "End Game" actually is.

"We are grateful to the *Washington Post*, the *New York Times*, *Time* magazine and other great publications, whose directors have attended our meetings and respected their promises of discretion for almost forty years. It would have been impossible for us to develop our plan for the world if we had been subjected to the lights of publicity during those years. But, the world is more sophisticated and prepared to march towards a world government. The supranational sovereignty of an intellectual elite and world bankers is surely preferable to the national auto-determination practiced in past centuries."[11]

For those of you who would like greater precision, Daniel Estulin's most recent book, *TransEvolution: The Coming Age of Human Deconstruction*, lists the interlocking juggernaut of global media control in detail on pages 107 to 113. His conclusion: every important English-language news outlet, either print or electronic, is either owned or controlled by a Bilderberger.

CHAPTER NINETEEN

A LITTLE POST-WORLD WAR II HISTORY

A very wise friend who is aware of most of the information in this chapter suggested that I should begin by saying how difficult it has been for me and many others to believe that the information that has come into my possession is true. We long for a better life and a better world, so therefore we don't want to see or accept evil or think that we could be controlled by evil people. But after a decade or more of searching for the facts, I have come to the painful conclusion that all is not well with our world, and I feel duty bound to share this unhappy truth because the future health and welfare of every one of us, and of our children's children, will inevitably by impacted by this reality.

Soon after I went public about the extraterrestrial phenomena in 2005 there were several very interesting people who signalled they would like to meet me. One of the most famous was Edgar Mitchell, an Apollo 14 astronaut. A mutual friend Mike Bird told me that Edgar was coming to Toronto to make a speech and would like to get together if we could work out our two schedules. My wife Sandra suggested dinner the evening before his speech on July 8, 2006, and that worked perfectly for us both.

I won't repeat the whole story told in *Light at the End of the Tunnel* here, but want to include the following as it is relevant to this chapter. Ed denied having seen UFOs on his trip to the moon, an answer that I had to respect. But at one point when he mentioned the alleged crash at Roswell I interjected: "Why do you use the word 'alleged?'" A tell-tale smile a mile wide came across his face. Seconds later he asked me how many species (of visitors) I thought there were. I replied, "Somewhere between two and 12." "That's what I think, too," Ed said in response.

An important area of agreement came when we discussed possible reasons for the extended cover-up. The two most obvious were religion and economics, and the power base associated with each. In Ed's words:

"You can make a good argument for that, it's hard to decide which; but it's certainly entrenched power in any of these areas. It's putting self-interest ahead of the common interest and that is exactly the mission we have (to overturn). I try to work at it every damn day." We agreed on that, and Edgar kept fighting the good fight until he died on February 4, 2016.

Edgar and I were both far too conservative in our estimate of the number of species. Sergeant Clifford Stone, who worked in a unit that retrieved crashed UFOs, said the U.S. army manual he had been given in association with his work listed 54 species and how each should be handled.[1] If you think of the billions of star systems that exist in our universe it is likely that there are thousands and perhaps millions of species.

A few of these that are mentioned most often are the Short Greys, the Tall Grays, Nordic Blonds, Semitics and Reptilians, each with their own characteristics.[2]

They come from Zeta Reticuli, the Pleiades, Orion, Andromeda and Altair star systems.[3]

Wikipedia has this to say about the Nordics. "They are a human-like species who first began appearing to contactees in the 1950s, claiming to be from the planet Venus and later the Pleiades star cluster. Whether either is the origin planet or system of the Nordics is debatable, and it is possible that they wish to keep their true home a secret for security reasons. Nordic aliens are also known as Tall Whites and Space Brothers."

As I mentioned at the beginning of my journey into these matters, my prime source had told me that there had been face-to-face meetings between U.S. officials and extraterrestrial visitors. But he didn't mention any particular species and it is quite possible that he didn't know.

According to Len Kasten, by 1952 the one survivor of the Roswell crash, Extraterrestrial Biological Entity #1 (EBE#1) was in contact with his home planet Serpo, and communications in English between Serpo and scientists at Los Alamos National Laboratory in New Mexico were beginning. But the ruling clique, the MJ12 group, thought it better to keep it all under wraps.[4]

In July 1952 a number of UFOs flew over Washington, D.C, and U.S. jets were sent in pursuit, but to no avail. The incident, however, which was intermittent for several days, created the kind of paranoia that supported the Pentagon's overwhelming pressure for secrecy.

A year and a half later, President Eisenhower did meet with extraterrestrials at Edwards Air Force Base in California, then called Muroc Air Base.[5] The full story can be read in Len Kasten's *The Secret History of Extraterrestrials*. Apparently the meeting was with one of the benign species representing the Galactic Federation of Light, because Carol Lorenzen and her husband Jim, founders of Aerial Phenomena Research Organization (APRO) were convinced that the president would ignore the conflict between the various authorities and let the public in on the secret.

However, "the announcement never came because we made no agreement with the benevolent aliens. We turned down their offer of incredible new technology. All we had to do in return was to 'beat our swords into plowshares,' that is, give up our nuclear weapons. Apparently the top generals at the Pentagon believed this to be a ruse that would leave us defenseless in very dangerous times. So we had to say 'no thanks'"[6]

But, according to Len Kasten, who is one of the best and most thorough of ufologists, "Eisenhower's treaty with the Greys, signed at Holloman Air Force Base in 1954, gave the aliens permission to take humans up in their spaceships, ostensibly for genetic study, in return for alien technology. These abductions led to the creation of a hybrid race under Reptilian mind control."[7]

The U.S.S.R. would have learned that the U.S. had rejected the Galactic Federation offer of assistance in exchange for nuclear disarmament. The result has been an unprecedented arms race between the two major powers that includes both atomic weapons and the technology to master interplanetary travel. The U.S. and Russia both have sufficient atomic weapons to destroy all life on Earth. All it would take is one system malfunction, or a group of generals who actually believe that nuclear war is feasible, albeit with very heavy casualties, to launch this ultimate insanity.

A SECOND OPPORTUNITY LOST

In 1957, a Venusian commander named Valiant Thor landed in Virginia and was transported to the Pentagon, where he lived for more than three years. A Pentagon insider Nancy Warren, contacted Dr. Frank Stranges, Ph.D. at Val Thor's request.[8]

Thor, the benevolent alien with an IQ of 1,200, offered benefits, including the elimination of nearly all human diseases which, allegedly, was opposed by Vice President Richard Nixon because he had many close friends in the pharmaceutical business. And once again the chiefs turned down an offer of paradise on Earth at the cost of giving up their nuclear weapons, which should have been the highest priority if the interests of ordinary people mattered.

It was left to Thor's new friend Frank Stranges to write his story in a best-selling book, *Stranger at the Pentagon*, which was first published in 1967.[9]

Dr. Stranges seemed a rather curious figure in UFO circles. He was a dedicated UFO hunter and a freelance private investigator who apparently never had any trouble accepting the veracity of extraterrestrial activity. At the same time, he was an evangelical Christian preacher and founder of a group called the International Evangelism Crusaders.

PHIL SCHNEIDER, A PATRIOTIC AMERICAN

Of all the whistleblowers I have listened to there are none that influenced me more deeply than Phil Schneider. Therefore, I am taking the liberty of repeating a couple of pages from his lecture "Underground Bases and the New World Order." Post Falls, Idaho, May 10, 1995.[10]

"I love the country I am living in, more than I love my life, but I would not be standing before you now, risking my life, if I did not believe that there is something desperately wrong. The first part of this talk is going to concern deep underground military bases and the Black Budget. The Black Budget is a secretive budget that garners 25% of the gross national product of the United States. The Black Budget currently consumes $1.25 trillion per [2] years. At least this amount is used in black programs, like those concerned with deep underground military bases. Presently, there are 129 deep underground military bases in the United States.

"I have been building these 129 bases day and night, unceasingly, since the early 1940s. Some of them were built even earlier than that. These bases are basically large cities underground connected by high-speed magneto-leviton trains that have speeds up to Mach 2. Several books have been written about this activity. Al Bielek has my only copy of one of them. Richard Sauder, a Ph.D. architect, has risked his life by talking about this. He worked with a number of government agencies on deep underground military bases. In around where you live, in Idaho, there are 11 of them.

"The average depth of these bases is over a mile, and they again are basically whole cities underground. They all are between 2.66 and 4.25 cubic miles in size. They have laser drilling machines that can drill a tunnel 7 miles long in one day. The Black Projects sidestep the authority of Congress, which as we know is illegal. Right now, the New World Order is depending on these bases. If I had known at the time I was working on them that the NWO was involved, I would not have done it.

"I was lied to rather extensively."[11]

Schneider's Worries about Government Factions, Railroad Cars and Shackle Contracts

Phil goes on to speak about government activities. "Now, I am very worried bout the activities of the federal government. They have lied to the public, stonewalled senators, and have refused to tell the truth in regard to alien matters. I can go on and on. I can tell you that I am rather disgruntled. Recently, I knew someone who lived near where I live in Portland, Oregon. He worked at Gunderson Steel Fabrication, where they make railroad cars. Now, I knew this fellow for the better part of 30 years, and he was kind of a quiet type. He came to see me one day, excited, and he told me 'they're building prisoner cars.' He was nervous. 'Gunderson,' he said, 'had a contract with the federal government to build 10,720 full length railroad cars, each with 143 pairs of shackles.'"[12]

What are these cars and shackles going to be used for? If I were an American I would certainly want to know.

Star Wars and Apparent Alien Threat

"Still, 68% of the military budget is directly or indirectly affected by the Black Budget. Star Wars relies heavily upon stealth weaponry. By the way, none of the stealth program would have been available if we had not taken apart crashed alien disks. None of it.

"Some of you might ask what the 'space shuttle' is 'shuttling;' large ingots of special metals that are milled in space and cannot be produced on the surface of the Earth. They need the near vacuum of outer space to produce them.

"We are not even being told anything close to the truth. I believe our government officials have sold us down the drain — lock, stock and barrel. Up until several weeks ago, I was employed by the U.S. government with a Ryolite-38 clearance factor — one of the highest in the world. I believe the Star Wars program is there solely to act as a buffer to prevent alien attack — it has nothing to do with the 'Cold War,' which was only a ploy to garner money from all the people — for what?"[13]

Some Statistics on the Black Helicopter Presence

"The black helicopters. There are over 64,000 black helicopters in the United States. For every hour that goes by, there is one being built. Is this the proper use of our money? What does the federal government need 64,000 tactical helicopters for, if they are not trying to enslave us? I doubt if the entire military needs 64,000 worldwide with Lidar and computer-enhanced imaging radar. They can see you walking from room to room when they fly over your house. They see objects in the house from the air with a variation of 1 inch to 30,000 miles. That's how accurate that is. Now, I worked in the federal government for a long time, and I know exactly how they handle their business."[14]

Government Earthquake Device

"The federal government has now invented an earthquake device. I am a geologist, and I know what I am talking about. With the Kobe earthquake in Japan, there was no pulse wave as in a normal earthquake. None. In 1989, there was an earthquake in San Francisco. There was no pulse wave with that one either. It is a Tesla device that is being used for evil purposes. The Black Budget programs have subverted science as we know it."[15]

Phil Schneider was a true patriot who became deeply concerned about what was really going on in the U.S. shadow government. He handed in his extreme high-security pass and started to speak the truth publicly. What he revealed is more than enough to demand immediate full disclosure. Seven months after giving one of the lectures quoted here he was found strangled. The "official" cause of death was "suicide." The NWO deals harshly with whistleblowers.

A RACE FOR CONTROL OF SPACE

Although the U.S. and the U.S.S.R. reached a rough equilibrium in atomic weapons – two stockpiles so great that a nuclear war would make the Earth uninhabitable – the contest has moved to another dimension, space. Both powers, with the help of their extraterrestrial accomplices, have achieved a space capability. This was confirmed by Ben Rich, former CEO of Lockheed's Skunk Works, where many Black Ops have been developed, when he told an alumni reunion at the University of California, Los Angeles in 1993, "we now have the technology to take ET home."

This technology was subsequently used to establish bases on the Moon and Mars. I don't have an exact date, but the base on Mars had been operating for some time before Laura Magdalene Eisenhower, great-granddaughter of former President Dwight David Eisenhower made her public statement exposing her attempted recruitment from April 2006 through January 2007 by a secret Mars colony project.

Ms. Eisenhower's account of being targeted by time travel surveillance and the attempted manipulation by trained intelligence agents attached to a Mars colony project were revealed in an ExopoliticsRadio.org interview, and in an extensive written statement on her website.

Ki' Lia, a Stanford-educated artist, futurist and colleague of Ms. Eisenhower, has provided a corroborating first-hand witness account of the attempted recruitment of both Ms. Eisenhower and herself into a secret human survival colony on Mars, available at Ki'Lia's website.[16]

The alleged purpose of the secret Mars colony was to provide a survival civilization for the human race on Earth in the event of a planned catastrophe (such as HAARP or bio-weapon induced) or natural cataclysm (such as solar flares) that might depopulate the Earth.

In revealing these secret Mars colony plans, Ms. Eisenhower and Ki'Lia have emerged to join a growing cadre of independent whistle blowers disclosing secret technologies and extraterrestrial-related covert operations of U.S. military-intelligence agencies and corporate entities.

It is alleged that the Russians participated in the Mars Colony Project, at least for a while, but the cooperation may have ended as the U.S. appeared to be getting the upper hand through new developments in the Star Wars Initiative. The initiative was originally passed off as a defense against rogue missiles but that was only a cover story. Its purpose was always much broader and included a wide range of hypothetical threats from both Earth and sky.

THE HAARP – CHEMTRAILS COMBO

If you want to see someone's eyes glaze over just ask them what they know about chemtrails. The odds are about 20 to one that they will never have heard about them. I was one of those people until three or four years ago when I was having my ears tested for new more sophisticated hearing aids. My audiologist was the one that clued me into the picture, giving me half a dozen of her photographs of chemtrails above our City of Toronto, including one right over the Hospital for Sick Children.

She asked me to get a copy of Elana Freeland's book *Chemtrails, HAARP, and the Full Spectrum Dominance of Planet Earth*,[17] which I read with a combination of acute interest and horror. When I finished, my fury knew no bounds.

My previous book, *The Money Mafia*, had been published before I was aware of chemtrails, so the most I could do was tack the subject onto the end of a YouTube presentation, where I described HAARP and chemtrails as Satan's illegitimate twins of death. I was a little bit familiar with HAARP (High Frequency Active Auroral Research Program) but I was clueless about the chemtrails that affect every one of us personally. When I saw the list of toxic substances being dropped on us seven days a week, and the long list of serious health hazards they produce, I recognized several of the symptoms. These poisonous substances are bad enough for an old man like me, but when I think of what they are doing to my grandchildren and great-grandchildren I can barely control my anger! The following is some very important information for you to consider.

WHAT CHEMTRAILS ARE DOING TO YOUR BRAIN — NEUROSURGEON DR. RUSSELL BLAYLOCK REVEALS SHOCKING FACTS[18]

"The Internet is littered with stories of 'chemtrails' and geo-engineering to combat "global warming" and until recently I took these stories with a grain of salt. One of the main reasons for my skepticism was that I rarely saw what they were describing in the skies. But over the past several years I have noticed a great number of these trails and I have to admit they are not like the contrails I grew up seeing in the skies. They are extensive, quite broad, are laid in a definite pattern and slowly evolve into artificial clouds. Of particular concern is that there are now so many dozens every day that are littering the skies.

"My major concern is that there is evidence that they are spraying tons of nanosized aluminum compounds. It has been demonstrated in the scientific and medical literature that nanosized particles are infinitely more reactive and induce intense inflammation in a number of tissues. Of special concern is the effect of these nanoparticles on the brain and spinal cord, as a growing list of neurodegenerative diseases, including Alzheimer's dementia, Parkinson's disease and Lou Gehrig's disease (ALS) are strongly related to exposure to environmental aluminum.

"Nanoparticles of aluminum are not only infinitely more inflammatory, they also easily penetrate the brain by a number of routes, including the blood and olfactory nerves (the small nerves in the nose). Studies have shown that these particles pass along the olfactory neural tracts, which connect directly to the area of the brain that is not only most effected by Alzheimer's disease, but also the earliest affected in the course of the disease. It also has the highest level of brain aluminum in Alzheimer's cases.

"The intranasal route of exposure makes spraying of massive amounts of nanoaluminum into the skies especially hazardous, as it will be inhaled by people of all ages, including babies and small children for many hours. We know that older people have the greatest reaction to this airborne aluminum. Because of the nanosizing of the aluminum particles being used, home filtering system will not remove the aluminum, thus prolonging exposure, even indoors.

"In addition to inhaling nanoaluminum, such spraying will saturate the ground, water and vegetation with high levels of aluminum. Normally, aluminum is poorly absorbed from the GI tract, but nanoaluminum is absorbed in much higher amounts. This absorbed aluminum has been shown to be distributed to a number of organs and tissues including the brain and spinal cord. Inhaling this environmentally suspended nanoaluminum will also produce tremendous inflammatory reaction within the lungs, which will pose a significant hazard to children and adults with asthma and pulmonary diseases.

"I pray that the pilots who are spraying this dangerous substance fully understand that they are destroying the life and health of their families as well. This is also true of our political officials. Once the soil, plants and water sources are heavily contaminated there will be no way to reverse the damage that has been done.

"Steps need to be taken now to prevent an impending health disaster of enormous proportions if this project is not stopped immediately. Otherwise we will see an explosive increase in neurodegenerative diseases occurring in adults and the elderly in unprecedented rates as well as neurodevelopmental disorders in our children. We are already seeing a dramatic increase in these neurological disorders and it is occurring in younger people than ever before."[19]

The use of chemtrails to decrease the effects of global warming has been denied, but it is clearly happening as outlined by Dr. Blaylock above. And this seems even clearer with the increasing rates of Alzheimer's, ALS, MS and other debilitating diseases, which can be linked to the increase in aluminum in our environment. Coupled with the evidence of ETs that has been covered up and the bases that exist on our Moon and Mars, alongside the Star Wars Initiative, there is an overwhelming amount of evidence that we are being controlled by forces that can only be described as evil.

CHAPTER TWENTY

A Strategy Of Lies And Deceit

After considerable research, much of which can be found in my book *The Money Mafia*, I am convinced that the Nazis never accepted defeat at the end of World War II in 1945. They simply surrendered, went underground, and started planning for the next time. They would have learned from their mistakes and resolved not to repeat them. Even an amateur strategist would remember that attacking one small country after another raised the ire of those powers sitting on the sidelines and, ultimately, persuaded them to unite as allies against the Germans.

The Nazis had a major stroke of good luck when large numbers of them were brought to the U.S. in the early post-World War II years to help the American forces in the Cold War fight with the U.S.R.R. This was exactly the opportunity the Nazis needed to build the world's most powerful military force under a cloak of secrecy. At the same time they were able to recruit the rich elite under the guise of a New World Order (NWO). The latter dreamed up the idea of uniting the world economically and persuading nation states to give up much of their sovereignty. Greg Palast, author of *The Best Democracy Money Can Buy* and whistle-blower extraordinaire, tells us the idea of globalization originated with the rich elite, the captains of industry and finance. He even managed to get minutes of some of their meetings. In an interview with *Acres USA*, Palast had this to say:

"One of the most amazing things in one of these meetings is when they talk about how to sell globalization to the public. They can't figure out how to sell this thing to the public because they can't figure out what the benefits of globalization really are to the average person. They actually sat there and said: 'Why don't we pay some professors a bunch of money, and get them to come up with a study that globalization is good for people?'

"Then the officer for Reuters, the big news service that's in every big paper on the planet, said: 'You come up with the material and we'll help you get it out, we'll place the stories in the papers.' It really freaked me out to find this propaganda system to sell people on the means of their own economic destruction."[1]

And it freaked me out as well to discover that Reuters, with its reputation as a totally responsible and reliable news agency, would be willing to collaborate in disseminating ideas that are propaganda at best and subversive at worst. Then I found the name of the CEO of Reuters on the list of Bilderberg attendees, and it all made perfect sense.

From about 1970 until 2005 I kept extensive economic files that I clipped from various newspapers. Consequently, I read many of the articles written by these hired professors. They seemed to assume that globalization was good in principle, but did not prove that it would be good for the people. In fact, the majority noted that it would result in greater disparity of income between individuals within countries, and between poor and rich countries. There was not one single instance in which one of the "learned" professors suggested how this problem could be solved, and it never has been.

The word "globalization" became the "cool" word however, and soon it was impossible to have a conversation with anyone for more than a few minutes without the word being used in the positive sense of offering hope. It was a classic case of brainwashing from which the world has never recovered.

Thus, the "free trade" craze began. Except the agreements were never actually "free trade" agreements. They were investment agreements whereby national sovereignty was transferred to trans-national corporations beholden to the banking cartel. Foreign corporations were given greater rights than citizens of the host country. For example, when the Government of Quebec put a moratorium on fracking for oil, a U.S. company sued the Government of Canada for damages. No Canadian company would have had that same right. Each round of the so-called "free trade" agreements has become more comprehensive in an economic "conquest" that is almost total as a result of constant brainwashing by the controlled press.

The world without economic borders has negative benefits to the majority of people, while providing great benefits for the big and powerful. It is a vehicle for the cartelization of the world, leading to dramatically higher prices that the poor can simply not afford.

For example, when a handful of corporations established an oligopoly in food the prices approximately doubled. I intended to name the companies but Forbes has delisted them in conformity to some new European Union (EU) privacy law. What happened to the promises of greater transparency in government? The flip side of this concentration of power is that small countries have lost many of their biggest and best corporations and the professional support jobs that were necessary for the head offices. In Canada, for instance, global companies like International Nickel, Alcan Manufacturing, and MacMillan Bloedel forest products have been bought out and all of our steel manufacturers are foreign owned. In boxing terms, the lightweights are getting in the ring with the heavyweights and you don't need to guess who gets pummelled.

While the Cabal has been concentrating on economic integration and building invincible military power, it has totally neglected the two most urgent issues affecting ordinary citizens – global warming and a dysfunctional financial system. The first is the most important so let's take a look at it first, and leave money for the next chapter.

OUR HOUSE IS ON FIRE

On April 26, 2018 I received an e-mail titled 'We're doomed': Mayer Hillman on the climate reality no one else will dare mention.

"We're doomed," says Mayer Hillman with such a beaming smile that it takes a moment for the words to sink in. "The outcome is death, and it's the end of most life on the planet because we're so dependent on the burning of fossil fuels. There are no means of reversing the process which is melting the polar ice caps. And very few appear to be prepared to say so."[2]

Hillman, an 86-year old social scientist and senior fellow emeritus of the Policy Studies Institute, in fact does say so. His bleak forecast of the consequences of runaway climate change, he states without fanfare, is his "last will and testament." His last intervention in public life. "I'm not going to write anymore because there's nothing more that can be said."

There are people saying the same thing as Hillman and I am one of them! It was the lead chapter in my book *Light at the End of the Tunnel* when it was first published eight years ago. I repeated the warning as forcefully as I knew how when *The Money Mafia* was first published four years ago. There are many, many concerned Earthlings who are singing the same song. The problem is that no one in a position of great power is listening.[3]

THE WORLD'S 20 NEROS FIDDLE WHILE PLANET EARTH BURNS

One is sadly reminded of the story of the Roman Emperor Nero, who is alleged to have played his lyre while the city of Rome was burning. In the absence of evidence to the contrary one must assume that the leaders of the G20 group of countries are still fiddling with offshore drilling, additional fracking, taxing carbon dioxide, and building pipelines that will require 20 or 30 years to amortize in order to export more heavy oil from the tar sands.

Where have our leaders been for the last decade? They just didn't get it! It is absolutely futile to hold conferences to set emission reduction targets for 20 or 30 years from now. The fire is almost out of control now. In 20 or 30 years there may be little left but the ashes of one of the most beautiful planets in the universe. I agree with Mayer Hillman that there is no more that can be said. But I disagree totally with his fatalist notion that there is nothing more that can be done.

Eight years ago, I said we had 10 years to turn the situation around to the extent of arresting global warming, and preventing the worst case scenario of a total disaster. I think that I allowed a year or two for the inertia of getting started, so today I estimate that we have five years to win the major battle with victory clearly visible. I am not talking about a world cluttered with ugly windmills and acres of equally distasteful solar panels.

A WAR FOR THE SURVIVAL OF OUR LIVING BREATHING WORLD

I hope that by the time you finish reading this book you will conclude, as I have, that wars as we have known them for thousands of years are obsolete. Each succeeding era has seen the introduction of weapons more deadly than those used previously, and the number of casualties has increased proportionately. A World War III using weapons of mass destruction that are almost beyond belief could kill billions of innocent civilians. Enough is enough, and the worldwide armaments producers are redundant.

A war for the survival of the world simply requires a reversal of the tactics used by the Allies in World War II. Every automobile factory, every refrigerator, stove and appliance factory was converted to the production of armaments. Eventually the tide turned, and the seemingly unbeatable Nazis were forced to surrender.

Now we must do the exact opposite and mobilize the entire military-industrial complex worldwide to manufacture zero-point engines to replace the internal combustion engines in every car, truck, tractor, motorcycle, motorboat, ship, factory, and house in the world. Of course this is a tall order, but billions of people can be mobilized in thousands of factories, in dozens of countries and millions more as the installers and converters.

The necessary technology has existed for decades, certainly in the United States, and probably in Russia as well. Dr. Michael Wolf, who had worked in laboratories in Areas 51 and S4, Wright-Patterson Air Force Base (Foreign Technology Division), Indian Springs and Dulce, said, "Satellite government scientists have successfully created zero-point energy and cold fusion.[4] This was in the 1960s. I personally prefer zero-point energy even though I am not a physicist, and can't explain it adequately. I know that it is the energy that exists everywhere in our universe, and it is just a case of harnessing it in what is comparable to a perpetual motion machine.

There have been many successful models, but they have all been suppressed one way or another, often with violence, because they pose a genuine threat to the oil industry that probably holds numerous patents. No industry has the right to jeopardize the future habitability of the planet, so Congress will have to override the patents and make them available at little or no cost. This can be a down-payment on the trillions of damage that has already taken place as a result of the irrationality of artificially extending the oil-burning era.

The U.S. Shadow Government Policy

The clandestine government that has also been called the "alternative government," or the "military-industrial complex" has been implementing policies that are neither well known, nor well understood due to near absolute secrecy. Fortunately, one of the scientists who came to the U.S. in Operation Paperclip, Dr. Werner von Braun, the world-famous rocket scientist, mellowed and wanted the world to know what his Nazi colleagues were planning to do.

Early in 1974 when Von Braun was old and appeared to be near death, he asked Dr. Carol Rosin his trusted assistant, to speak for him. He said that because the U.S. didn't have an enemy that could challenge them, the military-industrial complex would have to create enemies to justify the huge military expenditures required to create the vast military machine that would be needed to implement their plan. According to Carol, von Braun said that the first enemy would be the communists, then it would be terrorists and, finally, it would be the extraterrestrials. That, of course, is the progression that we have seen in real life, and now we are moving from terrorists to extraterrestrials, which is supposed to be the final chapter.

Project for a New American Century

The initial draft of the Pentagon document "Defense Planning Guidance on Post-Cold War Strategy" (PNAC) was dated February 18, 1992. A leaked copy of the document prepared under the supervision of Paul Wolfowitz, then the Pentagon's Undersecretary for Policy, was disclosed by the *New York Times* in March 1992. The negative reaction from both the White House and foreign capitals was so strong that it had to be redrafted. The revised version, though in less offensive language, still envisaged an empire bigger and better than any other since the Roman Empire.

It may have been assumed that when the time came it would be relatively easy to persuade President Bush to abandon his stated policy of not getting America more deeply involved in international affairs, but persuading the American people would be more difficult. Ordinary Americans would question such a giant sea change in policy on the part of the Pentagon.

The authors of PNAC recognized this difficulty from the outset because their document contained the following sentence. "Further, the process of transformation, even if it brings revolutionary changes, is likely to be a long one, absent some catastrophic and catalyzing event – like a new Pearl Harbor.[5]

Well, it wasn't too long before they got their catastrophic event. Terrorists struck the World Trade Center in New York and the Pentagon in Washington, D.C. on September 11, 2001.

SEPTEMBER 11, 2001, THE GREATEST DECEPTION IN HISTORY?

As I sat in my office and watched the television images of flames emerging from one tower of the World Trade Center in New York City and later from a second tower, I was filled with horror. What a dastardly thing to do. Who were the perpetrators?

Great sympathy was near universal. The Muslim community, with the exception of a few hard-core terrorists, were in lockstep with everyone else. Many churches held memorial services including ours, Metropolitan United in Toronto. We mourned the loss of so many innocent people, and shared some of the pain that we knew their relatives were feeling.

The consequences were quick and far-reaching. Airport security was tightened to an extent that had never been experienced before. Everyone had to add half-an-hour to the time necessary to catch every flight. And some of the items banned from being carried with you on an aircraft were highly questionable. Fortunately, a little more common sense has been applied as the years passed.

In the U.S., a new department of Homeland Security was established and some very macabre rules applied, such as the right to confiscate phones within 100 miles of any border. The CIA suspended *habeas corpus* and the rule of law was abandoned whenever "in the interest of national security" could be invoked. Subtly, but irrevocably, America was being transformed into a police state.

Almost immediately after the 2001 attack, defense appropriations were doubled. The U.S. was already so powerful militarily that no country on Earth would dare attack it. It can only be assumed that the military seized the opportunity to grab twice as many tax dollars to accelerate their space capability, and the black operations associated with it.

The other immediate decision after the 9/11 attacks was to declare war on Iraq in accordance with the Plan for a New American Century. This was hard to defend because Iraq had absolutely no connection to the attack on the Twin Towers. Osama bin Laden, the leader of al-Qaeda who was rightly or wrongly, probably wrongly, credited with masterminding the attack, was in Afghanistan, while the men involved in the atrocity were from Saudi Arabia.

Consequently, it was very difficult to find an excuse to single out Iraq and, allegedly, possession of weapons of mass destruction was the only choice they could agree on, even if there was no evidence to substantiate it. But it did facilitate the Cabal's policy of continuous war in order to justify obscene military expenditures.

The 9/11 attacks also provided President George W. Bush with the excuse to declare that the U.S. had been attacked, without naming any country in particular. In my opinion that failed to meet the test required in order to claim that NATO members were bound to come to America's aid.

This extremely questionable maneuver upset me immensely. I remembered that Robert (Bob) McNamara had tried on more than one occasion to persuade me that Canada should join the U.S. in the Vietnam War. My answer was always a firm no for a number of reasons, the most important being that NATO was a defensive alliance, not a "ready aye ready" task force for the U.S. I still lament that decades later someone was able to pull it off.

The war on terrorism was lost the day that U.S. bombs started falling on Baghdad. The whole Muslim world that had been sympathetic or neutral about 9/11 was outraged. Where there had been a few terrorists, a number small enough to be manageable by intelligence groups working in concert with the police, there were soon thousands backed by whole populations sympathetic to their cause.

Christianity was given a bad name and soon many had to flee from places where they had lived in relative safety for centuries. Others, including some in Egypt where they had been part of the landscape, became casualties at the hands of an angry mob. It is no comfort for those of us who care about these matters that American Southern Baptists had endorsed George Bush's attack on Iraq.

By the time I wrote *Light at the End of the Tunnel* and had it published in 2010, I was having haunting doubts about the official story concerning September 11, 2001. I remembered enough mechanics to know that two aircraft did not produce sufficient kinetic or heat energy to bring down those sturdy towers, but I didn't spend a lot of time thinking about it, so I hedged my bets by saying that, although doubts had been raised about the official story it was likely the truth would never be known. I was wrong. The truth is now known, and it was the biggest con job in history.

In *The Money Mafia* I tell the story in detail and will not repeat it here, but simply relate a few key points. I had seen a presentation by Major General Albert Stubblebine III (Ret.) whose final assignment before retirement was responsibility for all of the U.S. Army's strategic intelligence forces around the world. At the instigation of his wife he began connecting the dots, and finally came to the very, very unhappy conclusion that the towers had been subject to controlled demolition.[6]

In 2010 I received a copy of First Edition: v.1.1. of the *9/11 Investigator: Exposing the Explosive WTC Evidence*, wherein 1,000 architects and engineers challenged the Official Report of WTC Destruction.[7]

A page 4 "Summary of Evidence: A Call to Action" by Pete Denney follows:

"The destruction of the Twin Towers and WTC Building 7 were the largest structural failures in modern history. The official story, as told by the 9/11 Commission and NIST, claims that fires weakened the structures, causing all three buildings to collapse. However, the evidence, most of which was omitted from official reports, supports a very different conclusion: explosive controlled demolition.

Summary of the evidence:

1. Rapid onset of destruction with unnatural symmetry of debris.

2. Constant acceleration at or near free-fall through the path of what should have been greatest resistance.

3. 118 witnesses to explosions and flashes of light, and foreknowledge of WTC 7's collapse.

4. Lateral ejection of multi-ton steel sections 600 feet at more than 60 mph.

5. Mid-air pulverization of 90,000 tons of concrete, and massive volumes of expanding pyroclastic-like dust clouds.

6. Isolated explosive ejections 20-60 stories below 'crush zone.'

7. Total destruction of all three buildings, with 220 missing floors from the Twin Towers – each an acre in size.

8. Several tons of molten steel/iron found in the debris pile.

9. Evidence of thermite incendiaries on steel beams.

10. Nanothermite composites found in WTC dust.

11. Destruction of evidence by those in charge of the investigation.

"The above constitutes overwhelming evidence supporting the hypothesis of engineered destruction. Demolition experts agree that the preparation to execute the controlled demolition of a high-rise building takes months to plan and carry out. Several credible reports of foreknowledge have come forth. It is only reasonable to suspect that powerful insiders, not just the 19 alleged hijackers, were behind the destruction."[8]

THE CLINCHER

In November 2012, I was a presenter at the Breakthrough Energy Movement in Hilversum, the Netherlands. Another speaker was Judy Wood, B.S., M.S., Ph.D., an engineer whose PowerPoint presentation was mind-boggling. She dispelled any notion that the two tall towers could have been taken down by fires started by the two terrorist aircraft that had ploughed into them. The towers were designed to withstand more stress than the suicide attack could have created. Even my wife Sandra, who automatically tunes out at the slightest whiff of the notion of conspiracy, said Judy made her re-think the situation by not making accusations but showing facts.

I got a copy of her book *Where Did The Towers Go?*[9] and ploughed through its 540 pages of evidence including over 860 images and diagrams. The book takes the reader through the evidence in a methodical way, show-ing them what happened rather than asking them to believe a theory.

The amazing thing was that although each floor appeared to collapse on the next floor the buildings did not collapse. They may have been rigged for controlled demolition to get the process started, but thousands of tons of steel and concrete were reduced to dust before they hit the ground. This could only have happened with the use of a new directed energy weapon.

The Arabs, who were merely bit players in this tragedy of tragedies, were vilified by the American press. The condemnation was so compelling that a very significant proportion of Americans were ready to "nuke them," according to a poll I saw at the time. Yet, despite the truth becoming ob-vious, there has been no effort to set the record straight. And the reason seems clear.

This world-shaking event is consistent with the *modus vivendi* of the "shadow government" which, apparently, has not told American taxpayers the truth about anything of significance from July 1947 to the end of 2017.

That truth means that the U.S. has forfeited any claim to moral leader-ship in a world in turmoil.

CHAPTER TWENTY-ONE

THE LOVE OF MONEY
IS THE ROOT OF ALL EVIL

This chapter is very close to my heart. I mentioned early in the book that it was the totally irrational boom-bust financial system that propelled me into political life at age 25. My economics professors confirmed that our system was cyclical but accepted this reality without question. There was no hint of looking for a solution. Now, 70 years later, nothing has changed except the situation seems even more perilous, something like trying to walk across the Niagara River gorge on a tightrope.

At that time, I was appalled, did my own homework, and concluded that the problem was a highly leveraged banking system that created too much money (credit), which would then create a boom, followed by too little, resulting in a recession or depression with horrendous consequences. Thus, I began a life-long journey to try to do something about an absolutely insane system that is little more than a monstrous fraud. It is a gargantuan Ponzi scheme that would have landed all of its perpetrators in jail if the bankers had not persuaded generations of politicians to grant them legislative licenses to commit grand larceny.

Although I understood the basics when I was first elected in 1949, I still had a great deal to learn, and I had to refine my ideas. At the outset, my guide was the first and, in my opinion the brightest Governor of the Bank of Canada (BoC) Graham Towers. He was able to explain the basics of banking to members of the parliamentary committee on banking and commerce in terms so simple and straightforward that anyone with a Grade 10 education could understand. Towers was able to confirm everything that I believed.

Years later, John Hotson, professor of economics at the University of Waterloo became a mentor and friend. John and William (Bill) Krehm launched an organization called the Committee on Economic and Monetary Reform (COMER). A few years ago, Bill, COMER, and Ann Emmett, the long-time president of COMER and one of the several members who had run as candidates for the Canadian Action Party when I was its leader, launched a court challenge against the BoC for abandoning its shareholders in favor of new international rules detrimental to the public interest.

They engaged the outstanding Rocco Galati, an exceptionally good constitutional lawyer to present the case. Those of us who sat in the courtroom thought that Rocco's presentation was much superior to the government's lawyer. Ultimately, however, the case was lost on appeal.

My final mentor was Keith Wilde, a former Government of Canada economist, perhaps one in a thousand, who really understood money and banking. Keith, before his death, helped me write the proposal for reform, endorsed by 40 of us, that was first presented to Canadian Finance Minister James Flaherty on March 21, 2013. It was ignored by the Conservative government and again ignored when re-submitted to the new Liberal government of Justin Trudeau in the early days of his regime. I was not even given the courtesy of an acknowledgment. He also appears to be taking his advice from the world-without-borders supporters including two or three Bilderbergers.

If either the Conservative or Liberal governments, or indeed the Government of the U.S., would send an intelligent critique they could at least be credited with due diligence. To reject new ideas with glazed eyes during a period of worldwide turmoil, however, is just not good enough! Money and banking is one of the three most important problem areas for the human species and by far the most urgent. If your eyes have been glazing over as you read this, please have another cup of tea or coffee and pay attention. Your job, your retirement income and maybe, just maybe, the future of the human species may be at stake.

MONEY AND BANKING

The first question is who actually owns the right to print, create or manufacture money?

ANSWER: We the people. At one time it was the prerogative of kings and queens, but that power has passed from the monarch to citizens. In countries that are constitutional monarchies such as Canada, the right is held by the Crown (Parliament) on behalf of the people. In the U.S. it is the Congress on behalf of the people.

Who actually creates or manufactures money?

ANSWER: Private banks with charters have a virtual monopoly on "money creation." In Canada, the BoC, which is publicly owned, prints just enough paper money to meet the day-to-day needs of the private banks to supply us, their customers, with enough cash for casual needs, perhaps one to two percent of their deposits.

In the U.S., more than 100 years ago, Congress gave the people's right to create money to private bankers through a central bank called the Federal Reserve System. It is neither federal nor reserve. It is a central bank owned by several of the biggest, most powerful banks in the world. In *The Money*

Mafia, I call it "The Biggest Heist in History." This privately owned bank has the right to print Federal Reserve notes that are the common currency in use in the U.S., and as a reserve currency for many other central banks.

Where do private banks get the money they lend to you?

ANSWER: In nearly every case they create it out of thin air. It isn't actually money that they lend you. They don't have any money (legal tender) to lend. What they do lend is their credit. The system works this way.

If you want to borrow $35,000 to buy a car, you visit your friendly banker and ask for a loan. He or she will ask you for collateral, some stocks or bonds or a second mortgage on your house or cottage. If you have none of these things you will be asked for a signature of guarantee by a well-to-do family member or friend.

Once your banker is satisfied with the collateral, you will be asked to sign a note at the current prime rate plus a premium of one or two percent. Once the note is signed the banker will make the appropriate entries on their computer and presto, a credit of $35,000 will appear in your account that you can use to buy the car. Seconds earlier that "money" did not exist. It was created out of thin air, so to speak.

Meanwhile, if you read something that convinces you that a new model car coming out in a few months would be worth waiting for and you leave the "money" in the bank, you might be paid zero interest or a fraction of one percent. The way the banks make their money is on what they call "the spread" between what, if anything, they pay on your deposit while you leave the money in the bank, and the significant interest you pay on your note. So, obviously, it is in the interest of the bank to make as many loans as possible and collect as much interest as possible.

PROBLEMS WITH THE PRESENT SYSTEM

What is the problem with how this system works? The answer, in a short phrase: "Just about everything." The first and fundamental problem is that bank-created money (BCM) is all created as debt. All banks lend to individuals to meet their needs, or to a business to expand or buy out a competitor, or to a government that provides a bond as collateral have to be repaid, with interest. But no one creates any money with which to repay either the principal or interest. So, it's a dead-end system from the outset.

You would think that people who can put a man on the Moon, establish a colony on Mars and develop artificial intelligence (AI) would be able to understand such a basic dilemma. What is the point in spending millions on AI if we don't use the intelligence we were born with to solve problems like global warming and financial stalemate.

The consequence of allowing private banks and the central banks, which in the majority of cases they control, determine the rate of increasing the money supply is a cyclical system that creates uncertainty on the one hand and devastating consequences for ordinary people on the other hand when a recession or depression results. Jobs will be lost, as will homes and businesses. Dreams will be unfulfilled and lives ruined.

According to *The Fortune Encyclopedia of Economics* there were 45 recessions or depressions in the U.S. between 1790 and 1991, and every one of them was the result of the highly leveraged debt money system.[1] Two or three were deliberate on the part of the big banks including the Great Depression of the 1930s and the Great Recession of 2007-2017, when most economies were about back to the level where they had been years earlier.

In the latest debacle the bankers threw themselves a lifeline to resuscitate a moribund economy. They reduced interest rates to rock bottom so that millions of people who would otherwise not qualify for mortgage loans would be tempted to take a chance on buying a home that was bigger and more expensive than they needed. It's an old trick called bait-and-switch. As soon as the economy begins to show signs of life the banks raise interest rates to control incipient inflation. (This after homes and apartments and the mortgages on them have already increased excessively, due to low interest rates.) Some homeowners will default on their mortgages. The banks will foreclose, make a tidy unearned profit, and ultimately start the whole cycle over again.

UNDERFUNDING BY GOVERNMENT

By any measurement, the major tragic consequence of our present system is underfunding of essential services by governments at all levels. When they have to rely exclusively on taxation and borrowing they simply do not have the cash flow necessary to meet the needs of health, education, welfare, and infrastructure. The numbers do not add up, especially when a first charge on revenues is interest on existing debt.

The result is that corners are cut in multiple areas that should not be cut, and infrastructure repairs and new installations are postponed, sometimes at the risk of public safety. Other remedies include plastering public property such as new streetcars and buses with grotesque commercial advertising, and the reliance on casinos to supplement government coffers. Politicians turn a blind eye to the human consequences of casinos and gambling that result in lost savings, broken families, and more suicides than we realize, as they are not reported.

THE DISPARITY OF INCOME

The disparity of income that the present system has produced is beyond comprehension. A 2016 Oxfam report said that in 2010, the 388 richest people owned the same wealth as the poorest 50 percent. This dropped to the 80 richest in 2014, before falling again in 2015.

"The vast and growing gap between rich and poor has been laid bare in a new Oxfam report showing that the 62 richest billionaires own as much wealth as the poorer half of the world's population." The report called for urgent action to deal with a trend showing that one percent of the people own more wealth than the other 99 percent combined.[2]

Those figures are mind-boggling! And no remedial measures have been taken. A combination of globalization and a financial system that defies any kind of logic has divided the world between the super-rich, many of whom have succeeded in finding tax havens for large quantities of money in order to avoid paying their fair share of taxes, and the millions of people who are living on starvation diets. Millions more are living just one paycheck away from defaulting on rent or mortgage payments.

Searching for Solutions

The long years of austerity budgets and high levels of unemployment following the meltdown of 2007-08 have finally re-awakened interest in finding new solutions for a seemingly intractable problem. There have been many proposals, some much better than others, so I will only mention two examples to illustrate the trends.

In November 2017, the International Movement on Monetary Reform published a paper "The Swiss Sovereign Money Initiative: Five Questions & Answers." I don't have space to repeat the questions and answers here, but the objective is to have the Swiss central bank create all of the new money coming into circulation as opposed to the present system where 90 percent is created by the banks at the click of a button. The current system does not comply with Article 99 of the Swiss constitution that states: "The Money and Currency System is a matter of the State."[3]

My other example is more current. In February 2018, an article entitled "The Venezuelan 'Petro' – Towards a New World Reserve Currency?" was circulated. "As this article goes to print, *Globovision TV* quotes Venezuelan President Nicolas Maduro announcing the launch of a new cryptocurrency, the 'Petro Oro.' It will be backed by precious metals."[4]

I don't think there is any possibility of the Petro becoming the new world reserve currency to replace the U.S. dollar, although the need is obvious and the other major powers will insist that it happen. My concern with the "Petro Oro" is calling it a cryptocurrency. That designation can be confused with the bitcoin and the many new cryptocurrencies that are sprouting up like mushrooms. Like toxic mushrooms, they should be harvested and destroyed. *Cryptocurrencies should be totally banned!*

THE ANTIDOTE FOR A WORLD DROWNING IN DEBT

The best antidote for a world drowning in debt, is debt-free money. Many of the ideas being considered and/or implemented are a big improvement on the *status quo*, but all of them I prefer and strongly recommend the collegial effort that I included in *The Money Mafia*.

The first requirement, of course, is for nation-states to nationalize their central banks as Canada did in 1938. The price paid, especially in the case of the U.S. Federal Reserve System, should be harshly determined to compensate American citizens for the vast sums that the bankers have extracted since 1805, when ownership of the money-creation system was transferred from the government to the richest of the elite bankers.

The banking industry is a very large industry employing many thousands of people, so the plan that my colleagues and I designed provides for a gradual transition with a minimum disruption in the lives of ordinary people. This can be achieved in addition to the following universal objectives:

1. Inject very large sums of government-created, debt-free money into every national economy suffering from high unemployment and low growth. This includes the eurozone, where the actual mechanics are a bit more complicated due to existing treaties. Appropriate legislation would be necessary to allow the European Central Bank to accept shares from member countries as collateral for the creation of currency. One of the goals would be reducing the level of world unemployment by one-half in less than two years. Increased activity on this scale should provide new hope to the middle class who have been subjected to systemic reduction.

2. Provide nation-states with the fiscal flexibility to address global warming pretty damn quickly, before the magnitude of the damage becomes calamitous.

3. First cap and then reduce federal net debt as well as those of states, provinces, and municipalities.

4. End immediately the power of the Bank for International Settlements (BIS), the International Monetary Fund (IMF), the World Bank, the U.S. Fed and other central banks to destroy democratic institutions and "in the process" Western civilization.

5. End the power of the BIS and the international banking cartel to run the world and, in particular, reduce the leverage of private banks from their present larcenous levels, often equal to 20:1 or more, to 2:1 over a period of seven years. That means banks would be able

to create $200.00 in loans or acquire that amount of interest-bearing assets for every $100.00 in cash that they have in their vaults or on deposit with their central banks.

6. Replace an unstable and unsustainable monetary and financial system with one that is both stable and sustainable.

7. Revive the concept of government of, by, and for the people before it is snuffed out completely.

A SOCIAL CONTRACT BETWEEN THE GOVERNMENT AND PEOPLE

Central banks have been designed in such a way that their books must balance. Consequently, they must have collateral equal to the money they would print for the government. Therefore, I am suggesting that instead of giving the central banks bonds, which would show on the books as debt, governments should provide non-transferrable, non-convertible, non-redeemable share certificates with a nominal value appropriate to the amount of money being created. For Canada, I am recommending $10 billion nominal value share certificates. For the U.S., $100 billion would be more appropriate.

This approach would facilitate the seven objectives that I listed above. If properly executed, this new sharing of power between the banks and the people should work like a charm. It would eliminate all of the disadvantages associated with the present system, and business cycles, booms, and busts would be gone forever. For anyone wanting a little or a lot more detail, read Appendix A, or Chapters 7 and 8 in *The Money Mafia*.

I was hoping that Canada's Prime Minister Justin Trudeau would be open to the above proposal, so I wrote to him the day he was sworn in to point out that there was a Canadian precedent that proved the efficacy of sharing the money creation function between the Government of Canada and the private banks.

"From 1939 to 1974 the Bank of Canada printed very large sums of near-zero cost money for the federal government. This system got us out of the Great Depression, helped finance World War II, helped finance all of the great post-war infrastructure projects including the St. Lawrence Seaway, the Trans-Canada highway, the great new air terminals as well as many provincial and municipal projects, in addition to our enviable social security system. From a public relations point of view all you have to say is that you have decided to introduce a slightly more sophisticated version of the policy that served Canadians so well for so long."[5]

I asked him if he would be content to pursue his advertised Keynesian plan, or if he was prepared to think outside the box and create a modern miracle that would set him on the path to become one of Canada's greatest prime ministers and achieve a reputation as a world leader to be reckoned with in time of crisis.

Unfortunately, he stuck with an outdated orthodoxy, appointed a minister of finance who was even more conservative, increased Canada's debt substantially, and robbed the Canadian people of the $450 billion that they could have drawn down at the rate of $150 billion a year. That would have been more than enough to meet all of Canada's immediate needs, including infrastructure, while leaving sufficient to pay down some of the existing heavy debt.

My letter also reminded him that of major problems, banking reform is the most urgent because without it, nation-states will not have the liquidity to finance the rapid transformation from an oil economy to a zero-point energy economy essential to save the planet from overheating. Drilling and fracking for oil and building pipelines is like looking in a rear-view mirror and not seeing the yawning chasm straight ahead. Building factories and zero-point energy machines would provide more than enough jobs to employ everyone displaced by abandoning oil.

With one more year left in his mandate, Justin Trudeau still has time to start looking ahead, cleaning house, and acting boldly as a twenty-first-century leader should.

CHAPTER TWENTY-TWO

REMOTE VIEWING

It is quite likely that most readers will not previously have heard of a new scientific field called "remote viewing." This is because for many years the practice was primarily used for highly classified military purposes. I strongly suspect that it is still being used for military purposes due to its usefulness as a tool for espionage. The military does not walk away from anything that works, especially when it enables them to reliably obtain information without the risk of a person who could get caught.

Remote viewing is a mental process that allows a highly trained individual to perceive things, places, events, and people across time and place. Remote viewers only work under totally blind conditions, meaning that they are not told what it is that they are expected to perceive. They are told nothing other than there is a target. The remote viewer then uses specialized procedures to read images and other sensory information that appears to them. They then end up with very detailed and accurate descriptions of what is termed a "target," which is what they are supposed to perceive, but is unknown to them consciously when they do their work. To someone who is new to remote viewing, it looks magical. But it has long been known to work, even though physicists have yet to figure out why it works. From the military's perspective, the fact that it does work is more important than knowing why it works. Remote viewing also works under any number of blind conditions, including double-blind experiments, where no one who is in contact with the remote viewer has any idea of what the target is either. For those who are interested in how this is done, there are free lessons available online, such as at the web site for The Farsight Institute (http://farsight.org/SRV/index.html).

The fact that remote viewing ability exists, and has been used by the U.S. and Russian military authorities, has been acknowledged numerous times, including by the official CIA release on 2001/04/03 of a previously classified 92-page paper written in 1993 by Captain Michael E. Zarbo, United States Army, and "Submitted to the Faculty of the Defense Intelligence College in partial fulfillment of the requirements for the degree of Master of Science of Strategic Intelligence."[1] That particular document contains photographs and remote viewers drawings, many of them of very mundane targets.

PSYCHIC WARRIOR

Psychic Warrior by David Morehouse[2] is the true story of a highly decorated army officer, special operations infantryman, and one of the army's elite airborne ranger company commanders who was destined by his superiors to wear "stars." Its release is the culmination of a battle with the military who tried to kill Morehouse to prevent him from writing it.

Morehouse's airborne company was sent to the Kingdom of Jordan for an exercise where he was hit in the head by a stray machine gun bullet. Soon he began to have strange visions and haunting nightmares. Instead of treating these dreadful symptoms, the army earmarked him for recruitment into Stargate, a top-secret clan of psychic spies called "remote viewers" where he became one of their top operatives. Morehouse was able to "travel" to unknown worlds to experience the pain, anguish and horror of Dachau; to the searing heat of ground-zero in Hiroshima; to the exhilaration of discovering the Ark of the Covenant; and to the choking smoke of Desert Storm's aftermath.

When Morehouse realized that remote viewing was to be primarily used as an instrument of war his spirit rebelled, and he decided to let the world know of the phenomenon and the fact that it was going to be used as a method of warfare. Inevitably, his superiors found out and someone tried to have him killed.

First, he had a tire blow out at high speed. He survived, but when the tire was examined it had been cut on the inside. Even worse was an attempt to kill his entire family. During a winter storm, he and his long-suffering wife Debby put their generator on the driveway to provide enough power for a light, the refrigerator, etc. A few hours later they were barely conscious when the fire department arrived. Someone had moved the generator into the garage and shut the door, so it was only by the grace of God that the Morehouse family escaped annihilation.

Ultimately, Morehouse had to resign his commission at extremely great cost to himself and his family, as a result of his less then honorable discharge. He lost his pension and all of his benefits. On the basis of a higher spiritual standard, he might have been awarded a Congressional Medal of Honor. Eventually, as the months and years passed and memories dimmed, the tide turned for Major Morehouse and his family and they began to receive the love and respect they had earned at inestimable cost.

COSMIC VOYAGE

My exposure to the details of remote viewing methods is primarily through a version known as "Scientific Remote Viewing" (SRV). This version is used primarily on the civilian side and is derivative of some of the methods used by the military. More specifically, from reading two books by Courtney Brown, Ph.D., *Cosmic Voyage* published in 1996,[3] and the follow-up *Cosmic Explorers*[4] published four years later, I gained an appreciation of how much remote viewing can be used to explore elements related to extraterrestrial life. I mentioned earlier that I had met Courtney in June 2008 at the Society for Exploration Conference in Boulder, Colorado. I acquired a copy of *Cosmic Voyage*, but I didn't read it until recently. My first attempt to read it failed because there was quite a bit of historical background and a preliminary section on the techniques used. I guess I just wasn't ready for it.

One has to first develop an appreciation of the vast nature of our universe, its uncountable suns and planets and the names of at least some of the species who inhabit them. That leads inexorably to the fact that some species have been visiting Earth for thousands of years and have played active roles in our development. It was only when I had reached this stage in my personal journey that I developed a healthy appetite to learn more.

THE PHOENIX LIGHTS

For several years I had been a bit skeptical about remote viewing because I was aware of a couple of attempts to view the future, and this was unreliable because the future keeps changing, although my understanding is that experiments are still ongoing in this regard. When it comes to the present or past, however, remote viewing is proving to be as accurate as an eye witness, and this can easily be seen with respect to many of the projects conducted at The Farsight Institute. The first case that convinced me was in respect to an incident with which I was familiar as a result of first-hand reports from many of the UFO enthusiasts that I regard as friends. This was a Farsight remote-viewing project to study the well-known incident of The Phoenix Lights.

On Thursday, March 13, 1997, an anomalous series of lights flew in steady formation over the American southwest, eventually settling over Phoenix, Arizona. The lights appeared to be connected to a large craft, and the underbelly of that craft was so big it blocked out much of the sky above it. The event was witnessed by thousands of people for a number of hours, including the governor of Arizona, who at first denied knowledge of the incident but later confirmed that he had been an eye witness.

From Farsight's project description: "Utilizing new data from two of the best remote viewers on the planet today, Dick Allgire and Daz Smith, and using methodology derived from techniques developed by the U.S. military for espionage, we now know that this event involved at least one huge extraterrestrial spacecraft. But there is more. The data for this project, recorded live on video, includes stunningly corroborating data, and what appears to be a direct communication between a being on the craft and one of the remote viewers, a communication that spans the years 1997 to 2015."[5]

I watched the entire video of this revolutionary documentary conducted at the Farsight Institute, of which Courtney Brown is Director. I was sufficiently convinced to read his book *Cosmic Voyage* from cover to cover in wide-eyed fascination. The 36 chapters cover a broad range of subjects including information about several ET species, the Galactic Federation, Jesus, the Buddha, Guru Dev, and God, and some of the interaction between ETs and Earthlings and how we have been influenced by them. I will only include one example here, which is of primary interest to me.

THE GREYS

I have to admit that the Greys have been my biggest quandary in respect to ETs. My good friend Paola Harris thinks they are good, and the late Dr. Michael Wolf who actually worked with them said, "I have never met a Grey that I didn't like." Despite these impressive credentials, they were reported to have had human hostages in the lower levels of the seven-level underground Dulce Base that the U.S. built as a joint operation with them, and in the lowest below-surface level they were allegedly performing genetic experiments that were grotesque by any known human standard.

Cosmic Voyage has given me the broader picture. They are not homogeneous. Like humans, they have good apples and a few bad apples, but many more good than bad, and they are members in good standing of the Galactic Federation of Light. Courtney tells us a lot about the Greys, who have had their own problems. But as space is so limited I would just like to include an excerpt from his discussion of the Grey Mind that paints a broad picture and provides good advice.

From *Cosmic Voyage*: "Given the scope and the substance of Grey interactions with humans as reported in the abduction literature (see especially Jacobs 1992; and Mack 1994), it is easy to see how the activities and intentions of Greys could be misunderstood as hostile from a human perspective. But it may turn out that the Greys are less of an invading army than a rescuing cavalry. They may do things to us that we do not understand or like, but they are not evil, of this I am now certain. We simply do not yet understand this species.

"Nothing in my experience as a remote viewer suggests that Greys see us as an enemy. They may be afraid both of us and of what we represent, but they need us, spiritually as well as physically. And lest we judge too quickly, we may need them for our own evolutionary survival just as dearly.

"In short, we need to know more, much more, about them, ourselves, and the role that we should play in this intensely interesting drama. I suggest that it may be wise to postpone our judgements of all nonhuman species until we advance a bit more in our own understanding of the broader galactic community."[6]

THE MOSES PROJECT

Another Farsight project involves the historical subject, Moses. This project is typical of Farsight projects that seem to question nearly everything that we normally take for granted, especially with respect to history. From Farsight's website: "Never in the history of human civilization has there been a more enigmatic individual. According to legend, he led the Israelites to freedom from slavery in Egypt by releasing God's wrath on the Egyptians with a series of plagues. And then he met with God in the mountains, where God gave Moses the Ten Commandments, the artifact that was eventually carried in the Ark of the Covenant and which was used to defeat the enemies of the Israelites in battle after battle using mysterious powers. And Moses had God split the Red Sea so that the Israelites could make their final escape from the land of Egypt. Those are among the most astounding accomplishments of any human ever told. But they happened so long ago, some historians now doubt that any of that ever happened, or whether Moses even existed.

"Now, finally, the amazing story of Moses can be explained with remote viewing recorded live for all to see. Yes, Moses really did exist. And yes, those amazing things really did happen. But how they happened is quite a different story from the story told in the Judeo/Christian Bible. The bottom line is that Moses had outside help, a lot of it. And it was help that even he may not have understood. We now know more about who actually did it, who pulled off one of the most important civilization redirections in the history of humanity.

"Finally the artifact known as the Ten Commandments still exists today, hidden, but without obvious protection in a war torn area. Now we can offer descriptions of where it is. But we also know why it is terribly dangerous to search for it at the present time.

"Here, told through riveting remote viewing recorded live on video for the first time are three eye witness accounts of what really happened in the distant past. We now know what caused the great plagues that affected Egypt. And we now know that there really was an artifact that we call the Ten Commandments. We know where it came from, and we know that it held off-world technology. We know that the Israelites really did cross the Red Sea to escape from the Egyptians. But now we know how it happened. We know how the Red Sea parted so that the Israelites could run across. These are no longer mysteries. It all makes sense, once one looks at these remote-viewing sessions."

In summary, "Moses: Beyond Exodus" finds that:

1. The Ten Commandments artifact contained alien technology.

2. The first of the great plagues that affected Egypt was a result of an extraterrestrial biological and chemical attack that affected the water supply.

3. Extraterrestrials directed a meteor or asteroid to hit the Red Sea, creating a gap in the water that allowed the Israelites to cross to the other side.

4. The artifact known as the Ten Commandments still exists today, in a war-torn region.

5. Extraterrestrials were fundamentally involved in creating the Moses legend, thereby transforming human society through the centuries in ways that seem miraculous even today."[7] For a more detailed, full account, readers can go to the Farsight website.

This chapter has been an introduction to a relatively new science that has been used for decades by the Russian and U.S. military. The Farsight Institute has adopted the same high technical standards more compatible with the wishes of the Creator.

CHAPTER TWENTY-THREE

GOD IS ALIVE, WELL, AND EVERYWHERE

This is by far the most important chapter I have ever written in any of my books.

It is about my walk with God, which has been getting closer and closer as the years have passed. It isn't necessary for me to confide in Him because he knows my every thought and action. Increasingly, however, he has confided in me and has never refused to answer one of my questions. He has also showered me with blessings.

2017 A YEAR OF MOMENTOUS REVELATION

I was walking along the street one day in the early part of 2017 when the thought occurred to me that it was surprising that God always responded to my questions instantly at any time of the day or night. This seemed strange as I assumed that there were thousands or millions of other people who were in need of help or who had questions to ask of Him.

There was only one way to find out, and that was to ask. I said, "Are you a Guardian Angel the Lord has sent to watch over me? Or are you the real thing." "I am the real thing," was the instant reply. Immediately, the words "Universal Consciousness" came into my mind. God is everywhere at the same time. This was interesting because I remembered Jesus saying "Even the hairs of your head are numbered." I must admit that I considered that a bit of a stretch. It might not be difficult to count the hairs in my nearly bald head because I am old. The people with gorgeous thick hair, however, would pose a greater challenge. Jesus may have been exaggerating a bit to make his point, but with universal consciousness the problem is solved. Ironically Don Inkpen, a member of the Seniors Bible Class that I taught in the 1950s, who had been suffering from cancer for a long while and had been told there was no further treatment that would help, wrote me an urgent e-mail. He recommended that I read a book titled *Beyond Biocentrism*, by Robert Lanza, M.D. with Bob Berman. He admitted that it was not written from a religious point of view. It was pure science but very thought provoking.

I ordered the book and read it on the way to Sandra's family reunion that was held in Crete in June 2017. It was as stimulating as Don had promised. One of Dr. Lanza's postulates was universal consciousness, although he ended his book without any hint of where his belief in universal consciousness originated.[1]

Meanwhile my friend, mentor, and spiritual collaborator Pierre Juneau, who was responsible for exposing me to what I call "The Broader Reality" sent me an excerpt from Courtney Brown's book *Cosmic Explorers*. The following section is from a chapter entitled "With the Eyes of God."[2]

With the Eyes of God

This section is one that had a profound influence on me. Courtney Brown perceived what he believed to be the essential beginning of the universe. There was a shape of light that somewhat resembled a spinning cloud or vortex. In the middle of the session, he wondered what to do next. He cued on the idea of a suggestion, inviting his subspace mind to offer a hint as to the meaning of this experience. The response was immediate. He sensed that he was to cue on God. The following is his account.

> The conscious mind was confused by this suggestion, and probably as a consequence of this, the idea came to me that I should cue on someone who could explain this to me. I then cued on Jesus in the matrix. For reasons that I will explain, I have long considered him our older brother, in a literal sense. I suppose I intuitively felt that he would be sufficiently experienced and wise to know what to do in this situation. Instantly I sensed my awareness shift to include this being's flavor of consciousness, and I sensed him suggest to me that I should abandon fear and plunge into the vortex that I perceived.
>
> I did so.
>
> The vortex was alive. There was the sense of a huge consciousness, and as I extended my mind across this consciousness, I felt stretched like the skin of a balloon, although not uncomfortably so. It then became clear to me that this being was terribly alone, and sad beyond measure. It had spent an eternity by itself, slowly evolving, until it finally grew to a point at which it could end its pain.
>
> Then, in one sudden burst, I experienced this being's solution. The being essentially blew itself up, or at least much of itself. As I followed the outward rush of the being's fragmenting expansion, I perceived that it experienced a new joy that nearly overwhelmed me. The being did not die.
>
> At first the bits and pieces of the larger being were too small and immature to even be aware of themselves. Neither were they aware of their own origin. From this point began the most profound evolution of the original being. It had become a parent to the fragments of itself.

The fragmented parts began to experience existence in a way that seemed independent of the parent. Initially they did not understand that they were literally part of a single larger being. Yet as they continued to grow in experience, they matured and developed an intense need to know how they came to exist, and indeed, the reason for their existence. This led them eventually to seek and discover the reality of their parent, their loving creator. It was at this moment of realization that they understood that they were their parent, and that their own growth and evolution was also the growth and evolution of their parent. The parent had created a way to look back at itself through a mirror of a multitude of individual consciousnesses."

I had inadvertently mislaid Pierre Juneau's e-mail, but I remembered the gist of it. The concept was so vast that I had difficulty getting my mind around it. So I let it lie fallow for a while. One day when I felt especially close to my Heavenly Father, I decided to ask the question directly but reverently:

Q. Is it true that you blew yourself up?

Source: Something like that.

That was enough to satisfy me for several weeks, although I thought the answer was less than definitive. As time went by, and because I had already concluded that I was being encouraged to write another book to complete the trilogy of inspired books, I decided that I had to have the courage to ask the question again.

Q. The last time we discussed the question as to whether or not you had blown yourself up you said "something like that." I would like to know whether you did or didn't, yes or no?

Source: The answer is yes.

Needless to say I was grateful for the candor because it put a whole new light on the greatest mystery in the universe. Some weeks later while I was still in Crete vacationing with Sandra's family, the subject came up one more time when I was praying silently.

Q. You said you blew yourself up?

Source: Yes.

Q. This was a conscious, deliberate decision on your part?

Source: It was.

Q. You know that I will quote you?

Source: That is what you are supposed to do.

I was neither the first nor the only one to come to the conclusion that God was the omnipresent Creator. My mind went back to the night Apollo astronaut Edgar Mitchell had dinner at our condo. Sandra had asked him directly if he believed in God. He said no, if you mean an old man with a beard somewhere in the sky. Later, however, he added, "I believe that the universe is God's body."

Another coincidence occurred when I was looking for a reference in one of Shirley MacLaine's books. Shirley was one of the very interesting people I had met as a result of my interest in UFOs and ETs. She had tracked me down through the Canadian Action Party office in Vancouver and called me when she was visiting Toronto. She broke bread with Sandra and me more than once, and we became friends.

When I was writing this chapter I consulted her book *Going Within* and couldn't find the information I was searching for. Skimming to the end, however, I came across her interview with the late Stephen Hawking where she recorded this: "If, as Hawking and many other scientists say, the Big Bang explosion resulted in life as we know it today, then the seeds of all things, ourselves included, were present at the birth of creation ..."[4]

THE DIVINE CREATION OF INFINITE VARIETY AND BEAUTY

It is true that the God particles flew out of the vortex into the void, but not before they had received precise instructions as to how they should act, interact with each other and grow to become the stars that give us light and warmth, the water that is essential to life, and a plethora of trees, plants, and animals to aid us and sustain us.

Our Creator must have a love of beauty. Anyone who has seen pictures taken by the Hubble telescope will appreciate that the cosmos is infinitely beautiful. There is nothing comparable. Closer to home, our planet is a joy to behold. In the course of writing my first book about 50 years ago I had the good fortune to visit 26 different countries. My unforgettable impression is that every one of those countries was beautiful, each in its own way.

My wife Sandra and I have always felt close to God when we watched the sun rise or set, when we viewed the stars in the sky, or walked in the woods, or enjoyed the thunder and lightning of a summer storm. What we did not know was that every hill and mountain, every field and forest, every stream and river, every tree and flower, every stone and thistle as well as every calm or raging ocean is God incarnate. They all consist of God particles as do our cities and factories. All particulate matter in the cosmos comprises God's body.

Paramount to Earthlings is that we are all God's children and made in His image. That does not mean that we look like him, but that we are part of Him and He is part of us. It doesn't matter about the color of our skin, we are all equal. We are brothers and sisters. There is no doubt in my mind that our Father is not pleased when those of us with white skin either think or act as if we are in some way superior to our siblings. We are not!

The same might be said when any of us treat LGBTQ+ with less respect than we would expect from others. Regardless of sexual orientation all of us are equally God's children. Consequently, as I said in *Light at the End of the Tunnel*, "What God has created let no man (or woman) disdain."

In addition to a common heritage, our bodies are temples of the living God. He has arranged for each of us to be provided with a soul that becomes our eternal consciousness at the exact moment when we utter our first cry or take our first breath as babies. Our souls remain with us through good times and bad, and leave our bodies at the exact moment when we take our final breath. Our souls are immortal but our bodies have then served their purpose and can be recycled. There is no particular point in making elaborate arrangements to preserve them, especially at the expense of diverting arable land from its intended purpose.

A life on Earth is a gift from God and should be treasured. While we are temples of God, we should avoid ingesting or inhaling substances that harm our bodies and may cause us pain in later years. We don't need drugs to make us happy. We can get our "highs" from the beauty of nature or from providing aid and comfort to others. Every human has a role to play, from something as humble as a perennial smile to dedicating one's life to a search for a cure to a disabling disease. There are a thousand ways to serve others and be happy in our work.

We can show our appreciation to our father, God, by loving him with all our heart and soul, strength and mind, and by treating our neighbors as we would have them treat us. While I have been writing about all of the dreadful things that have been going on in the world, it has often occurred to me that there is not a single problem that couldn't be solved by the application of the Golden Rule, which requires us to love our neighbors as ourselves. All of Earth's major religions adhere to the principle, but none practice it. That is the real problem!

Finally, to my scientific friends who may be sceptical about the above story of creation, and believe that we have reached our present state of development by chance alone, I would like to quote a paragraph from Dr. Robert Lanza's book *Beyond Biocentrism*.

"This takes us inescapably to considering chance as it tries to create some sort of universe. The problem is, our universe has an exquisite set of priorities that are Goldilocks-perfect for life to exist. We live in an extraordinary fine-tuned cosmos. It's a place where any random tweaking that conjured even slightly different parameters in hundreds of independent ways would not do the job of allowing any kind of life to arise. Let the gravitational constant be two percent different, or change the power of the Planck length or Boltzmann's constant or the atomic mass unit, and you'd never have stars, or life."[5]

Lanza goes on to say that as an explanation, randomness is close to idiotic. Yet the truth is we live in a cosmos teeming with life, both animate and inanimate. It was conceived and is being executed by the greatest mind of all time. So, for me, it doesn't matter that I can't explain how energy particles can evolve into stars and moons, planets and people. I haven't asked because my mind couldn't grasp such complexities.

ALLEGORIES IN THE BIBLE

To understand Biblical allegories, it is necessary to look back at the Jewish Bible, especially the early chapters. The creation stories, as told in Genesis, are allegories. The world was not created in six of our days as a half dozen of my literalist friends still insist. The several functions described took millions or billions of our years to complete. Also, of course, human life did not begin with Adam and Eve. There was human life on Earth thousands of years before their recorded arrival. In one of his sessions, Courtney Brown discovered that Adam and Eve were project managers in a "genetic uplift" program for humans on Earth.[6]

There is some evidence that Adam and Eve displeased God, and that their original sin was disobedience rather than illicit sex. In that respect little seems to have changed in the intervening years. The fact of extraterrestrial interference in human affairs underlines the complexity of trying to unravel human history.

My favorite book is the Bible. I have read it from cover to cover three times, and continue to read it daily when circumstances permit. At church on Sunday mornings when I was young, when passages from the scriptures were read, the reader would invariably end by saying: "This is the word of the Lord." The congregational response would be: "Thanks be to God."

As I now believe, the allegories in the early chapters of the Old Testament were not the word of the Lord. Neither were those that portrayed God as a ruthless warmonger counseling the massacre of men, women, and children before stealing their land. I believe that these words are not those of the God of Creation. They are the words of the Elohim, a highly advanced group from another planet or star system who, when they arrived on Earth in their space vehicles, were perceived as gods and received as such. They played a role in creation but it was a subordinate role. In the process the Elohim painted a false picture of God, who picked Jesus, a favored son, to come to Earth and set the record straight.

JESUS' ROLE IN HISTORY

It was God's plan that Jesus' arrival on Earth should be a lesson on humility. Instead of arriving on a spaceship with trumpets sounding, Jesus arrived as a baby, lying in a manger. The Bible has little to say about Jesus' early life and I am not going to speculate. We do know that as a young adult under the tutelage of John the Baptist, he was well prepared for his short but powerful ministry. Jesus was able to mingle not only with the leaders in the synagogues, but also with prostitutes and sinners in a demonstration that God the Father loves all of his children unconditionally. Jesus was particularly comfortable with the poor, and had a love of children, who are special in God's sight.

Jesus gave us a new and accurate portrait of God the Creator of Life. He erased the black and grey of the Old Testament historians and unveiled the real God of love and light. What a contrast. I had always had trouble explaining the God of the Old Testament and took refuge in the possibility that he had changed his mind as he had when he decided to have Saul replaced by David as the King of Israel. What a wonderful relief it was to discover that Jesus was putting a spotlight on the truth when he said, as recorded in the Gospel of Matthew, "Blessed are the peacemakers for they shall be called the sons of God."[7]

The only record of violence was when Jesus and his close associates overturned the tables of the money-changers in the Temple, saying to them, "Is it not written. 'My house shall be called a house of prayer for all nations? But you have made it a 'den of thieves.'"[8]

Holiness and justice were both key issues, but Jesus' fate was sealed for confronting the elite rulers. He was arrested, tried, beaten, and executed on a wooden cross, the most humiliating of deaths. In doing so, he fulfilled his own prophecy of: "Greater love hath no man than this, that he lay down his life for his friends."

With deference to my friend Len Kasten, one of the best ufologists, he states that Jesus did not actually die on the cross. I have been directed by the Creator to say that is incorrect. Jesus did die that day. On the third day he was raised from the dead, but in the fourth dimension not the third dimension, in which he had lived on Earth. In the fourth dimension he was able to walk through walls, materialize, and dematerialize, which would have appeared as magic at the time, but are characteristics of our ET friends the Greys, which they enjoy at their stage of development. Jesus did save us from our sins, but only if we obey his commandments, i.e. to love one another as he loved us.

The Doctrine of the Trinity

I have long entertained doubts about the doctrine of the Trinity. It somehow didn't make sense to me – too abstract and convoluted. As the years passed, the idea has seemed less and less credible, so I searched the synoptic gospels for evidence and read books written by Christian theologians who appeared to be attempting to reconcile the irreconcilable. First, I gathered evidence from the Gospel of Mark, which most scholars agree was the first of the gospels to be written.

I began with chapter one, where John baptized Jesus in the Jordan River. And immediately coming from the water, Jesus saw the heavens parting and the Spirit descending upon Him like a dove. Then a voice came from heaven, "You are My beloved Son, in whom I am well pleased."[9]

Later, in the same chapter, when Jesus was teaching in the synagogue at Capernaum, a man possessed with an evil spirit cried out: "What do you want with us, Jesus of Nazareth? Have you come to destroy us? I know who you are - the Holy One of God."[10]

In chapter eight, when Jesus and his disciples were visiting the villages around Caesarea Philippi, he asked them: "Who do people say that I am?" They replied, "Some say John the Baptist; others say Elijah; and still others, one of the prophets."

"But what about you?" he asked. "Who do you say that I am?"

Peter answered, "You are the Christ." ("The Christ" (Greek) and "the Messiah" (Hebrew) both mean "the Anointed One.")[11]

In the following chapter, Jesus took Peter, James, and John to a high mountain where he was transfigured in the company of Elijah and Moses. The disciples were frightened out of their wits and didn't know what to say. A cloud appeared and enveloped them, and a voice came from the cloud: "This is My Beloved Son, hear Him."[12]

The next reference taken from chapter ten, I find even more compelling. "As Jesus started on his way, a man ran up to him and fell on his knees before him. 'Good teacher,' he asked, 'what must I do to inherit eternal life?'

" 'Why do you call me good?' Jesus answered. 'No one is good – except God' "[13]

Surely Jesus would not have said that if he had been God incarnate!

Later, in speaking of the end of the age, which he seemed to think was not far off, Jesus said: "No one knows about that day or hour, not even the angels in heaven, nor the Son, but only the Father."[14] It is inconceivable to me that Jesus would say that if he had been God in a human body.

And on the night of his arrest, when his soul was "overwhelmed to the point of death," he petitioned God and prayed that if possible, the hour might pass from him. "Abba, Father," he said, "everything is possible for you. Take this cup from me. Yet not what I will, but what you will."[15]

The clincher for me came as Jesus hung near death on the cross, when he said: "My God, my God, why have you forsaken me?"[16] To me it is quite inconceivable that Jesus would have uttered these words had he been God incarnate.

Nor, too, was he "the only begotten son of the Father." There are billions of us. Notwithstanding the fact that he is one of our brothers, Jesus is very special. In fact, he is unique because he is the one the Creator chose to let us know how he wanted us to live. He was the one who was willing to go the second mile and die on the cross to get our attention and encourage us to learn the message God had asked him to deliver to us. It was not intended to be exclusive for Jews and later Christians. It is a message for the world.

When my wife Sandra and I, with our friends Kay and Kent Hotaling from Oregon, U.S.A., went to the Middle East in 2006 to get a snapshot of what was going on there, our host in Beirut was Samir Kreidie, a Muslim businessman who treated us royally. He had written a piece entitled "The Jesus for the World," which gets to the root of our problems. I asked Samir for permission to use it in *Light at the End of the Tunnel*, the first book in my trilogy, and I thought it was sufficiently compelling that I should reprint it here.

THE JESUS FOR THE WORLD

The Lebanese Muslim friends we met when we visited Beirut in 2006 were quite open about their willingness to work with us in building a better world in the Spirit of Jesus. Not, they made clear, the Christian Jesus, whose name had been invoked during the Crusades and the Inquisition, but by the historical Jesus, one of the five Islamic prophets, who preached peace, justice, and humility, and who eschewed violence. His message is one that makes sense in a war-torn, insecure, and troubled world. Therefore, it is one they can endorse without abandoning their own religion and culture.

Samir Kreidie, who coined the phrase "The Jesus for the World" pointed out the many similarities between the Qur'an and the Bible. There are differences, of course, but the point was that in significant ways we have common beliefs that are more important than our differences. Here is some of what he said.

"As a child I studied in the Evangelical School of Beirut. I studied the Bible and I was very impressed by the stories of all the prophets, especially by the teachings of Jesus. My father also put me into the tutelage of a sheikh in order to study our religion, which is Islam. I found I was studying the same stories, the same prophets, the same teachings, and the same principles. One day the sheikh told me that all Christians would go to hell and all Muslims who pray would go to heaven. [Sounds familiar.] It meant my good teacher Mrs. Smith, who I loved so much, was going to hell only because she was born a Christian, while Abu Ali, the butcher who was cruel to me and my friends, was going to heaven just because he happened to be a Muslim who prayed. I cried a lot for Mrs. Smith.

"As I was growing up this question was always in my mind. I started observing the world go into conflicts and wars and noted that one of their basic causes was religion. So I searched for the religion of God. I asked: Is he a Muslim, a Christian, a Jew, a Buddhist or what? I thoroughly studied the Qur'an, the Tawrat and the Bible. Again I found I was studying the same stories, the same prophets, the same teachings, and the same principles. I came to a conclusion that God does not have a religion. God is universal. He is for all the world. He is love. He is mercy. He is giving. I concluded that most conflicts and wars result from our ignorance, from not knowing our own religion and the religion of others. Religion as practiced by many today is a misrepresentation of the real spiritual idea and teaching of God. It is coated and surrounded with ignorance, with cultural, political and economic motives. If we removed all these coatings we are going to reach the same God, the same prophets, the same teachings and the same principles.

"Today many Muslims and Christians live together, study together, work together, and some even get married to each other. In spite of this, many of them do not know about the religion of each other. If only they really knew their own religion and the religion of the others, they would discover that they believe in the same prophets, the same teachings, the same principles, the same God. They would also discover that they agree on a much wider range of issues than it seems on the surface. They share the same religious history, philosophy and values although they differ in religious practices. The two sides think they disagree while actually they agree with each other.

"Let me give you an example that happened to me personally. Four months ago I gave a lecture in Lebanon in English. The topic was 'I am a Muslim and a Follower of Jesus.' The day following the lecture the newspapers wrote, 'Kreidie is a Muslim and a believer in Issa (the Arab name of Jesus in the Qur'an).' Many of my Muslim friends called me and congratulated me. They said it is good that I told the Christians that Jesus is not only for them but for the whole world. The second day another newspaper wrote, 'Kreidie is a Muslim and a believer in Yassoua (the Arab name of Jesus in the Gospel).' So all my Muslim friends called me, criticizing me for believing in the Christian Jesus."

CHAPTER TWENTY-FOUR

Blessed Are The Peacemakers For They Shall See God

Every one of us has to choose between our Creator God who cares about the poor, the sick and the outcasts of society, and the Evil One, or Dragon who, with his willing helpers, is largely responsible for the current crisis here on Earth.

As Richard Rohr said in his Daily Meditation of February 6, 2018, "In Jesus' teaching and in his life, we see modeled nonviolent, peaceful action. He encourages us to likewise 'turn the other cheek' and not return vengeance with vengeance. There is no way to peace other than through peacemaking itself."[1]

The other option of meeting force with force is never a long-term solution. How many nations have tried to kill radical Islam as portrayed by the Islamic state in Iraq and Syria (commonly referred to as ISIS) by escalating the use of increasingly lethal force. But you can't "kill" an ideology. The only cure is the presentation of a better way of life. This can be best achieved by getting to know each other, and breaking bread together.

Let the United Nations convene a disarmament conference at once. The UN has not achieved much that is noteworthy for quite a long time. Two of its agencies are exceptions to this generality. The UN High Commissioner for Refugees (UNHCR) and the UN Children's Emergency Fund (UNICEF) are both producing noteworthy results. The General Assembly, however, must abandon its comfortable acceptance of the status quo and demonstrate its unquestionable potential by tackling the hot issues that undermine any hope of a peaceful world and, perhaps, the survival of the human species.

At the top of the list is a disarmament conference. The first item on the agenda should be de-nuclearization. It is not only North Korea that should be de-nuclearized, but all nations in possession of nuclear weapons. Russia and the U.S. each have enough nuclear weapons to destroy the world. All it would take is one uncontrollable clash of personalities, or one malfunction of the surveillance system, to cause a catastrophe.

It is the real and legitimate fear of an irreversible accident that encouraged our extraterrestrial cousins to visit Earth in unprecedental numbers after the U.S. exploded its first atomic weapon in 1945. They know that the universe is God incarnate, and consequently is a whole and completely interconnected entity. Consequently what happens on one planet, though seemingly remote and insignificant, has repercussions that affect the whole cosmos. That is the reason the ETs made such generous offers of their technology to allow us to achieve "the good life," if we would only give up our atomic weapons.

The ETs would also know about of the war in Heaven that took place eons ago, as referenced in the Bible, Revelation, Chapter 12, vs 7, "And there was war in heaven. Michael and his angels fought against the dragon; and the dragon and his angels fought."[2] Thanks to Remote Viewing and the Farsight Institute we now know that a real war took place in our solar system. It was an atomic war, and all that remains of the one planet that was destroyed as a result of the war between that planet and Mars, is an Asteroid Belt. The surface of Mars was made uninhabitable, so survivors had to live underground or emigrate to another planet.[3] This should be warning enough for Earthlings to de-nuclearize while it is still possible.

ATTEMPT TO RECONCILE AND ENLIGHTEN ALL MAJOR RELIGIONS

In *Light at the End of the Tunnel*, I recalled when Canadian Prime Minister Lester Pearson showed me a top secret letter from Canada's ambassador to the Union of Soviet Socialist Republics (U.S.S.R.) expressing the view that organized religions were responsible for many of the world's conflicts. My instant reaction was one of denial because I considered myself to be modestly religious. When I became better acquainted with the history of the world I had to conclude that there is not one of the major religions that does not have blood on its hands as a result of conflicts or adventures of one kind or another.

It is a matter of great regret that the problem continues unabated, although there has been a miraculous reconciliation between Catholics and Protestants in the Christian faith. That is a good news story. The continuing conflict between Shias and Sunni Muslims is a blot on the history of Islam. The problem is deeply rooted in power and politics even though both worship the same God, and revere the same holy book, the Quran. It is shameful that both the U.S. and Russia pick sides and provide armaments to nations or factions without which the various conflicts would be more difficult, if not impossible, to continue.

The UN needs to initiate two open-ended conferences. The first should include all of the major religions sitting down at the same table and getting to know each other. They can look for commonality of purpose. They can

223

also look for out-dated anomalies such as honor killing and death for apos-
tasy. The Israelites have adapted many of their ancient practices to reflect a
more modern view of the Creator's wishes and the Muslims should look at
some of their rules and regulations with equally open hearts.

The second conference should be for Sunnis and Shias only. They simply must end their age-old conflict and effect a reconciliation that would
allow them to work hand-in-hand to help build God's kingdom here on
Earth. I would suggest that former U.S. Congressman Mark Siljander who
has learned Arabic in order to build bridges between Christians and Islam,
act as a neutral chair. He has told me that he could recruit one moderate
Shia Imam and one moderate Sunni Imam to assist him in one of the greatest, most important challenges of our time.[4]

THE ISRAELI-PALESTINIAN CONFLICT

The late Osama bin Laden advised U.S. President George W. Bush as
follows: "As to America, I say to it and its people a few words: I swear
to God that America will not live in peace before peace reigns in Palestine,
and before all the army of infidels depart the land of Muhammad, peace be
upon him."[5] There is little doubt that the warning, which was ignored by
George Bush, is still valid. There is no evidence that the Israeli government
really wants peace. My conclusion is that the Israeli strategy is a slow and
steady encroachment on the Palestinian land in the occupied territories until there isn't enough land for a viable Palestine state, at which time they
will attempt to push their boundary to the Jordan River. This insidious plan
must end, and a fair and final peace must be established.

If President Jimmy Carter is physically able to chair the negotiations
he would be the ideal choice. If not, African Bishop Desmond Tutu
might be a happy alternative. All interested parties including Hezbollah
and Hamas should have a seat at the conference table. Only the United
States should sit on the sidelines. Its long record of providing very large
amounts of financial and military aid to the Israelis and very little help
of any kind to the Palestinians reveals an inherent bias that must not be
injected into the negotiations. U.S. domestic politics has often trumped
neutrality as appeared self-evident in that country's recent recognition of
Jerusalem as Israel's capital.

If an agreed settlement of the perennial Israeli-Palestinian dispute can
ever be negotiated that would be the perfect solution. If that is not possible
the chair should write a report setting out what is considered to be a fair and
just solution and send it to the UN General Assembly for consideration. A
simple majority of the votes cast should make the agreement binding on
both parties and have the force of law, and not subject to veto by the Security Council.

In the unlikely event that the General Assembly vote is negative, a new chair should be appointed and the negotiations begun again. The dispute that has been a thorn in the flesh of the world's body politic for decades must be removed, and peace established as a precursor to peace and justice on Earth.

SOME GOOD NEWS FOR A CHANGE

It is the bad, shocking and heartbreaking news that we read about most often in the daily press and listen to on television or radio. But there are some wonderful things going on in the world at the micro level, thousands of them that provide inspiration and encouragement to the rest of us.

This morning June 1, 2018, we had our dear friend Peg Herbert, Ph.D., founder and CEO of Help Lesotho, join us for breakfast as she begins a two-day visit to meet with some of her faithful donors to account for her stewardship, and bring them up to date on the extraordinary value they are getting for their financial support. I mentioned Peg in my latest book, *The Money Mafia*, but thought the story was worth repeating for what I hope will be a wider audience.

A little more than a decade ago in the course of a vacation in Lesotho, Peg felt God's call to establish a mission to help orphan children whose parents had both died due to HIVAIDS. Since that humble beginning, her work has grown a hundred-fold, and education has been provided to thousands of young people who are taught the benefit of a good lifestyle. The two buildings she was able to erect have become the headquarters for myriad activities including computer training, which is so popular that members of the local police force are lining up for admission. All of the employees are Africans and their ability to change and enrich lives is a modern miracle. It is a team effort that only exists because Peg responded positively when called by God.

* * *

An article by Barbara Sheffield in the *United Church Observer* November/December 2017 edition reads as follows.

> "How can we show Muslims in our communities and in our country that we, as Christians stand with them in solidarity against expression of religious intolerance and acts of religious terrorism? The congregation at Islington United Church [Toronto] is demonstrating its commitment to interfaith solidarity in creative and compassionate ways.
>
> "The congregation recently invited its Muslim neighbors into the church for an interfaith service. The service included the bless-

ing of 54 prayer shawls and the dedication of a memorial bench in the church garden – an act of honoring the families who lost loved ones in the horrific act of terror committed in January 29, 2017 at the Centre Cultural Islamique de Québec.

Mary Bradley, one of the many knitters in the prayer shawl project, said, "Knitting is a form of prayer. When we knit we are making a difference in this turbulent world. We hope our prayers bring comfort and peace to the Mosque families."[6]

* * *

Not all of the good news stories claim religious connection. Avaaz, a global web movement, sponsors many important initiatives. Danny, Alice, Allison, Marigona, Ricken, Iain and the rest of their team are world leaders in drawing attention to injustices, industrial excess and world problems of all kinds. One of their appeals really got my attention.

Dear Friends,

15,000 scientists just sent out an SOS – a "warning to humanity" that if we don't stop polluting, our planet is doomed.

The facts are terrifying: species are going extinct at 1,000 times the natural rate. 90% of the Great Barrier Reef is dead or dying. Oceans are so choked with plastic that fish are addicted to eating it.

But scientists have discovered something else – a kind of miracle that could save us. If we can protect 50% or our planet from human exploitation, our ecosystem will be able to stabilise and regenerate. Life on Earth will recover!

Our governments have already promised to protect a quarter of the planet, so we know it's possible. But no other global movement is championing this miracle recovery plan! The Avaaz organization is trying to raise money for the next critical 25%.

It's up to us.

If 50,000 of us chip in just the cost of a cup of coffee a week, we can make the proposal famous, face down the polluters and poachers, and campaign to get leaders to drive through a deal to save the planet at the Global Summit on Biodiversity.

* * *

ONE CHANGED LIFE IMPACTS MANY

In 1987, a young man, Michael Timmis, stopped in Washington, D.C. on his way to experience Africa. While in D.C. he met a Zulu pastor from South Africa who helped him begin to follow Jesus. Shortly after this life-changing experience he arrived in Uganda. This was Uganda shortly after the Idi Amin years, and he was overwhelmed with the devastation in this once-beautiful country. Soon after, with funds from his family and in partnership with John Riordan and Tim Kreutter, a work was begun focusing on under-privileged children with an emphasis on youth leadership development. In the past 30 years over 2,000 young men and women have been part of this program.

In the character development curriculum, young people are taught the timeless and universal principles of forgiveness, honesty, integrity, compassion, kindness, hard work, humility, and service to the less fortunate – as exemplified in the teachings of Jesus and the perennial wisdom of all traditions – without affiliation to any one institutional religious group.

These communities are a living model of unity in diversity in that they are composed of all the different tribes, nationalities, political groupings, cultures and religious backgrounds found in each country. These are the divisions that are behind the wars and conflicts that have torn Africa apart for years.

The emphasis has been on developing the next generation of leaders for Africa. This has been done through creating a family culture of support as the young people live together and engage in the various programs of education, sports, and creating homes for homeless kids. The core focus is on developing the cornerstone of Africa's next generation. The purpose is to raise up future leaders with a shared vision of positively transforming their communities and nations as an outgrowth of their own personal transformation. Today there are 250 staff members, almost all Africans, who lead this transformative work in Uganda, Kenya, Tanzania, Rwanda and South Sudan.[7]

CREATING OPPORTUNITIES – A VOLUNTEER'S MEMOIR

Creating Opportunities, by my dear friend Chris Snyder, is a late entry in my book. Chris gave me a copy to read while crossing the Atlantic Ocean on the way home from a desperately needed eight-day river cruise holiday. I had only read a few pages before being convinced that he deserved an honorable mention.

Chris is not a particularly religious person but he "walks the talk" better than just about anyone I know. He has been involved in "sweat equity" (volunteer labor) projects in Malawi, India, Burkina Faso, Tanzania, Cambodia, and with the Indigenous peoples of Canada. I would like to quote a paragraph from his "Acknowledgments" that outlines the scope of his activities.

"In my capacity as a volunteer, I have worked with so many people around the world who have helped to create opportunities and improve the lives of others. Many of these people are mentioned in the book, however there are countless others who are not named. I want you to know how thankful I am to have worked and learned from you all! This includes an exhaustive list of family, friends, sports coaches, camp counsellors, mentors and teachers. It also includes men at the end of a shovel in Tanzania digging trenches, grannies in Malawi looking after their grandchildren, limbless people in Cambodia who have shown their resilience despite having a leg blown off by a landmine, people in Africa living with AIDS, and Indigenous peoples who have struggled with the after-effects of residential schools but are committed to survival. You have helped me learn how things and places and people and passions and causes can all be connected."[8]

Each and every one of these groups, and thousands more, has been making a significant difference in making our world a better, kinder, more loving place for us and our neighbors wherever they may be. What we need is a tsunami of similar initiatives to tip the balance in God's favor.

* * *

Of all the things that have happened in recent years none has given me renewed hope as much as the reaction of American students in the aftermath of mass shootings. "We are the students, we are the victims, we are change, fight gun violence now! student organizers wrote for one of the planned events."[9]

On a number of occasions American students have demonstrated that they are much more mature and better qualified to govern than the politicians who not only tolerate, but protect the right of the public to buy and use automatic rifles. Wouldn't it be wonderful if these students could elect a Congress that would make possession illegal, compensate owners for surrendering these lethal weapons, and then literally melt them down and use the metal to make hand tools for the poor people of the world. An exercise of common sense of that magnitude would restore hope everywhere.

A WORLD OF PEACE, JUSTICE AND BEAUTY

These three fundamental goals pretty well cover the agenda. Peace is the prerequisite for survival. The maintenance and modernization of nuclear arsenals will inevitably lead to the decimation of our species, which is alleged to have already occurred in an earlier epoch when Atlantis and Lemuria couldn't co-exist.

Justice would be a principal by-product of peace. Is it right for us as a species to spend hundreds of millions on weapons to kill each other when thousands of children are denied the basics in education, food and potable water? Justice is a basic tenet of both the Jewish and Christian Bibles, yet we callously ignore it, to our shame.

Beauty can be another by-product of peace and common sense. A drastic reduction in defense spending when added to a massive infusion of government-created money would provide enough purchasing power to solve many problems including an immediate transition from an oil economy to a zero-point energy economy. Some will ask what will be done to occupy the labor force and how will the funds that would become available in a few years be used? The answer: beautify the planet.

Old cities would benefit from eradicating their slums, building new parks, constructing transportation systems that eliminate the frustration of travel we experience now daily, due to traffic congestion.

One solution would be to build some new cities to reduce the over-crowding in our present cities. Half a century ago I was proposing a new city to take the pressure off Toronto. It would have been designed in modular fashion of communities within the city, where any of the ultimately two million inhabitants could travel to any other place within the city in 20 minutes.

JEANNE WHITE EAGLE'S VISION

Jeanne White Eagle and her husband John Pehrson visited Sandra and me at our cottage in Muskoka, the Lake District north of Toronto, for a couple of days in the summer of 2017. I had read her book, *Eyes Open: Looking for the Twelve*,[10] but that was the only introduction we had before they arrived.

We were so favorably impressed by these two extraordinary people, their charm, musical talent and joy, in addition to their spirituality and Jeanne's vision, that I promised to mention her in the book I was about to write. One of her admirers wrote the following.

"*Eyes Open* opens us to the possibility of a radically new way of learning and communicating: beyond the boundaries set by race, religion, political persuasion, nation state or even planet of origin. The author, Jeanne White Eagle, extends an invitation for the reader to join her in manifesting a shared dream of creating the physical, environmental and systems structures needed to enable and nurture an enlightened international and interplanetary community."[11]

I am not a Utopian. I don't think perfection is an attainable goal. However, I do believe that the dedicated pursuit of peace, justice and beauty by a few million inspired Earthlings would create a world so much better than the world we know today that it would seem like a dream come true.

I regret to say, however, that our hopes and aspirations may be crushed if our American friends don't wrest control of their country from the Cabal which hold an opposite set of core values.

CHAPTER TWENTY-FIVE

How Can Americans Retrieve Control Of Their Country?

It is now or never for Americans to recover control of their country from those who espouse an ideology that is totally foreign to their history, their core beliefs, and their interests. To be blunt, it is time to wrest control from the Cabal I described in Chapter 18, which is also known as the shadow or alternative government that is now dominated by the Nazi party.

The situation in the world in 2018 is similar to the one that existed in 1939 with one critical exception. At that time, Hitler's military juggernaut was in full sight for everyone to see, and to fear the ominous consequences.

Today, the situation is even more frightening. The near invincible military might of the Nazis does not consist of storm troopers and tanks, fighter aircraft, and missiles. The primary source of military power consists of an armada of space ships equipped with weapons that make the ones used in World War II, prior to August 6, 1945, when the first atomic bomb was dropped on Hiroshima, look like toys.

The tragic irony of the present crisis is that the military power intended to be used against the United States and its Allies has been built by American scientists, engineers, and laborers under the noses of American citizens and financed by them. Secrecy has been maintained by a truth embargo so rigorous that patriots who might want to speak the truth, remain silent because they have been warned that their lives would be in danger if they talk about the situation.

President Eisenhower sounded the alarm in his fmal address to the nation when he warned Americans to beware of the military-industrial complex. It would have been helpful if his language had been more specific, because he already knew that the UFO-ET file had fallen into the wrong hands.

The extent to which this is true can be gauged by the fact that even though, as Dr. Michael Wolf explained, the underground base at Area 51 is a sprawling city the size of Rhode Island, and it continues to grow, with a sister base called S4, some 12 miles away, and another named Indian Springs,[1] only President Obama has been allowed to land at Nelles Air Force Base, and to the best of our knowledge no American president has ever been allowed to visit or inspect the vast installations in the area.

The incredible fact that the president of the United States, who is legally the Commander-in-Chief of all its armed forces, has not been fully privy to the plans and projects of those forces is 100-percent proof that something smells in the heart of the Republic, and a faint whiff of that odor has just begun to be detected.

I mentioned earlier that the power of the enemy within is almost invincible. The only hope lies in the word "almost." Unlike the situation in 1939, the idea of an extended mobilization would be ridiculous in the extreme. There are, however, a few steps that if taken before the U.S. mid-term election in November 2018, would prevent the Nazi coup from ever happening. This is the final call to action stations!

Before listing the specific actions that must be taken, however, I think it may be useful to review the circumstances that have led to the crisis.

When Germany surrendered to the Allies in May 1945, it was assumed that the war with the Nazis was over. The British and Americans were both paranoid about their Russian Allies and considered extending the conflict by invading the U.S.S.R. Their respective chiefs of staff warned that they didn't have the resources for a quick or easy victory, so common sense prevailed. But the U.S. in particular never lost its desire to conquer the communists. That meant that an all-out effort was made to recruit the top German scientists to move to America before the Russians could make them an offer.

One of the projects was known as "Operation Paperclip," which brought hundreds of Nazi scientists and technicians to the U.S. where they were given American citizenship, new names, and credentials, and then appointed to important jobs in both civil and military establishments. President Truman, who had approved the plan, decreed that no one who had been active in the Nazi Party would be eligible, but this provision was largely ignored.

Many more specialists were hired by the military-industrial complex and when Allen Dulles finally became director of the Central Intelligence Agency (CIA) he, with the support of his brother John Foster Dulles, managed to bring an additional wave of Nazi immigrants who, in concert with those who had come before them, managed to infiltrate many branches of the U.S. establishment.

For a time there were two distinct branches of the CIA. One was chasing down former Nazis who had entered the U.S. illegally, while the other was bringing them in and giving them new identities.

Anyone who has read my book *The Money Mafia, A World in Crisis* may have reached the conclusion that the Nazis never really accepted defeat in World War II. They simply surrendered and went underground after making elaborate plans to keep their supremacist ideology alive. Long before the war had ended they established a self-contained base in Antartica, that was fully equipped as a government in exile. It was manned by many of their top scientists with the staff to support them. They called it the New Berlin, and the Americans were well aware of its existence. They decided to attack and eliminate it by dispatching the equivalent of a naval armada.

Operation Highjump

Wikipedia describes the plan as "a United States Navy operation organized by Rear Admiral Richard E. Byrd, Jr., USN (Ret), Officer in Charge, Task Force 68, and lead by Rear Admiral Richard H. Cruzen, USN, Commanding Officer, Task Force 68. Operation Highjump commenced 26 August 1946 and ended in late February 1947. Task Force 68 included 4,700 men, 13 ships, and 33 aircraft.

This much of the report is the truth. But it is wedged between a title "Operation Highjump, officially titled The United States Navy Antarctic Developments Program, 1946-47" and the closing sentence,"Operation Highjump's primary mission was to establish the Antarctic research base Little America IV." both of which are blatant lies![2]

The truth is that the task force was forced to retreat when it was repelled by flying discs that could have been either German or Reptillian, the one ET species that has been regarded as hostile, which had been collaborating with the Nazis before and during World War II. The discs destroyed an American ship and killed 68 men in a brief engagement that forced Byrd to retreat and terminate the operation.

Admiral Byrd was so angry that he suggested using nuclear weapons to eliminate the enemy base in Antarctica. By the winter of 1947, however, the Nazi influence on American policy was such that nothing was done.

One has to assume that the Nazi headquarters in Antartica has spent the intervening decades preparing to support the coup planned by their American collaborators to establish a Fourth Reich to "settle the score" with the Americans for joining the allied forces and contributing greatly to the Nazi's humiliating defeat in 1945.

The extent of the corruption of the U.S. government is stated brilliantly by John Loftus, a former US government prosecutor and army officer in his illuminating book *America's Nazi Secret*. Two paragraphs from the back cover tell the story:

> The Nuremburg trials were fixed. The US Justice Department did it. Some of America's most influential families funded Hitler. Ambitious lawyers in Washington covered it up under a cloak of national security. The Justice Department brought Nazis into America by the thousand to be trained as cold war spies.
>
> The Attorney General personally sponsored some of the worst war criminals for immigration to the USA, including the chief of the

Ukrainian security service, Mykola Lebed. His troops murdered tens of thousands of Poles, Ukrainians and Jews, including Simon Wiesenthal's mother.

In 1985 the Justice Department pawned this Ukrainian mass murderer off to Congress as an innocent leader of the Anti-Nazi resistance. Almost everything the Justice Department has ever told Congress about Nazis in America has been a conscious and deliberate lie.The hunt for Nazi war criminals has been a mere public relations effort to placate Jews and WWII veterans.

Need I say more? There is nothing more to say!

An Action Plan for Americans to Take Back Control of America

1. The Centra Intelligence Agency

The CIA is at the top of the list of "An Action Plan for Americans to Take Back Control Of America." When I think of the CIA I am reminded of Baron Stamp's description of the Bank of England of which he was a director from1928-1941. He said: " Banking was conceived in iniquity and was born in sin."

I would say the same was true of the CIA. The whole idea of fighting a worldwide clandestine war to impose the ill-defined ideological precepts of a single country is anathema to our God-given freedom of choice. Worse, such a war was doomed from its inception. Tim Weiner's monumental book, *Legacy of Ashes*, tells the story.

To paraphrase Sir Winston Churchill you might conclude that never in the annals of human history have so many people spent so much time and tax payers' money in illegal acts of bribery, murder, mayhem, political interference on behalf of the candidate of choice, the undermining of democratically elected leaders and myriad other misdemeanours outside the law with so little positive and lasting results to show for it.

The CIA introduced torture, which is one of Satan's tools. It has promoted the policy of continual war. It has also, according to various accounts, been one of the biggest, if not the biggest, drug dealer in America, despite the U.S. war against drugs. I listened to a youtube session describing the CIA importing drugs in the bodies of dead service men. Also, not long ago, I had a long chat with a former USAF F104 pilot who flew as escort for a CIA Dreamlifter cargo plane filled with drugs. How many young lives have been ruined by using the drugs the CIA has been peddling to raise money for its' Black Operations?

In his latest book titled *Unacknowledged*, Dr. Stephen Greer, one of the world's top UFOlogists, states that the CIA is now running a night-time shuttle of anti-gravity discs to the Middle East carrying payloads of weapons and drugs that are sold for cash. These operations and other illegalities are kept out of the courts by the CIA simply designating them as a matter of national security.

Does the U.S. need a genuine intelligence organization to collect legitimate information? Yes. But it already has so many intelligence agencies that they are difficult to count. The CIA is totally redundant as well as dangerous in more ways than one can imagine. It has been the headquarters for the evil empire, at least at the covert level.

The CIA should be locked and shuttered before any documents can be removed and shredded. Employees should be given three months separation pay and the organization, and the inestimable damage it has done, pass into history. .

2. THE NATIONAL SECURITY AGENCY

The National Security Agency (NSA) should be shut down at once, but only on an interim basis until the war is over. Putting the massive spy agency in mothballs will level the playing field and make it impossible for the Nazis to know who among their numbers has opted to tell the truth and who has not. At least the massive spying organization will become inert until the situation has become sufficiently stabilized, so that the Congress can decide how much universal spying should end, and how many selective targets, if any, remain.

3. DEFENSE ADVANCED RESEARCH PROJECTS AGENCY

The Defense Advanced Research Projects Agency (DARPA) should be completely shut down until the Congress can examine and review all of its advanced projects from a moral and ethical point of view. Is DARPA involved in experiments to develop beings that are half human and half machine? If so what is the purpose of its experiments, and is it one that our Creator God would approve?

The same question can be asked of artificial intelligence. Building robots to do the "dirty work" like mining, for example, is perfectly rational. But why develop machines to do our creative thinking for us when we don't use the common sense that is part of our inheritance?

Some of the projects that DARPA is alleged to be working on appear to be quite grotesque and totally out of sync with a world of peace, justice, and beauty, which should be the standard by which the Congress should determine its suitability for public funding.

234

4. The Fed

Of all the targets mentioned here, the Federal Reserve System should be on a par with the CIA. It must be nationalized at once, before the congressmen and congresswomen start thinking about campaign funds for the 2020 election.

In my book *The Money Mafia,* I refer to the Fed as "The Biggest Heist in History." That is exactly what it is. The power to create money is the most valuable financial asset that any country possesses. Yet it was given away, yes, given away, to a handful of the richest bankers in the world. The legislation to establish the Fed was introduced just before Christmas, and the Congress may have had other things on its mind; but, allowing this legislation to be passed and implemented was one of the most irresponsible actions imaginable.

Just three years after the Federal Reserve Act of 1913 was passed into law, President Woodrow Wilson wrote: "A great industrial nation is controlled by its system of credit. Our system is concentrated in the Federal Reserve System. The growth of the nation, therefore, and all our activities are in the hands of a few men ... We have come to be one of the worst ruled, one of the most completely controlled and dominated governments in the civilized world.[3]

If President Wilson were alive today he might add, "In no other system could a handful of men usurp the people's power and make them slaves to a ruthless foreign ideology."

Congress must act immediately to right a 105-year-old injustice, and dissolve the system that has given the Cabal its nearly absolute power! Anyone who has read *Lucifer's Banker* by Bradley C. Birkenfeld[4] will conclude that the present banking system is rotten to the core, and should be redesigned from the ground up, preferably along the lines I have outlined in Chapter Twenty-One.

It should also be recognized that international trade, despite its many benefits in providing a wide range of products to pander to many different tastes, is not an economic panacea. It might increase GDP infinitesimally if it results in increasing the velocity of turnover of the existing money supply. But generations of depressions, recessions, and austerity budgets are all due to inadequate domestic demand, and the only way of filling that perennial void is government-created money.

The Chemtrail - HAARP Duo

The U.S. president should order the armed forces to cease and desist from using chemtrails-HAARP, this most evil of projects. In one fell swoop he would eliminate their ability to use weather as a weapon. Global warming is creating more than enough extreme variations in weather patterns without adding to it artificially.

The devastating medical and health problems related to our daily dose of nanoparticles of aluminum, barium, strontium, and other unknown elements has already been noted in a previous chapter. This chapter is about survival and the balance of power between nations, and between the military and innocent civilians.

The chemtrail-HAARP fence has been designed to encourage psychotic generals into believing that the U.S. could wage a nuclear war with Russia and suffer only acceptable casualties. This is sheer madness, of course, but when generals are subject to mind control they cease to be rational. This same "fence" is designed to discourage any good ETs who might consider coming to our rescue from doing so.

Finally, if Phil Schneider was correct when he said that part of the Cabal agenda is a drastic reduction in the world's population, the fascists would only have to insert a lethal virus in their chemtrail mix to kill millions of people within 48 hours. So those countries, including Canada, who have been duped into believing that the chemtrails are related to climate control, I say tear up your agreement with the U.S. and act immediately. No need for studies or commissions of inquiry, the health and possibly the lives of your citizens are in danger until you end this horrific system.

Ground Space Command

The U.S. president should issue an order grounding all space vehicles of every kind until the question of who will represent Earth in space has been agreed by all the major powers, including Russia and China in particular. Another arms race is inevitable in the absence of a diplomatic solution, which must become the norm.

Certainly the Nazi-controlled U.S. fleet should sit on the ground until all crews have been screened for allegiance to the U.S. constitution and the people of America. Space travel offers an exciting new frontier, but we are not welcome in deep space until we abandon our frontier mentality of shoot first and ask questions after, which has been our *modus vivendi* until now.

Ban Automatic Rifles Except for the Military

I have added this one in honor of those wonderful young people who I admire so much. They are concerned about their lives and safety and so should we all be! As I suggested earlier it would be wonderful to outlaw the automatics, compensate the owners, and convert the metal into hand tools for the people who need them most.

The Potential Miracle Can only Happen from the Bottom Up

There is no way that America can be saved for Americans if you expect the miracle to begin at the top. It will only happen if many million ordinary Americans are sufficiently motivated to save their country from the Nazis that they contact the president, their Congressman or Congresswoman and their Senator, if he or she is one of those up for re-election, and say to each one of them: We will vote against you, regardless of party affiliation, if you don't initiate and enact the agenda set out above before the election.

Promises of action after the election won't do. Only action now will earn you my vote because it is the survival of my country as an independent entity that is at stake.

A Joint Congressional Committee

It would be good to have a joint congressional committee established immediately to seek the truth in these matters. But first it would be necessary to enact a general amnesty under the National Security Act. There are many patriots that would love to tell the truth, but the cost is too high without an amnesty.

Spiritual Revolution

I ended both of my other books on world affairs by stating that spirituality has been the missing link. I am not promoting any specific religion, because I know that there are many rivers that run into the sea. Instead, I suggest to young and old alike, fill the churches, the mosques, the synagogues, and the temples. But not to listen to long-winded theological homilies or practice ancient rituals. Instead, to praise our Creator God for life and all his wondrous works. Then spend the rest of the time together planning on how to help the sick, the homeless, the hungry, the handicapped, the aged, and the lonely.

May God save us all from the scourge of Nazism. Meanwhile, we can pray for our leaders and our enemies that at least some of them may see the light.

This is a condensed version of my life until June 2018. It has been a good life and I have much to be thankful for. There is more that could be said about the potential for the human species, but that will only be realized if we abandon our wicked ways and learn to live in the light. The Creator gave us the power of choice, so we can write our own future history

NOTES

CHAPTER ONE

1. Louise Veninga, *The Ginseng Book*. (California: Big Tree Press, 1973, p. 63.
2. Ibid., p. 64-65.
3. May Quale Innis, *An Economic History of Canada*. (Toronto: The Ryerson Press, 1935 (Fourth Edition 1948), p. 43.
4. Louse Veninga, *The Ginseng Book*, op. cit., p. 66.
5. Ibid., p. 67.
6. Ibid., p. 69.
7. John S. Martin was the local member of the Ontario Provincial Parliament from 1923 until 1931. He held the Agriculture portfolio at the time of his death that year.

CHAPTER TWO

1. Irving Berlin Publishing Company, 1941.
2. Letter from my mother, December 10, 1941. Hellyer Papers, Toronto, Ontario.

CHAPTER THREE

1. Letter from Doug Zeller, January 9, 1942. Hellyer Papers, Toronto, Ontario.
2. Letter addressed to me by Sgt. L.R. Silver from the Royal Canadian Air Force Overseas Headquarters, 2 Cockspur Street (Trafalgar Square), London SW1, January 29, 1942. Hellyer Papers, Toronto, Ontario.
3. Letter from Margaret Nelson, April 10, 1944. Hellyer Papers, Toronto, Ontario.
4. Major G. Fay Davies, ed., "Airmen Treated as Zombies," Editorial Page, Canadian Corp Association, 1944, p. 18.

CHAPTER FOUR

1. Rose MacDonald, *The Telegram*, Toronto, March 7, 1949.
2. Court Stone, *The Globe and Mail*, Toronto, March 7,1949.

CHAPTER FIVE

1. Letter from Hon. Brooke Claxton, Minister of National Defence, November 26, 1953.
2. For a full account of the St. Laurent trip see Dale C. Thompson, *Louis St. Laurent: Canadian*. (Toronto: MacMillan of Canada, 1967).

CHAPTER SIX

1. Editorial, "Toronto's Apprentice Minister," *Toronto Daily Star*, February 10, 1956.
2. For details of Comet crashes in 1952 and 1953 see Andrè J. Launay, *Historic Air Disasters*. (London: Ian Allen Ltd., 1967), pp. 32-46.
3. Private & Confidential letter to the Hon. Brooke Claxton, Minister of National Defence, November 23, 1953.
4. Letter from Brooke Claxton, Minister of National Defence, November 26, 1953.

5. Pocket Calendar, May 24, 1956. Hellyer Papers, Toronto, Ontario.

6. Thomson, Dale C., *Louis St. Laurent: Canadian*. (Toronto: Macmillan of Canada, 1967), p. 498.

7. Ibid., p. 499.

8. Prime Minister Mackenzie King and Postmaster General William Mulock had been elected from one of the York constituencies, and James Murdock, who was King's Minister of Labour and MP for Kent County, ran in High Park in 1925 but was soundly defeated.

9. Editorial, *Toronto Evening Telegram*, April 26, 1957.

10. *Toronto Daily Star*, April 26, 1957.

11. *Globe and Mail*, April 26, 1957.

12. Date Book, May 9, 1957. Hellyer Papers, Toronto, Ontario.

13. *Toronto Daily Star*, May 28, 1957.

14. Senior Liberals reading the manuscript recall the Liberal figure as 108. The difference can be accounted for if you included Liberal Labour, Independent Liberal and Independent MPs who supported the Liberals.

Chapter Seven

1. Lisa Duperreault, "Midland Park: The Modern Place to Live." An information kit for neighbors and public officials in support of an heritage designation for Midland Park.

Chapter Nine

1. James Plomer, "The Gold-braid Mind is Destroying Our Navy," *Maclean's* magazine, September 7, 1963.

2. Ibid.

3. Postscript to a letter from a Mr. Justice Donald Keith of the Superior Court of Ontario, Osgoode Hall, Toronto, December 17, 1980.

4. *Toronto Star*, "Sensible Defence to a Point," March 28, 1964.

5. Ibid., March 28, 1964, p. 7.

6. "Defense for a Decade Ahead," the Canadian edition of *Time* magazine, April 3, 1964, pp. 11-12.

7. "A Force To Fit Canada's Needs," *Montreal Star*, March 20, 1964.

8. "Nothing but Praise for Defence Minister Hellyer," *Canadian Aviation*, Vol. 37, No. 5, May 1964.

9. Lubor J. Zink, "Clear Thinking on Our Defense," *Toronto Telegram*, March 30, 1964, p. 7.

10. *Maclean's* magazine, January 3, 1965, pp. 7-11.

11. Canada, Cabinet Minutes, June 18, 1963.

12. Lester B. Pearson, *Mike: The Memoirs of the Rt. Hon. Lester B. Pearson*, eds. John A. Munro and Alex I. Inglis, Vol. 3. (Toronto: University of Toronto Press), p. 107.

13. Hellyer diary, February 24, 1964.

14. Ibid., April 9, 1964.

15. Ibid., April 13, 1964.

16. Judy LaMarsh, *Memoirs of a Bird in a Gilded Cage*. (Toronto: McClelland & Stewart, 1968), p. 91.

17. Ibid.

18. Ibid.

19. Hellyer diary, May 6, 1964.

20. Letter from Graham Towers, Rockcliffe Park, Ottawa, April 12, 1964. [HP/T]

Chapter Ten

1. Hellyer diary, February 3, 1964.

2. Martin, Paul, *A Very Public Life*, Vol. 2. (Toronto: Deneau, 1985), pp. 547-8.

3. Pearson, Lester B., *Mike: The Memoirs of the Rt. Hon. Lester B. Pearson,* ed. John A. Munro and Alex I. Inglis, Vol. 3. (Toronto: University of Toronto Press, 1975), p. 135.

4. Canada, Cabinet, Minutes, February 16, 1965.

5. Hellyer diary, November 13, 1965.

6. Ibid.

7. Gordon, Walter, *A Political Memoir.* (Toronto: McClelland & Stewart 1977), p. 233.

8. *Montreal Gazette,* June 2, 1967.

9. Story as recounted by Prime Minister Pearson.

10. *Ottawa Citizen,* June 27, 1967.

11. Canada, Cabinet, Minutes, June 29, 1967.

12. Ibid., July 25, 1967.

13. Ibid., July 26, 1967.

14. *Ottawa Journal,* August 22, 1967.

15. Hellyer diary, September 11, 1967.

16. Ibid., September 16, 1967.

CHAPTER ELEVEN

1. Hellyer diary, March 17, 1969.

2. Ibid., March 29, 1969.

3. Ibid., March 30, 1969.

4. English, John, *Citizen of the World: The Life of Pierre Elliott Trudeau,* Volume One: 1919-1968. (Alfred A. Knoff Canada, 2006), pp. 108-109.

5. Hellyer diary, April 23, 1969.

6. This information was provided by Hon. Leo Cadieux personally during a flight from Brussels to Ottawa.

CHAPTER TWELVE

1. Peter Desbarats, *Ottawa Journal,* October 4, 1971.

2. David Owens, "Political manifest," *Winnipeg Free Press,* November 6, 1971

3. Hellyer notebook, 1971.

CHAPTER THIRTEEN

1. Hellyer papers, Toronto.

2. A telephone conversation between Bill Lee and Bill Neville as reported to me by Bill Lee.

3. As reported to me by Sean O'Sullivan.

4. Hellyer diary, February 21, 1976.

5. Hellyer papers, Toronto.

CHAPTER FOURTEEN

1. Actual figures for the U.S. and Canada were included in my book *Funny Money* that was published in 1994.

2. Hellyer diary, April 14, 1993.

3. Ibid., April 15, 1993.

4. Ibid., May 26, 1993.

5. Ibid., October 27, 1993.

CHAPTER FIFTEEN

1. Hellyer diary

2. Ibid.

3. Metropolitan United Church

4. Hellyer diary
5. Ibid.
6. Ibid.
7. Ibid.

Chapter Sixteen

1. Senator Daniel K. Inouye at the Intra-Contra public hearings 1987. Chaired the Senate Select Committee on secret military assistance to Iran and the Nicaraguan opposition.
2. Chris Styles and Graham Simms, *Impact to Contact: The Shag Harbour Incident.* (Halifax: Arcadia House Publishing, 2013).
3. Downgraded to Confidential, September 15, 1969. Hellyer papers, Toronto.
4. Wilbert B. Smith, "What we are doing in Ottawa," an address to the Vancouver area UFO Club, March 14, 1961.

Chapter Seventeen

1. Paul Hellyer interview with Leo Pearce, January 6, 2008.
2. E-mail from Stan Fulham, October 31, 2007.
3. Nickolas Evanoff e-mail to Ray Stone, July 13, 2007.
4. Col. Philip J. Corso with William J. Birnes, *The Day after Roswell.* (New York: Pocket Books, 1997), p. 125.
5. Ryan S. Wood, *Majic Eyes Only: Earth's Encounters with Extraterrestrial Technology.* (Colorado: Wood & Wood Enterprises, 2005).
6. Jim Sparks, *The Keepers: An Alien Message for the Human Race.* (Taylor: Granite Publishing, 2008).

Chapter Eighteen

1. Memorandum E-A10, 19 October 1940, Council on Foreign Relations, War-Peace Studies, Baldwin Papers, Box 117.
2. J.H. Retinger, the European Continent, London's Hodge, 1946.
3. "The Crisis of Democracy: Report on the Governability of Democracies to the Trilateral Commission," New York University Press, 1975.
4. "The Camel's Nose in the Tent," by permission, Roger Berry.
5. Dr. Michael Wolf, former NSA consultant in an interview with Chris Stoner.
6. Ibid.
7. Senator Daniel K. Inouye at the Intra-Contra public hearings 1987. Chaired the Senate Select Committee on secret military assistance to Iran and the Nicaraguan opposition.
8. Steven M. Greer, *Hidden Truth, Forbidden Knowledge: It is time for you to know.* (Crozet: Crossing Point, Inc. 2006).
9. "Joint Intelligence Objectives Agency," National Archives and Records Administration. (http://gov/iwg/declassified-records/rg-330-defense-secretary/). Retrieved October 9, 2008.
10. Brian Johnson, *The Secret War.* (London: Methuen Inc., 1978), p. 184.
11. Daniel Estulin, *The True Story of the Bilderberg Group,* (Walterville: TrineDay LLC, 2007), pp. 92-93.

Chapter Nineteen

1. Telephone conversation with Clifford Stone June 2018.
2. Chris Stoner in an interview with Dr. Michael Wolf, former U.S. National Security Council's Special Studies (UFO) Group and Jim Sparks in The Keepers.
3. Ibid.
4. Len Kasten, *The Secret History of Extraterrestrials: Advanced Technology and the Coming*

New Race. (Rochester: Bear & Company, 2010), p. 6.

5. Ibid., p. 7.

6. Ibid.

7. Ibid.

8. Valiant Thor, *The Benevolent Alien With An IQ of 1200*, Dislose.tv, March 23, 2017.

9. Dr. Frank Stranges, *Stranger at the Pentagon.* (Revised) (CreateSpace Independent Publishing Platform), 2001.

10. Phil Schneider lecture "Underground Bases and the New World Order, Post Falls, Idaho, May 8,1995.

11. Ibid.

12. Ibid.

13. Ibid.

14. Ibid.

15. Ibid.

16. Full Interview Here: http://www.ufo-blogger.com/2010/02/eisenhower-survival-secret-mars-colony.html

17. Elana Freeland, *Chemtrails, HAARP, and the Full Spectrum Dominance of Planet Earth.* (Port Townsend: Feral House, 2014).

18. What Chemtrails Are Doing To Your Brain – Neurosurgeon Dr. Russell Blaylock Reveals Shocking Facts: https://youtube.com/watch?feature=player_embedded&v=X31W-TG-G1k0

19. Ibid.

CHAPTER TWENTY

1. Greg Palast in an interview with Acres USA, June 2003.

2. Mayer Hillman: Excerpt from address to the University of Anglia in late 2017.

3. Ibid.

4. Dr. Michael Wolf, Former NSA Consultant in an interview with Chris Stoner. "Defence Planning Guidance on Post-Cold War Strategy."

5. "Rebuilding America's Defenses: Strategy, Forces and Resources for a New Century. Published by the New Investigation, www.wheredidthetowersgo.com September 2000."

6. Major General Albert Stubbleine III, www.veteranstoday.com/ ... /i-can-prove-that-it-was-not-an-airplane-that-hit-the-pentagon.

7. Architects and Engineers for 9/11 Truth, Peter Denney, "A Summary of Evidence: A Call to Action," August 24, 2010. First Edition: v.1.1 of the 9/11 Investigator: Exposing the Explosive WTC Evidence, 2010.

8. Ibid.

9. Judy Wood, *Where Did The Towers Go?: Evidence of Directed Free-Energy   Technology on 9/11,* (The New Investigation, 2010).

CHAPTER TWENTY-ONE

1. David R. Henderson (Editor), *The Fortune Encyclopedia of Economics.* (New York City: Grand Central Publishing, 1993).

2. Larry Elliott Economics (Editor) *The Guardian,* "Richest 62 people as wealthy as half of the world's population, says Oxfam," January 18, 2016.

3. International Movement for Monetary Reform, "The Swiss Sovereign Money Initiative: Five Questions & Answers," by Brandi Geurkink, November 2017.

4. Peter Koenig, "The Venezuelan 'Petro' – Towards a New World Reserve Currency?" February 23, 2018. Dispatches from Peter Koenig.

5. My letter to Prime Minister Justin Trudeau, November 4, 2015.

Chapter Twenty-Two

1. Michael E. Zarbo, Captain, United States Army. Thesis submitted to the Faculty of the Defense Intelligence College in partial fulfillment of the requirements for the degree of Master of Science of Strategic Intelligence, November 1992.
2. David Morehouse, *Psychic Warrior: Inside the CIA's Stargate Program: The True Story of a Soldier's Espionage and Awakening.* (New York: St. Martin's Press, 1996).
3. Courtney Brown, *Cosmic Voyage: A Scientific Discovery of Extraterrestrials Visiting Earth.* (New York: Penguin Books USA Inc., 1996).
4. Courtney Brown, *Cosmic Explorers: Scientific Remote Viewing, Extraterrestrials, and a Message for Mankind.* (New York: Penguin Putman Inc., 2000).
5. Courtney Brown, Dick Allgire, Daz Smith, *The Phoenix Lights: A Farsight Remote-Viewing Project.* Published by Farsight Press, July 10, 2015.
6. *Cosmic Voyage*, op. cit., Chapter 11, p. 103.
7. "The Moses Project," Farsight Institute. http://farsight.org/FarsightPress/Moses_Beyond_Exodus_Farsight_Project_main-page.html

Chapter Twenty-Three

1. Robert Lanza with Bob Berman, *Beyond Biocentrism: Rethinking Time, Space, Consciousness, and the Illusion of Death.* (Dallas: BenBella Books, Inc., 2016).
2. Courtney Brown, *Cosmic Explorers: Scientific Remote Viewing, Extraterrestrials, and a Message for Mankind.* (New York: Penguin Putman, Inc., 2000).
3. Ibid., Chapter 35, pp. 348-350.
4. Shirley Maclaine, *Going Within: A Guide for Inner Transformation.* (New York: Bantam Books, 1989), p. 259.
5. *Beyond Biocentrism*, op. cit., p. 98.
6. Courtney Brown, *Cosmic Voyage: A Scientific Discovery of Extraterrestrials Visiting Earth.* (New York: Penguin Books Ltd., 1996), pp. 163-164.
7. The Bible, The New King James Version, Matthew, Chapter 5 vs 9.
8. Ibid., Matthew, Chapter 21 vs 13
9. Ibid., Mark, Chapter 1 vs 11
10. Ibid., Mark 1 vs 24
11 .Ibid., Mark 8 vs 27-29
12. Ibid., Mark 9 vs 2-7
13. Ibid., Mark 10 vs 18
14. Ibid., Mark 13 vs 32
15. Ibid., Mark 14 vs 36
16. Ibid., Mark 15 vs 34
17. An account written by Samir Kreidie and sent to the author August 28, 2008

Chapter Twenty-Four

1. Richard Rohr, *Daily Meditation*, "Blessed Are the Peacemakers," Tuesday, February 6, 2018.
2. Summary of "The War in Heaven" project as available on the Farsight Institute video-on-demand forwarded to author May 13, 2018.
3. Ibid.
4. Telephone conversation with Mark Siljander June 22, 2018.
5. From a translated text of Osama bin Laden's broadcast taken from *The New York Times*, October 2, 2001.
6. Barbara Sheffield, *United Church Observer* November/December 2017.
7. Story as related by Kent Hotaling, a friend of the Timmis family, June 19, 2018.
8. Chris Snyder, *Creating Opportunities – A Volunteer's Memoir.* (Toronto: Civil Sector

Press, 2018), Acknowledgments, pp. xvii– xviii.

9. Christal Hayes, "Students plan to walk out of schools to protest gun laws," *USA Today*, February 17, 2018.

10. Jeanne White Eagle, *Eyes Open: Looking for the Twelve – Blueprint for a New World.* (CreateSpace Independent Publishing Platform, 2014.)

11. Herman Maynard, business executive and co-author of *The Fourth Wave: Business in the 21st Century.*

Chapter Twenty-Five

1. Dr. Michael Wolf, former NSA consultant in an interview with Chris Stoner.

2. Wikipedia, "Operation Highjump, June 23, 2018.

3. Jack Metcalf, *The Two Hundred Year Debate: Who Shall Issue the Nation's Money.* (Olympia: An Honest Money for America Publication, 1986), p. 92.

4. Bradley C. Birkenfeld, *Lucifer's Banker: The Untold Story of How I Destroyed Swiss Bank Secrecy.* (Austin: Greenleaf Book Group Press, 2016).

PHOTOGRAPHS

A young Paul providing transportation for his cousin Walter

Paul in army uniform after being demobilized from The Royal Canadian Air Force

Paul and his young family, David, his wife Ellen, Mary Elizabeth and Peter

Defence Minister Hellyer with his deputy-minister, chairman of the Defence Research Board, the chiefs of staff, and Associate Minister Lucien Cardin after a meeting with General Lyman Lemnitzer, Commander in Chief of Allied Forces in Europe

Paul with some of his supporters at the 1968 National Liberal Leadership Convention won by Pierre Trudeau who became prime minister

Paul with Defense Secretary Robert McNamara watching an air demonstration

Paul and his bride Sandra on their wedding day October 1st 2005

Paul with Sandra Hellyer and Kay Hotaling in Lebanon, on a tour of the Middle East.

Paul presenting a copy of his book *Light at the End of the Tunnel: A Survival Plan for the Human Species*, and a bottle of good Canadian ice wine to President Jimmy Carter at a reception in Plains Georgia.

253

Dr. Edgar Mitchell, Apollo 14 astronaut, arrives at the Hellyer residence for dinner, July 7, 2006, accompanied by his friend, Susan Swing and Susan Boyne (later Bird) wife of Mike Bird who took the picture.

The Hellyers at lunch with international journalist Paola Harris, and Dr. Courtney Brown, Director of The Farsight Institute, at the Society for Exploration Conference, Boulder, Colorado, June 2008.

Paul singing the role of Peter in the opera Hansel and Gretel at the Banff School of Fine Arts during the parliamentary recess, summer 1954.

Paul dropping in to say hello to President Gerald Ford at a formal dinner in Toronto.

Chemtrails originating from Billy Bishop Airport being released directly over the world famous Toronto Sick Children's Hospital

If you look up and see the chemtrails in the sky you will become aware of a dangerous practice.

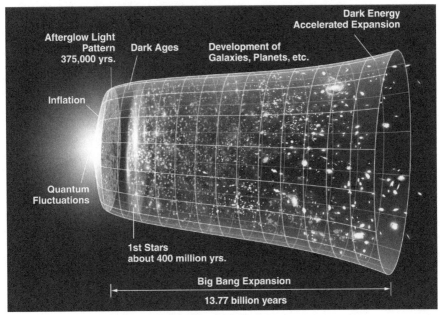

A sketch of the Big Bang

Valiant Thor, the Benevolent Venutian Alien with an I.Q. of 1200, who offered Earthlings a better, richer, healthier life in exchange for giving up our nuclear weapons. His offer was not accepted.

257

About the Author

Paul Hellyer is Canada's Senior Privy Councillor, having been appointed to the cabinet of Prime Minister Louis S. St. Laurent in 1957, just eight years after his first election to the House of Commons in 1949 at the age of 25. He subsequently held senior posts in the governments of Lester B. Pearson and Pierre E. Trudeau, who defeated him for the Liberal Party leadership in 1968. The following year, after achieving the rank of senior minister, which was later designated Deputy Prime Minister, Hellyer resigned from the Trudeau cabinet on a question of principle related to housing.

Although Hellyer is best known for the unification of the Canadian Armed Forces, and for his 1968 chairmanship of the Task Force on Housing and Urban Development, he has maintained a life-long interest in macroeconomics. Through the years, as a journalist and political commentator, he has continued to fight for economic reforms and has written several books on the subject.

A man of many interests, Hellyer's ideas are not classroom abstractions. He was born and raised on a farm and his business experience includes manufacturing, retailing, construction, land development, tourism and publishing. He has also been active in community affairs including the arts, and studied voice at the Royal Conservatory of Music in Toronto. His multi-faceted career, in addition to a near-lifetime in politics, gives Hellyer a rare perspective on what has gone wrong in the critical fields of both world politics and economics.

In recent years he has become interested in the extraterrestrial presence and their superior technology that we have been emulating. In September 2005 he became the first person of cabinet rank in the G8 group of countries to state unequivocally "UFO's are as real as the airplanes flying overhead." He continues to take an interest in these areas and provides a bit of basic information about them in this book.

APPENDIX A

The amount of money created would be approximately 5% of total bank deposits in the country. When the share certificates are presented to the central bank it would print a corresponding amount of cash for deposit to federal government accounts. The federal government would then divide the money 50/50 with the states and the municipalities. The ratio of division is arbitrary but the 50/50 was considered appropriate to fund needs at all levels, and leave the federal government with significant funds for debt reduction.

Legislation would be necessary to require all banks to increase their cash reserves at a rate of not less than 5% per annum until they reach 34 percent. This would guarantee that the government-created money (GCM) could not be leveraged by the private banks. This would guarantee that the GCM would not be inflationary.

The process would be repeated every year for seven years when all banks would have cash reserves of 34 percent. In each subsequent year the Governor of the Central Bank, in consultation with government, shall determine the amount of money to be created to keep the economy operating at its maximum without creating monetary inflation. Should there be disagreement between the Governor and the Secretary of the Treasury, or Finance Minister, the decision of the latter shall be final. The idea that central bank governors are somehow superior beings, and know best, is nothing but a cleverly created myth to protect the power of the banking cartel.

Index

Obama, Barack 230
O'Brien, Al 114
O'Dea, Frank 130
Office of Strategic Services (OSS) 178
Operation Highjump 232, 244
Operation Paperclip 178, 179, 193, 231
O'Sullivan, Sean 130, 134, 146, 240
Ottawa Citizen 48, 91, 96, 240
Ottawa Journal 100, 122, 240
Otter, George 19

P

Paish, Edith and George 42, 64
Palast, Greg 189, 242
Paton, Sam 63
Patterson, Irma 23
Pearce, Leo 166, 241
Pearkes, George 56, 71
Pearson, Lester B. (Mike) v, 40, 57, 65, 67,
    70, 71, 72, 73, 74, 75, 76, 77, 82, 84,
    86, 90, 92, 94, 96, 101, 102, 103,
    104, 113, 123, 223, 239, 240, 257
Pehrson, John 229
Peters, Doug 144
Picasso, Pablo 120
Pickersgill, Jack 48, 52, 53, 71, 74, 91, 92,
    98, 116
Pickford, Mary 14
Pitman, Walter 154
Plomer, James 78, 239
Pohran, Nicholas 123
Pope, Nick 168, 169
Power, Chubby 113, 116, 175
Poynter, Arthur 68
Prout, Terry 151
Psychic Warrior 207, 243

Q

Quail, Ollie 114

R

Race, John 8, 44, 60, 65, 159
Rae, Jim 28, 91
Raitt, John 14
Ralph, Al 37
Ralph, Betty 28, 30

Ralph, David 53
Ralph, Ellen Jean Valentine 24, 28, 30, 37,
    39, 40, 48, 53, 54, 65, 130
Ralph, Warren 130, 151
Ralston, James 23
Rattey, Aline 46
Regan, Vince 57
Retinger, Joseph 175, 241
Richardson, Jim 12, 116, 117
Ringier, Michael 2
Riordan, John 227
Rittingshausen, Eva 107
Road Back, The v, 67, 71
Robertson, Fred 46
Robertson, Gordon 46, 109, 113, 116
Robichaud, Hédard 74
Rockefeller, David 175, 180
Rockefeller, Nelson 164
Rogers, Buddy 15, 152
Rogers, Rix 149, 152
Rohr, Richard 222, 243
Rooney, James 38
Roosevelt, Franklin D. 2, 99
Rosen, William S. 32, 33
Rosin, Carol iv, 193
Ross, Edward 61
Ross, J.B. (Jock) 49, 65, 66
Rowley, R. 90
Royal Canadian Air Force (RCAF) 18, 20, 22,
    24, 27, 41, 50, 54, 76, 86, 87, 95, 166
Rudolph, Arthur 179
Rusk, Dean 79
Rykens, Paul 175

S

Safdie, Moshe 139
Salas, Marilyn 163
Salas, Robert 163
Salk, Jonas 120
Salla, Michael iv, 163
Sauder, Richard 184
Sauvé, Maurice 84
Schneider, Phil 183, 184, 185, 236, 242
Scott, Ted 150
Secret History of Extraterrestrials, The 172,
    182, 241